CARRYING QOHELETH'S *MAOTA* (HOUSE)

INTERNATIONAL VOICES IN BIBLICAL STUDIES

Editor
Pablo R. Andiñach
Jin Young Choi,
Lim Chin Ming, Stephen
Gerald O. West

Number 17

CARRYING QOHELETH'S *MAOTA* (HOUSE)

An Australian-Samoan Diasporic Reading

by
Brian Fiu Kolia

 PRESS

Atlanta

Copyright © 2024 by Brian Fiu Kolia

All rights reserved. No part of this work may be reproduced or transmitted in any form or by any means, electronic or mechanical, including photocopying and recording, or by means of any information storage or retrieval system, except as may be expressly permitted by the 1976 Copyright Act or in writing from the publisher. Requests for permission should be addressed in writing to the Rights and Permissions Office, SBL Press, 825 Houston Mill Road, Atlanta, GA 30329 USA.

Library of Congress Control Number: 2024944520

Contents

Acknowledgments		vii
Abbreviations		ix
Introduction		1
1.	Maota Tau Ave	7
	Contexts	7
	Diaspora	10
	Samoan Migration	12
	Maota Tau Ave	17
	Conclusion	26
2.	Talanoa Intertextually	29
	Intertextuality	29
	Talanoa	33
	Talanoa in the Hebrew Bible	36
	Where Qohelet Fits	50
	Conclusion	51
3.	House: From Homeland to Diaspora	53
	Preexilic *Bêt 'Āb*	53
	Bêt 'ēm (House of the Mother)	58
	Samoan Analogies	67
	Conclusion: The Diasporic Bayit	69
4.	Qohelet and Diaspora Studies	71
	A Case for a Diasporic Context	72
	Emergence of Diasporic Studies	73
	Diasporic Studies and Biblical Studies	83
	Conclusion	98

5.	Kingship	101
	Kingship in Qohelet	102
	Kingship in the Hebrew Bible	104
	Qohelet's Attitude to Kingship	116
	Conclusion	117
6.	God's Presence	119
	The Temple in Qohelet	119
	Temple and Presence of God in the Hebrew Bible	124
	Samoan Hermeneutics	136
7.	Moral Order	141
	Moral Order in Qohelet	141
	Moral Order in the Hebrew Bible	145
	Moral Chaos in Diaspora	156
	Samoan Diaspora Hermeneutics	158
8.	Qohelet's *Maota Tau Ave*	161
	Maota Tau Ave as Hermeneutical Lens	161
	Qohelet's Diasporic *Maota*	167
	Rereading Scepticism in Ecclesiastes	176
	Conclusion	177

Bibliography	179
Scriptural Index	197
Modern Author Index	201

Acknowledgments

I first give glory to God for the gifts of persistence and resilience, gifts that have allowed me to persevere and struggle, to push and to resist, to scrutinise and decolonise.

I acknowledge with the utmost gratitude the mentorship and friendship of my supervisor Prof. Mark G. Brett, whose advise, and insights helped shape the premise of this book. *Faafetai tele uso!*

I express my dear thanks to my second supervisor and friend, Dr. Jione Havea for his companionship and leadership, giving space for other Pasifika voices to follow his lead.

I give sincere thanks to the Principal, Rev Prof. Vaitusi Nofoaiga and the Faculty at Malua Theological College for their support and camaraderie while pushing forward with the book.

I want to express my gratitude to my church, the Congregational Christian Church Samoa for their prayers and support. *Afioga i le Taitaifono, Sui Taitaifono, Le Laulau a Fono o le Fono Tele, Afioga i le Taitaifono ma le Komiti Mamalu o Tamā o le Ekalesia, le paia i Faafeagaiga faapea le Ekalesia Aoao. Malo le tatalo, fa'afetai le tapuai!*

I thank my family and friends, in particular my siblings Tiresa, Victoria and Charin for their love and support.

To my parents, my father Rev Elder Kolia Fiu Kolia and my late mother Sootuli Kolia, thank you for your love and care, your prayers and support, and for your choice to migrate from Samoa to Australia that allowed for the perspectives that gave rise to this reading. I also thank my late mother-in-law Seila Leuluai for her love and prayers.

Last but not least, to my dear wife Ta'alefili Tanaria and my precious son Elichai Tupu, thank you both for your belief, love, patience, and for struggling *with* me. I dedicate this work, with the utmost love, to you both.

Abbreviations

AB	Anchor Bible
ABS	Archeology and Biblical Studies
AIL	Ancient Israel and Its Literature
BASOR	*Bulletin of the American Schools of Oriental Research*
BBRSup	Bulletin for Biblical Research Supplements
BETL	Bibliotheca Ephemeridum Theologicarum Lovaniensium
Bib	*Biblica*
BibInt	*Biblical Interpretation*
BN	*Biblische Notizen*
BN-NF	*Biblische Notizen – Neue Folge*
BWANT	Beiträge zur Wissenschaft vom Alten und Neuen Testament
CBQ	*Catholic Biblical Quarterly*
CurBR	*Currents in Biblical Research*
CurBS	*Currents in Research: Biblical Studies*
ExpTim	*Expository Times*
FAT	Forschungen zum Alten Testament
FRLANT	Forschungen zur Religion und Literatur des Alten und Neuen Testaments
HS	*Hebrew Studies*
IVBS	International Voices in Biblical Studies
JBL	*Journal of Biblical Literature*
JBRec	*Journal of the Bible and Its Reception*
JPS	Jewish Publication Society
JSOT	*Journal for the Study of the Old Testament*
JSOTSup	Journal for the Study of the Old Testament Supplement Series
KAT	Kommentar zum Alten Testament
LAI	Library of Ancient Israel
LBS	Library of Biblical Studies
LHBOTS	Library of Hebrew Bible/Old Testament Studies
m.	mishnah
MT	Masoretic Text (of the Hebrew Bible)

NCB	New Century Bible
NIB	*New Interpreter's Bible*
NICOT	New International Commentary on the Old Testament
NRSV	New Revised Standard Version
OTE	*Old Testament Essays*
OTL	Old Testament Library
OTM	Old Testament Message
OtSt	Oudtestamentische Studiën
PzB	*Protokolle zur Bibel*
SBLDS	Society of Biblical Literature Dissertation Series
SBLSP	Society of Biblical Literature Seminar Papers
SBLSymS	Society of Biblical Literature Symposium Series
ScrHier	Scripta Hierosolymitana
SEA	*Svensk Exegetisk Årsbok*
SemeiaSt	Semeia Studies
TOTC	Tyndale Old Testament Commentaries
VT	*Vetus Tesatementum*
VTSup	Supplements to Vetus Testamentum
WAWSup	Writings from the Ancient World Supplement
WBC	Word Biblical Commentary
WMANT	Wissenschaftliche Monographien zum Alten und Neuen Testament
ZAW	*Zeitschrift für die alttestamentliche Wissenschaft*

Introduction

The prominence of "scepticism" in the book of Ecclesiastes is considered a feature of ancient Israelite wisdom traditions. Yet, it seems that attitudes of scepticism are not unique to the book, as similar notions of suspicion can be found throughout the rest of the Hebrew Bible.[1]

Qohelet,[2] the protagonist of the book, reveals his pessimism and disdain towards a variety of concepts, such as toiling (for example, Eccl 1:3; 2:18–23), wealth (e.g., 5:8–20), moral order (e.g., 8:14), and even wisdom itself, particularly the conventional form espoused in Proverbs. However, the form of scepticism in the book of Ecclesiastes is peculiar, and scholars have often been distracted by this peculiarity—to the extent that studies have not often considered how this voice of critique finds resonance with other forms of scepticism elsewhere in the Hebrew Bible. If Ecclesiastes were part of a walled-off genre of wisdom literature, then why does Qohelet's voice reflect the position of scepticism found in other books in the Hebrew Bible?

I propose an alternative way of considering the scepticism in Ecclesiastes—in relation to other forms found in legal, narrative, prophetic, and sapiential genres. What might connect these diverse strands of scepticism? Is there a common thread that might help illuminate Qohelet's own voice of dissonance?

The genre classification of Ecclesiastes as "wisdom," and in particular as a compendium of antithetical responses towards conventional wisdom and traditions, comes into question. Contemporary scholarship has often recognised the sapiential character of Ecclesiastes, and therefore classed it as part of a separate wisdom tradition within the Hebrew Bible.[3] Yet the idea of a distinct genre of wisdom was not an ancient phenomenon but "according to common accounts,

---

[1] All biblical references are from the NRSV unless otherwise stated.
[2] Qohelet is the Hebrew name of the book of Ecclesiastes, which comes from the Hebrew word קהל ("to assemble") as though the author is speaking in front of an assembly. The author of Ecclesiastes is referred to as Qohelet (with variant spellings among scholars) in modern scholarship and will be referred to as such throughout the remainder of this book.
[3] Choon-Leong Seow, *Ecclesiastes: A New Translation with Introduction and Commentary*, AB 18C (New Haven: Yale University Press, 1997), 67.

wisdom developed as a distinct subject with a corresponding corpus in the Hebrew Bible soon after the turn of the twentieth century."[4] James Crenshaw argues that Johannes Meinhold, in his book *Die Weisheit Israels in Spruch, Sage und Dichtung* of 1908, was the first to acknowledge a separate wisdom category.[5] Crenshaw, a strong advocate for the distinction of wisdom as a literary genre, argues that a professional class of sages were responsible for the production of Hebrew Wisdom literature.[6] Quoting Jer 18:18, Crenshaw refers to three classes of leaders, priests, prophets and sages. The priests give instruction (תורה), the prophets proclaim the divine word (דבר) while the sages give counsel (עצה).[7] Indeed, this separation of three classes distinguishes each as a separate tradition from the other.

Hermann Gunkel perhaps inspired Crenshaw, with the latter also quoting Jer 18:18 in reference to the sages, considering them as a social group which resulted in the emergence of the wisdom genre. Gunkel imagines that "the sages who practiced such wisdom were long-bearded men who sat together in open squares or in the gates (Prov. 1.20–21) exchanging the sayings they learned in their youth, while the young were to listen and to learn wisdom."[8] The effect of this distinction is reflected in "the view that Hebrew wisdom literature represents a worldview, tradition, and movement distinct from those of the priests and prophets and that it provides an alternative to Yahwism, that it is anti-revelatory."[9]

This view is rejected by Mark Sneed who argues that "the same authors who composed the wisdom literature are also responsible for the composition and/or preservation of other types of literature."[10] In other words, these authors were not "particularistic" but "studied and taught all the traditions, types of literature, and genres to their students." Sneed's preference therefore is for wisdom to be viewed as complementary to the rest of the Hebrew Bible and not a separate tradition.

Similarly, Will Kynes takes issue with wisdom as a separate tradition, and argues that the texts normally associated with wisdom are "not 'Wisdom Literature' in any definitive, categorical sense that would justify the assumption that

---

[4] Will Kynes, "The Modern Scholarly Wisdom Tradition and the Threat of Pan-Sapientialism: A Case Report," in *Was There a Wisdom Tradition? New Prospects in Israelite Wisdom Studies*, ed. Mark R. Sneed, AIL 23 (Atlanta: SBL Press, 2015), 12.
[5] James L. Crenshaw, "Prolegomenon," in *Studies in Ancient Israelite Wisdom*, ed. James L. Crenshaw, LBS (New York: Ktav, 1976), 3.
[6] James L. Crenshaw, *Old Testament Wisdom: An Introduction*, 3rd ed. (Louisville: Westminster John Knox, 2010), 24–25.
[7] Crenshaw, *Old Testament Wisdom*, 24.
[8] Hermann Gunkel, "The Literature of Ancient Israel," in *Relating to the Text: Interdisciplinary and Form-Critical Insights on the Bible*, ed. Timothy J. Sandoval and Carleen Mandolfo, JSOTSup 384 (London: T&T Clark International, 2003), 69–70. Also see Michael V. Fox, *Qohelet and His Contradictions*, JSOTSupp (Sheffield: Almond, 1989).
[9] Mark R. Sneed, "Is the 'Wisdom Tradition' a Tradition?," *CBQ* 73 (2011): 53–54.
[10] Sneed, "Is the "Wisdom Tradition," 54.

they were composed in a separate school with a distinctive theology that requires its own introductions, specialists, courses or conference sections."[11] Rather, Kynes believes that a new approach to genre that "reads texts, not in exclusive categories, but in multiple overlapping groupings ... will offer a more nuanced understanding of the so-called Wisdom texts' place in the intricated intertextual network of the canon and beyond."[12]

Further to the question of genre, is the topic of scepticism, as already indicated. What makes Ecclesiastes so distinctive as a sceptical text? I will argue that the answer to this question relates to the social location of the literature.

To address the problem of genre and to investigate the location of Qohelet's scepticism, I will answer these questions within a methodological framework that might be called "intertextuality"—in two senses. The first sense is a "hard" intertextuality which John Barton identifies with a theoretical approach that looks at the relationship between texts in general, quite regardless of the details of historical influences or interactions. The latter is the second sense—"soft" intertextuality.[13] I will utilise hard intertextuality to describe the potential relevance of diaspora theory for reading Ecclesiastes. Ultimately, I will use my Australian-Samoan background as a cultural text to engage with Ecclesiastes, to further underscore the diasporic implications from a soft intertextual reading. Accordingly, the book will take shape in the following format:

In chapter 1, I begin with a discussion of my reading position which feeds into a hermeneutic based on a Samoan proverb "*Maota Tau Ave*" ("the House that is Carried"). In this chapter, I will explain how *Maota Tau Ave* acts as a mandate for Samoan migration, with a focus on the movements of Samoans to their southwestern neighbours, Australia and New Zealand. This will highlight the tensions Samoan migrants experience with the application and relevance of Samoan cultural and religious traditions in foreign lands.

In chapter 2, I discuss a Pasifika way of interrogation and conversation known as *talanoa* as a method for reading, in conversation with another form of interrogation: intertextuality. For this discussion, I analyse the development between the original theoretical focus, as purported by Julia Kristeva, which mostly prescribed intertextuality as a way of looking at the relationship between texts, to how biblical scholars had considered its practical use as a way of analysing texts, to draw out historical and hermeneutical insights.

To consider the hermeneutical questions of this intertextual enterprise, I propose a (re)reading from a diasporic perspective, using my background as an

---

[11] Will Kynes, "The 'Wisdom Literature' Category: An Obituary," *The Journal of Theological Studies* 69 (2018): 24.
[12] Kynes, "'Wisdom Literature' Category," 1.
[13] I will explain John Barton's concept of "hard intertextuality" in more detail later. Also see John Barton, "*Déjà Lu:* Intertextuality, Method or Theory?," in *Reading Job Intertextually*, ed. Katharine Dell and Will Kynes, LHBOTS 574 (New York: Bloomsbury, 2013), 10.

Australian-born Samoan. Using the intertextual framework as well as my diasporic background, I will construct a hermeneutic of *Maota Tau Ave* to reread the text; a hermeneutic that brings *Maota Tau Ave* into focus to articulate the migration of Samoans to other villages and other lands, as though they are carrying their *maota* (house) with them to these lands. Thus, the motivation behind a *Maota Tau Ave* reading is to examine the possibility that Qohelet's voice of dissonance and defiance reflects a diasporic social location. Specifically, I ask the question of whether Qohelet was a member of the diaspora, who carried his *maota* (house) from homeland into a foreign land. Could the diaspora be where Qohelet voices his frustration and scepticism? This possibility has been identified tentatively in previous research[14] and this study will build a comprehensive case.

Moving forward from the Samoan discussion of *maota* (house) in chapter 1, I juxtapose that with the ancient Israelite concept of בית (house), as depicted in the Hebrew Bible, which will be explored in chapter 3. Although the concept is not mentioned explicitly in Ecclesiastes, I investigate possible assumptions in the book of a similar functional notion of carrying one's house in diaspora. To clarify, I survey the term בית in the Hebrew Bible in order to highlight its various nuances. For example, I will take up the common scholarly hypothesis that the monarchic concept of the "father's house" was modified under the conditions of exile.

The implications drawn from considering an exilic context for Qohelet's בית will be explored in chapter 4 by placing Qohelet in conversation with Diaspora Studies, through the works of Stuart Hall, Edward Said, Homi Bhabha, Frantz Fanon, Paul Gilroy, James Clifford, and Gayatri Spivak. Subsequently, I will analyse how diaspora theory had been applied to (re)read the biblical text through the works of Daniel L. Smith-Christopher, Fernando Segovia, and Gale A. Yee. This will allow us to see intersections between the experience of diasporic peoples with the lives of migrant biblical characters, on the way to considering a possible diasporic location for Qohelet.

Using the methodological framework formulated in the previous chapters, chapters 5 to 7 will include an intertextual talanoa between Ecclesiastes and other texts in the Hebrew Bible which resonate with a diasporic/exilic experience. Specifically, the discussion analyses three key themes: kingship, the presence of the divine in the temple, and moral order.

In chapter 5, I will review the issue of kingship in Ecclesiastes, in particular, the attitudes of scepticism towards kingship in dialogue with similar reactions of doubt towards kingship and leadership in other parts of the Hebrew Bible.

In chapter 6, I evaluate how the concept of divine presence in the temple receives scrutiny from Qohelet. To reflect on the implications of the scepticism

---

[14] Daniel L. Smith-Christopher who suggests that Ecclesiastes "is literature that makes the most 'sense' when read in the context of the Diaspora," in *A Biblical Theology of Exile, Overtures to Biblical Theology* (Minneapolis: Fortress, 2002), 168. Also see Stuart Weeks, *Ecclesiastes and Scepticism* (New York: T&T Clark International, 2012), 7.

Introduction   5

towards this concept, I bring Qohelet into conversation with other instances of critique of the divine presence found throughout the Hebrew Bible. For example, I look at the aetiology of Bet-El in Genesis, and the possible attitudes of scepticism towards Bethel as the place (מקום) of God's presence. Secondly, the discussion will illuminate the attitudes towards vows in Deut 23:22–24 [MT], raising the question whether a delay in fulfilling a vow would be problematic when living at a great distance from the Yahwist Temples. Finally, the analysis will look at the Departing Glory of God in Ezek 10. In particular, I discuss Ezekiel's shift from temple practice to the application of ethics for an exilic context as a way of considering God's presence from a diasporic perspective.

In chapter 7, I look at scepticism towards moral order. The question of moral order and moral chaos is troubling for those in diasporic and exilic conditions. From this standpoint, a review of such instances of moral order/chaos in the Hebrew Bible is warranted. First, I consider the unjust acts of Joseph's brothers. I note the problem that the brothers do not receive their just desserts as a result of their treatment of Joseph. Given the migrant nature of the story, the ethical dilemma may be understood from a diasporic perspective. Second, in further reckoning of moral order under exilic conditions, I extend the talanoa to an analysis of Ps 14. I will explore the attitude of the Psalmist in responding to the statement אין אלהים ("There is no God") and consider whether it points to a theological dilemma in relation to the delay of divine judgment on immoral behaviour. Finally, the talanoa will move to the Ninevites and Jonah, reimagined from a diasporic perspective. Bearing in mind that Jonah is an outsider—a "migrant"—does his final complaint articulate the moral injustices faced by those outside of the homeland? Ultimately, the aim of these intertextual readings is to provide further insight into Qohelet's critique of moral order—not considered as a unique critique, but one that may be shared in some ways with other genres and traditions.

In the final chapter, I will draw out further implications for Qohelet's location by reading intertextually using my own cultural texts as intertexts. In this chapter, I extend the implications drawn from previous chapters to reread Ecclesiastes from a diasporic Australian Samoan perspective. The experience of being a second-generation Australian-Samoan may have significant implications for understanding Qohelet. How might this affect the ability of diasporic people to fit their *maota* onto new lands? Or does Qohelet's scepticism illuminate the vanity of such practices, as well as the vanity of trying to fit in? Answering these questions, conversely, may also provide clues for determining where Ecclesiastes sits within the Hebrew Bible. Is Ecclesiastes a wisdom text? Is there a separate wisdom tradition? Or is Ecclesiastes better understood as a dissonant voice from afar, in conversation with the rest of the Hebrew Bible?

The ripples of this talanoa will help us reread and reimagine Ecclesiastes from an alternative (alter-native?) perspective. In terms of methodology, this book seeks to provide further dimensions of intertextuality and its application to biblical studies. From an historical point of view, a focus on the social conditions of

Qohelet may provide additional insight in conversation with social scientific scholarship. From a hermeneutical standpoint, the possibility of Qohelet voicing his concerns from outside Jerusalem provides room for reflection. Ultimately, we may be inclined to consider a diasporic understanding of scepticism in the Hebrew Bible, while reviewing the place of wisdom in the biblical canon.

1. Maota Tau Ave

An intriguing aspect of the book of Ecclesiastes is its unconventional attitude towards wisdom, compared to the conventional forms in other wisdom books such as Proverbs and Ben Sira. Even though we find less focus on Mosaic law in wisdom texts, there was nevertheless a broadly held agreement between Torah and wisdom traditions that good behaviour yields blessing, and wickedness brings affliction. It is a wonder, then, that in spite of these prominent ideals, there is a voice in the canon that stands in defiance. Where did this voice come from, and how did it manage to secure a place in the Hebrew canon? This is a key question for this study, which will explore the socio-historical context of Qohelet.

Contexts

Such a pessimistic voice among the priestly elite seems inconceivable. Could wisdom circles stretch to such extremes? Or could it be the voice of someone living in the Jewish diaspora who has found it difficult to accept the wisdom of the homeland, while acculturating in the host-land? This last question opens up the possibility of visualizing a diasporic setting for Qohelet.

Modern scholarship continues to grapple with the issue of Qohelet's defiant voice, including prominent modern figures such as James Crenshaw, R. Norman Whybray, Roland E. Murphy, Michael V. Fox and Choon-Leong Seow. They have been influential in trying to decipher the enigma of Qohelet's voice.

In his book *Ecclesiastes* (1987), Crenshaw views Qohelet as a pessimist and a sceptic.[1] To Crenshaw, the main theme of הבל is nothing more than a metaphor for emptiness or nothingness, a view that I will argue against. In *Harper's Bible Commentary* (1988), Crenshaw concludes that chapter 12, with its conventional tone, is a "polemical corrective" as though the main voice of Qohelet had been

---

[1] James L. Crenshaw, *Ecclesiastes: A Commentary*, OTL (Philadelphia: Fortress, 1987).

"corrected" to correlate with conventional thinking, and this might help to explain its inclusion in the Hebrew canon.[2]

Whybray wrote that the voice of Qohelet was an extension of "earlier doubts about the purposes of God and dissatisfaction about the human condition."[3] Like Crenshaw, it was evident to Whybray that there was a clear voice of disgruntlement against conventional accounts of toil and wealth.

Murphy claims that Qohelet had an "ambivalent attitude towards wisdom."[4] He argues that Qohelet refused to accept a simplified understanding of life, but acknowledged the enigma between the pleasure of life and the misery of death. For Murphy, "Life is much more complicated than the sages made it out to be."[5]

Seow, who produced an extensive commentary on Ecclesiastes in the Anchor Bible series (1997), argues that Qohelet "does not mean that everything is meaningless or insignificant, but that everything is beyond human apprehension and comprehension."[6] This is a statement that places divine wisdom out of reach of human reasoning. Perhaps this sounds more like resignation than defiance, however, it still renders humanity's position precarious.

Fox, a Jewish rabbi, was the first scholar to claim that Ecclesiastes has two voices. At first glance, this might seem to be a similar view to Crenshaw, who states that Ecclesiastes is the work of more than one author. However, for Fox, the voices are not a consequence of redaction in any conventional sense. Rather, as he argues in his JPS commentary on Ecclesiastes, the first voice is Qohelet in the first person, while the second is a frame narrator who is speaking *about* Qohelet.[7] Redaction is not a hidden attribute of the text, but a more explicit feature of the literary form of later reception.

These scholars provide a basis for which to consider another element of the defiant voice. I put forward an alternative hypothesis: What if the views provided by Qohelet in the core of his writings reflect attitudes found in the Jewish diaspora? What if the pessimistic outlook towards life is reminiscent of the grumblings of a people in exile?

In this study, I propose a diasporic reading of Ecclesiastes that arises from the experience of Samoans living in diaspora. I belong to the diaspora who, as Fernando Segovia writes, are a "growing segment of people from the Third World who are forced to live—for whatever reason, though usually involving a

---

[2] James L. Crenshaw, "Ecclesiastes," in *Harper's Bible Commentary*, ed. J. Crenshaw and J. Willis (San Francisco: Harper & Row, 1988), 518.
[3] R. N. Whybray, *Ecclesiastes*, OTG (Sheffield: Sheffield Academic, 1989), 60.
[4] Roland E. Murphy, *Ecclesiastes*, WBC 23A (Dallas: Word, 1992), lxiii.
[5] Murphy, *Ecclesiastes*, lxiii.
[6] Seow, *Ecclesiastes*, 59.
[7] Michael V. Fox, *Ecclesiastes: The Traditional Hebrew Text with the New JPS Translation Commentary*, The JPS Bible Commentary (Philadelphia: The Jewish Publication Society, 2004). See also Fox, *Qohelet and His Contradictions*, 311–12.

combination of sociopolitical and socioeconomic factors—in the First World."[8] For years, Samoans have left their homeland in search for better opportunities for work and education in New Zealand. From there, they dispersed into Australia, from suburb to suburb, state to state, in search of a better life. With the better lifestyle came a completely different experience—one where the values and insights of that different lifestyle came into conflict with the ethno-cultural values of the homeland.

The question that continues to challenge Samoans in the diaspora is whether or not they should maintain the culture and customs of the homeland. As Samoans continue to exist as an ethnic group in a multi-ethnic society like Australia, the relevance of the Samoan culture comes into question. Should they still uphold the *faa-Samoa*?[9]

From this perspective, I enter the scholarly debate regarding Qohelet's voice by arguing that his voice might resonate with a people detached from their homeland and dispersed into a foreign land. Most scholars agree with a Persian or Hellenistic date for Ecclesiastes and Stuart Weeks argues, "an origin in the diaspora cannot be excluded."[10] A key question within the inquiry is whether or not the pessimistic and defiant tone of Qohelet arises not just from frustration with Israelite Wisdom and Deuteronomic formulae, but also from an ambivalent acceptance of the inherited Israelite wisdom of the new land.

I bring into the discussion the concept of *Maota Tau Ave*. This concept arises from a well-known Samoan proverb, which literally means "the house that is carried." This proverb acts as a motto for Samoans wherever they go, whether they go to the next village, to the next island, or to another country and context altogether. The *maota* (house) embodies the Samoan's identity: their *aganu'u* (culture), their *suafa* (chiefly titles), their *tu ma aga* (customs), their *pa'ia* (dignitaries), their *gagana* (language), and their *'āiga* (kinship). So wherever a Samoan journeys, they take these things with them because these are the roots of their identity.

Modern Australia is a multicultural society, and as such, Samoans are granted a space to carry their *maota*. But like Qohelet, Samoan wisdom, as exemplified in the *faa-Samoa*, conflicts with *Australian norms* (*faa* Australian), in a way that leads second and third generation Australian Samoans to question the validity of upholding the ethno-cultural *faa-Samoa* in an Australian context where no single ethno-culture is dominant.

---

[8] Fernando Segovia, "Toward a Hermeneutics of the Diaspora: A Hermeneutics of Otherness and Engagement," in *Social Location and Biblical Interpretation in Global Perspective*, vol. 2 of *Reading from This Place*, ed. Fernando Segovia and Mary Ann Tolbert (Minneapolis: Fortress, 1995), 60.
[9] The *Faa-Samoa* (lit. "the Samoan way") is the name given to the Samoan culture, which encompasses the traditions, customs, and wisdom of the Samoan people.
[10] Weeks, *Ecclesiastes and Scepticism*, 7.

Ecclesiastes reflects a similar tension, one that exhibits contradictions between the established order and a new understanding/ new context.[11] In rereading Ecclesiastes, I use my experience as a framework for reading wisdom. In particular, I use the conflict between Samoans trying to uphold wisdom and those who choose to neglect the relevance of *faa-Samoa* in the Australian context.

Hence, the overall methodology is grounded in postcolonial theory and decolonial thought and enhanced by sociohistorical interrogation. Such an approach will allow me to provide a distinctive and alternative understanding of the voice of Qohelet, in dialogue with earlier contributions to the scholarly debate.

I named this chapter *Maota Tau Ave*, and I will expand on what it means later on in this chapter, but in brief, it refers to the Samoan mandate instituted upon Samoans to never forget their native identity as they migrate into new lands.[12] It is relevant for Samoans living in diaspora communities in Australia, New Zealand, and the United States, as Samoans have sought to maintain their culture and language abroad. As I will be using *Maota Tau Ave* as a hermeneutical lens for (re)reading Ecclesiastes, it is important that I discuss the concept of *Maota Tau Ave* outlining its significance for Samoan diaspora communities.

In this chapter therefore, I will discuss briefly what is meant by the term "diaspora" before embarking on a discussion of *Maota Tau Ave* and arguing that *Maota Tau Ave* can reimagine the notion of diaspora, particularly from an Australian-Samoan perspective.

Diaspora

The term *diaspora* comes from the Greek word διασπορά which is defined as "the region or area in which persons have been scattered (particularly a reference to the nation of Israel which had been scattered throughout the ancient world.)"[13] The word was first used in the Septuagint in Deut 28:25, when referring to the exiled Israelite community. The term "diaspora" was later applied to Jewish exilic communities which took form as a result of the Assyrian invasion of the Northern Kingdom (Israel) in 722 BCE and the Babylonian invasion of the Southern Kingdom (Judah) in 586 BCE.

The depiction of the Jewish diasporic communities is an intriguing discourse in the Old Testament. Erich S. Gruen argues that there "Two potent and recurrent

---

[11] Cf. Fox, *Qohelet and His Contradictions*, 86.
[12] Research on the Hebrew "house" will be discussed in chapter 3, notably Cynthia Chapman's work: Cynthia R. Chapman, *The House of the Mother: The Social Roles of Maternal Kin in Biblical Hebrew Narrative and Poetry* (New Haven: Yale University Press, 2016).
[13] Louw and Nida, *Greek-English Lexicon*, 199.

images, with quite distinct messages, dominate the discourse on this subject."[14] Gruen highlights these two distinct images through Psalms and Jeremiah.

FORCED DIASPORA

Specifically, Ps 137 alludes to the Babylonian exile as a forced diaspora characterized by "melancholy reverie" that "signals the lament of the exile crushed by enforced removal, incapable or unwilling to make peace with an alien environment, and pining away for Palestine as the authentic soul of his being."[15]

The term "diaspora" had been expanded by William Safran, who states that the term in recent times refers to "metaphoric designations for several categories of people—expatriates, expellees, political refugees, alien residents, immigrants, and ethnic and racial minorities *tout court*."[16] With a similar nuance to its use in the Septuagint, Safran implies that diaspora pertains to a sense of displacement and forced removal from their native homelands. This provides a platform for indifferent attitudes, particularly those of scepticism and pessimism, which are often associated with the philosophy of Ecclesiastes.

The connection between a diasporic context and such perspectives is not a new discovery, yet surprisingly, such a connection has not been emphasised by scholars, and in fact, it has largely been ignored. I contend that different diasporic attitudes evident in Ecclesiastes could help to explain the ambiguities of the book. I wish to highlight that Ecclesiastes resonates with the ambiguity of diaspora. Many nuances can spring forth from the concept of diaspora, not just displacement and forced removal.

VOLUNTARY DIASPORA

Ironically, Gruen states that Jeremiah portrays the exile as a voluntary settlement. At the very least, we may concede that Jeremiah projects the possibility of choice. In Jer 29 verses 5 and 7, the prophet says: "Build houses, settle down; plant gardens and eat what they produce.... Work for the good of the city to which I have exiled you, since on its welfare yours depends."[17] The emphasis on agency here is a far cry from the sorrow of Ps 137, highlighting a different character of the exile. Here in Jeremiah, "the prophet counsels adjustment and accommodation, a recipe for successful diaspora existence—an identification of Jewish interests with those of the community at large."[18]

---

[14] Erich S. Gruen, *Diaspora: Jews Amidst Greeks and Romans* (Cambridge, MA: Harvard University Press, 2002), 4.
[15] Gruen, *Diaspora*, 4–5.
[16] William Safran, "Diasporas in Modern Societies: Myths of Homeland and Return," *Diaspora: A Journal of Transnational Studies* 1 (1991): 83.
[17] Gruen, *Diaspora*, 4. Also see Numerator Ofo'ia who discusses migrant implications from a Samoan perspective in "Revisiting the Babylonian Exile in Jeremiah 29:1–14: A Samoan La-tō Reading Using an Oceanic Hermeneutic," MTh Thesis, University of Otago 2017, 99.
[18] Gruen, *Diaspora*, 5.

Scholars such as Fernando Segovia and Mary Ann Tolbert have also argued that diaspora communities include people that have migrated willingly to other countries in mass numbers, due to the pull of economic benefits and well-being.[19] Naturally, low income earners desire to be economically stable, and would seek this from elsewhere, leading to a pattern of migration from third-world to first-world.[20] Samoa falls into this category, as Samoans migrate to "first world" countries such as the United States, New Zealand and Australia. This pattern of migration continues today. I will focus mainly on the movement of Samoans to Australia although most of the literature on Samoan migration centres on the American and New Zealand diasporas.

SAMOAN MIGRATION

According to Felise Va'a, "Samoans have always wondered about what the rest of the world looked like."[21] Encounters with European traders and sailors piqued the interest of Samoans as they saw "the advantages in possessing the Europeans' goods."[22] Prior to the mass migrations of the early 1950s, which proceeded firstly from American Samoa, migration was largely an individual affair.

In Samoan history, the first known overseas traveller was Sio Vili, who travelled to Australia and other neighbouring Pacific islands on a whaling ship in the 1820s.[23] He returned to Samoa, bringing back, amongst other things, the Sio Vili cult, which was a distorted form of Christianity that Vili improvised from what he had learnt whilst travelling. Malama Meleisea notes that Jesus Christ was referred to by Vili as "'Seesah Elaisah' (a mispronunciation of Jesus Christ)."[24]

The next type of traveller according to Va'a was the theological scholar. In the 1860s and later, Catholic and Methodist theological students conducted their studies for advanced ministry in Australia, and in the French territory of Wallis and Futuna.[25] Also during this time, graduates of Malua Theological College, under the London Missionary Society, were sent to Sydney, Australia to prepare them for missionary work in the Torres Strait Islands and Papua New Guinea.[26]

During the World Wars in the first half of the twentieth century, the islands of Samoa were divided between the United States and Great Britain. The eastern islands consisting of Tutuila and Manu'a were taken over by the Americans, while

---

[19] Segovia, "Towards a Hermeneutics," 60.
[20] Segovia, "Towards a Hermeneutics," 60.
[21] Unasa L. F. Va'a, "Searching for the Good Life: Samoan International Migration" (paper presented at the Department of Anthropology Colloquium, University of Hawaii, Honolulu, 27 January, 2005), 1.
[22] Va'a, "Searching for the Good Life," 5.
[23] Malama Meleisea, *Lagaga: A Short History of Western Samoa* (Suva, Fiji: University of South Pacific, 1987), 52.
[24] Meleisea, *Lagaga*, 52.
[25] Va'a, "Searching for the Good Life," 3.
[26] Va'a, "Searching for the Good Life," 3.

the western islands consisting of Savaii, Upolu, Manono, and Apolima were colonised by the British. New Zealand was assigned as a British Mandate and became responsible for the western islands. Subsequently, the eastern islands were renamed "American Samoa" while the western islands became "Western Samoa."[27] The migration trend reflect this divide, as migrants from American Samoan would head for America (mainland and Hawaii), while migrants from Western Samoa would journey to Commonwealth nations New Zealand and Australia.

Consequently, another wave of migrants emerged in the early decades of the twentieth century, such as a group of Mormon missionaries who went to the dedication of the Hawaiian temple in 1919, and prisoners who were sent during the colonial period to serve jail time in Hawaii.[28] A large number from these groups chose to settle in these countries for the remainder of their lives after their respective terms had been served.[29] Also, Samoans who married colonial officers with their half-caste children travelled to the homes of their colonial spouses in Germany, United States and New Zealand.[30]

While the classes of people migrating differed, there was a common thread among these groups. The attraction of the "good life" which existed in European contexts highlighted the financial, political and social drawbacks in Samoa. The intrigue and curiosity may have lured these early Samoans to move away from home, but the distinction between home and the new land prompted them to stay. As such, the early history of Samoan migration led to a sustained pattern of migration which continues to this day.

SAMOAN DIASPORA IN NEW ZEALAND

The majority of Samoans in Australia emigrated from New Zealand. It is important therefore to point out that any conversation regarding Samoan migration to Australia should always reference, in the first instance, this movement of Samoan people to New Zealand.

The mass migration of Samoans to New Zealand commenced around the end of World War II from the 1940s to the 1950s.[31] Ian Fairbairn notes that the New Zealand census in 1956 listed persons born in Western Samoa at 2,995 which does not sound significant, until Fairburn concludes that the figure "meant that one out of every 30 persons born in Western Samoa was residing in New Zealand."[32] The growth rate from the end of World War II to the 1956 census was significant and pointed towards a piqued interest in what New Zealand had to offer. This pattern

---

[27] In 1997, Western Samoa was renamed "The Independent State of Samoa" or simply, "Samoa."
[28] Va'a, "Searching for the Good Life," 4.
[29] Va'a, "Searching for the Good Life," 4.
[30] Va'a, "Searching for the Good Life," 4.
[31] Ian Fairbairn, "Samoan Migration to New Zealand: The General Background and Some Economic Implications for Samoa," *The Journal of the Polynesian Society* 70.1 (1961): 19.
[32] Fairbairn, "Samoan Migration," 19.

of migration is even more intriguing given that it coincided with Samoa becoming an independent state in 1962. The irony of this is that after the efforts of seeking independence from British and New Zealand rule, when it was finally achieved, the exodus of Samoans began.

Yet perhaps the exodus was never intended to be a permanent one. Fairburn notes that "personal conversations with many of these 'new arrivals' leave the impression that the motive to return to Samoa after a temporary stay in New Zealand is very strong."[33] This sense of return is due mainly to the strong ties to family in Samoa. The evidence of this as Fairburn discovered lay in the "regularity and size of total remittances" transferred to family in Samoa.[34] This is still very much the sentiment to this day for migrants from Samoa. Some return, though a large number never remigrate back to Samoa to live. Those who do not return, plant their *maota* on New Zealand land.

Perhaps the most glaring changes are the economic and social implications of settling in New Zealand. Through migration, a new economic attitude evolved from the period of early European contact as Samoans abroad understood the importance of a cash economy and the benefits it had for the *'āiga* back home. From a sociological point of view, Samoans in New Zealand were now having to adapt to a new setting as their settlement became a permanent phenomenon.

The process of adapting had its issues. A. D. Trlin articulates through a series of interviews the negative attitude New Zealanders had towards Samoan migrants in the city of Auckland, who were not deemed tobe ideal neighbours and were found to be "noisy" and of "bad character."[35] The issue of acceptance was a consistent problem in the early years of Samoan mass migration, that is still faced, perhaps with less vigour yet greater subtlety, by Samoan migrants today.[36] In addition, Cluny Macpherson notes the effect that migration had on the Samoan worldview, particularly from an economic point of view. The new economic thinking had transpired to a questioning of the *faa-Samoa* and its ideologies, as in some instances, money had become more important than kinship.[37] This thinking, as Macpherson argues, had affected village life in Samoa:

> A neighbor was complaining to a group of friends, many of whom had returned from abroad, about the difficulties and costs she had faced in getting some repairs done to her house. She pointed out that in the 'old days' one could ask relations to come and do the work. As long, she noted, as you fed them and thanked them

---

[33] Fairbairn, "Samoan Migration," 23.
[34] Fairbairn, "Samoan Migration," 25.
[35] A. D. Trlin, "Attitudes Towards West Samoan Immigrants in Auckland, New Zealand," *The Australian Quarterly* 44.3 (1972): 51.
[36] Cf. Melani Anae, "O A'u/I—My Identity Journey," in *Making Our Place: Growing up Pi in New Zealand*, ed. Peggy Fairbairn-Dunlop and Gabrielle Sisifo Makisi (Palmerston North: Dunmore, 2003).
[37] Cluny Macpherson, and La'avasa Macpherson, *The Warm Winds of Change: Globalisation in Contemporary Sāmoa* (Auckland: Auckland University Press, 2009), 99.

appropriately, the work was done and everyone was happy. When those who had helped you needed assistance, you went and helped them in turn. That was the essence of fa'asāmoa, the Sāmoan way. Now, she noted, even kin wanted to be paid for their work and fed and thanked. The neighbour concluded that, in the 45 years she had been away from Sāmoa, people had come to see the world differently. People thought more and more about money and less and less about their obligations as kin. Money, she speculated, was now becoming more important than kinship in Sāmoa.[38]

Such attitudes were born in the diaspora. Exposure to new ideas, new cultures and a new context led to new attitudes of scepticism and perhaps reinterpretations of the *faa-Samoa* and Samoan cultural and religious ideologies. New Zealand offered more than economic benefits for their *aiga* and homeland, but it also provided a platform from which Samoans could self-reflect regarding their own cultural and religious identity. As Samoans took advantage of the new cash economy, the desire grew for new opportunities. Samoans, since the end of WWII but especially during the 1960s and 1970s, had been limited to unskilled labour and blue-collar work. But as the years progressed, they became settled and they and their children availed themselves of the New Zealand education system. With this, Samoans were now employed in skilled labour and presented with better job prospects. As Macpherson notes:

> Fifty years ago that donor roll included the names of about ten people who were working in factories in Auckland, Wellington and Pagopago. Now, the roll includes the names of soldiers and security contractors in Iraq, teachers in Denmark, postgraduate students in London, nurses in Edinburgh, professional rugby players in Wales, a professional gridiron player in California, customs officers in Melbourne, restaurateurs in Sydney, factory workers in Auckland, taxi drivers in Wellington, fruit-pickers in Hastings, and fishermen and gold miners in Fiji.[39]

The opportunities for greater economic benefits were diverse, and it was not long before Samoans took interest in the opportunities in Australia. Australia possesses much tighter immigration laws, but with New Zealand citizenship granted, it opened up a gateway for Samoans to move across the Tasman.

SAMOAN DIASPORA IN AUSTRALIA

Va'a comments that "studies on Samoan migration in Australia are few, no doubt because Samoans did not migrate there on a large scale until the 1980s."[40] The studies conducted since the 1980s had been focused on certain cities where there

---

[38] Macpherson, and Macpherson, *Warm Winds of Change*, 99.
[39] Macpherson, and Macpherson, *Warm Winds of Change*, 72.
[40] Felise Va'a, *Saili Matagi: Samoan Migrants in Australia* (Fiji: ISP, 2001), 39.

was a concentration of Samoans in residence. Alex Burns and Suzanne Morton[41] conducted a study on Samoans living in Newcastle in New South Wales, while John Connell and Grant McCall,[42] with a much broader focus on Pacific Island migrants including Samoans, focused on Blacktown, west of Sydney. Va'a focuses on the Canterbury-Bankstown area in Sydney. It must be noted that Va'a's study is the most comprehensive of the three studies given that it was his doctoral work, now turned into a book.

All three of these studies have been conducted in specific areas of New South Wales and therefore do not include Samoan diasporas that had existed in other parts. They do not account for Samoan settlements during that time in Queensland, Victoria, and the Australian Capital Territory and more recently, Western Australia and Northern Territory. For the purposes of this study, it would be difficult to account for all these Samoan settlements but carrying on from the New Zealand study, I will focus more on the motivations and the attitudes of Samoan migration to Australia.

Va'a notes that Samoans had migrated to Australia between the early 1900s and prior to the 1970s, not in mass numbers but on individual pursuits, and back when immigration laws were not as tight as they have become since. There was never a huge mass migration in those early years due to an initial suspicion towards the cash economy because "during colonial times, from 1900 onwards ... Samoan interest was limited to obtaining cash for their basic needs."[43]

However, since the 1970s, New Zealand would not be the final destination for a large number of Samoan migrants. With a larger economy and better job prospects available, New Zealand's closest neighbour Australia would eventually be targeted by Samoan migrants. Consequently, this led to the mass migration of Samoans to Australia, beginning in the late 1970s to the early 1980s. Va'a, who writes of the early years of mass Samoan migration to Australia in his book *Saili Matagi: Samoan Migrants in Australia*, emphasises the pull of economic wellbeing for both Samoan immigrants and their extended families back home, as being the impetus behind their migration.[44]

Similar to New Zealand, there was a tendency by Samoans to seek housing closer to areas where there were unskilled jobs available, such as coal mining and factory jobs and/or areas with cheap housing.[45] Over the years, other parts of NSW were settled, as well as Canberra in the Australian Capital Territory for the same reasons. Melbourne in Victoria and Brisbane in Queensland also became

---

[41] Alex Burns, Suzanne Morton, and Migrant Resource Centre of Newcastle and Hunter River Region (N.S.W.), *Samoan People of Newcastle N.S.W.* (Hamilton: Migrant Resource Centre, 1988).
[42] John Connell, and Grant McCall, *Islanders in the West: Pacific Island Migrants in Blacktown Local Government Area, Sydney* (Blacktown NSW: Blacktown Migrant Resource Centre, 1989).
[43] Va'a, *Saili Matagi*, 5.
[44] Va'a, *Saili Matagi*, 46.
[45] Va'a, *Saili Matagi*, 39.

areas of settlement during the 1980s as Samoans headed to other areas on the Eastern side of Australia where there were more jobs, and cheaper and newer housing as Sydney grew in population. The 1990s saw people head west towards Perth and Fremantle where the mines presented further job opportunities. The experience of living, working and being educated in New Zealand put Samoans in good stead to take advantage of these opportunities. The demographics of Samoan settlement were no longer restricted to New South Wales, but now extended to the rest of Australia.[46]

With the settlement of Samoans, churches became established, which subsequently provided evidence of Samoan settlement. The significance of the churches is that it gave the Samoan communities a form of identity that replicated the villages in Samoa. Macpherson and Macpherson argue that the identity of the village is synonymous with the church "as though the church has always been the foundation of the village, its history and its social organisation."[47] As such, Samoans in Australia not only set up churches to maintain their religious experience, but to establish continuity with village life in Samoa. Additionally, Va'a claims that the churches provided

> many of the socio-economic and political functions of the Samoan village. They provide new arrivals with assistance in finding suitable accommodation and employment, financial support for the first six months before they are entitled to welfare benefits, and a forum in which they can interact with other Samoans.[48]

In other words, the churches became the Samoan migrant's village away from Samoa. This provides an interesting analogy with *Maota Tau Ave* which will be explained below.

MAOTA TAU AVE

Samoans have always been a navigating people. The eighteenth century French explorer Louis-Antoine de Bougainville, who visited the islands in 1768, greatly admired the skill of the Samoans with their canoes, which led him to call his

---

[46] In New South Wales, outside of Metropolitan Sydney, Samoans settled in country towns that provided opportunity for agricultural employment such as Griffith, Wagga Wagga and Leeton. In Queensland, towns with cheap housing such as Logan City, Goodna, Deception Bay and Cairns were settled by Samoans. In Victoria, Samoans settled areas such as Broadmeadows, Craigieburn, Melton, Tarneit, Cranbourne, Frankston and Dandenong. In the Northern Territory, Alice Springs now has a Samoan community. In Western Australia, Perth and Swan Valley have Samoan communities as Samoans headed west to take advantage of jobs in the mining industry.

[47] Macpherson, and Macpherson, *Warm Winds of Change*, 62.

[48] Va'a, *Saili Matagi*, 244.

Samoan voyage "*l'Archipel des Navigateurs*, the 'Archipelago of the Navigators.'"[49] Yet, in the phrase *Maota Tau Ave*, there is an implication that Samoans are both navigators and settlers.

The term *maota* refers to the Samoan *fale*, or "house." It is a respectful term. In fact, *maota* is used for the house of the high chief (*alii*), the church minister (*faifeau*), or any other person besides the orator chief (*tulafale*). The house of the *tulafale* is known as *laoa*. Because of the high status of the *alii* and the *faifeau* in the Samoan setting, *maota* has more prestige.[50]

The use of *maota* in the phrase *Maota Tau Ave* is metaphorical. It refers to a metaphorical *maota* that *houses* the key elements of Samoan identity. The *maota* entails the Samoan's culture, language, family honorifics and heritage, and religion (*lotu*). A Samoan must show honour to their *maota*. Because Samoans are a proud people, they would never entertain the thought of bringing shame upon their family and village. Committing an offence against the village and the family has great consequences for the offender and the offender's family, for not only will dishonour be brought upon a Samoan's family and village, but they may also suffer heavy sanctions and in more extreme cases, banishment from the village. Depending on the severity of the offence, banishment from the village may also entail burning down of the family's premises (*mu le foaga*).

It is apparent that the metaphorical *maota* is significant for Samoans, wherever they go. The ramification of dishonour brought to a family is greater if the offence is witnessed by another village. Hence, the term *tau ave* is also important in *Maota Tau Ave*. *Tau* has an array of meanings in the Samoan language and can mean "pluck," "snatch," "strive" or "fight." *Ave* means "take" or "carry" but with the word *tau*, the meaning of *tau* as "strive" is more appropriate, and hence *tau ave* denotes "striving to carry." *Tau ave* implies responsibility to the *maota* and to the family. To strive to carry therefore means that a Samoan has a responsibility to represent their family wherever they journey. They carry the family name, their honorifics, and *lotu*, and therefore their conduct and behaviour must serve to honour the *maota* that they carry. They are expected to engage in cultural practice, and worship God wherever they migrate. They are expected to live according to Samoan customs and traditions, and uphold Samoan values and wisdom through cultural teachings. In this sense, *Maota Tau Ave* is imperative.

Diaspora as *Maota Tau Ave*: Carrying the House Abroad

It is intriguing to reimagine the diaspora through the lens of *Maota Tau Ave*. When Samoans migrate, their elders expect that their identities, customs, and religion

---

[49] Serge Tcherkézoff, *'First Contacts' in Polynesia: The Samoan Case (1722–1848): Western Misunderstandings about Sexuality and Divinity* (Canberra: ANU E Press, 2004), 23.

[50] Being of high status here does not diminish the status of the *tulafale*, but rather it stresses their role as a *matai* (chief) in the village context. Those *matai* of *alii* status serve an overseer role, while those of the *tulafale* status are the village orators.

are taken with them. In the *faa-Samoa*, these things are just as vital as economic well-being. Before discussing why this is so, it is important that I point out first, that these "things" which Samoans *carry* with them in migration, are known as their "*maota*."

Metaphorically speaking, the *maota* encompasses a Samoan's identity and heritage, customs, and religion. When speaking of identity, it includes a Samoan's dignitaries (*pa'ia*) pertaining to their family (*'āiga*) and village. *Pa'ia* in Samoan means "holy" or "sacred" whereby a Samoan's dignitaries signify the holiness or sacredness of his or her *'āiga*, and village. In Samoa, we can say that the *maota* is henceforth *paia*, or the house is sacred.[51]

Identity also includes chiefly titles which are known as *suafa matai*. *Matai* is the Samoan word for "chief" who are the leaders of the *'āiga*. In a village setting, they collectively preside at the village council or *Fono o le Nuu*, where they deliberate over matters concerning village welfare. The *matai* are powerful leaders, and their power is explained by a backstory emphasising the significance of the *'āiga* and *gafa* (lineage) from which the *matai* hails. Some *matai* come from families of oratory significance, and these *matai* are known as *tulafale*. Other *matai* come from high-ranking families in the village and are bestowed titles as high chiefs, and these *matai* are known as *alii*. Some *matai* have ties to royal families, known as *tafa'ifā* who were the traditional rulers of Samoa. Today, *matai* from the *tafa'ifā* are eligible to become Head of State of Samoa.

Yet, as Samoans carry their *maota* to lands such as New Zealand, Australia, and the United States including Hawaii, questions of *Maota Tau Ave* arise of its relevance in these foreign lands. Conflicting views between the old and the new generations seem to emerge which is typical of the Samoan diaspora. In fact, it is typical of most diasporic communities according to Clifford Geertz. It may be that, in Geertz's terms, *Maota Tau Ave* is "essentialist pride"[52] propagated by Samoan elders in order that the Samoan way or the *faa-Samoa* is maintained regardless of the location. I will qualify this view of essentialism in the next section.

ESSENTIALISM AND EPOCHALISM

Maota Tau Ave will cause tension. Trying to position a Samoan's *maota* onto foreign land can be intrusive especially if *Maota Tau Ave* is perceived as essential for the migrating Samoan. But is *Maota Tau Ave* mandatory for Samoans in a way that suggests conflict with the foreign *maota*? Or can there be a compromise to

---

[51] Visitors to a *maota* and its host often exchange pleasantries upon the visitor's arrival. The visitor would often say to the host: "Ua paia lenei maota" (this house is sacred) to acknowledge the sacredness of the host and their *'āiga*. The host will also say to the visitor: "Ua paia lenei maota" to acknowledge that the house is sacred due to the presence of the visitors. The *maota* therefore carries an inherent *paia* (sacredness), but is also *paia* as a result of the encounter between two 'holy' camps.

[52] Clifford Geertz, *The Interpretation of Cultures* (New York: Basic, 1973), 252.

allow one's *maota* to coexist with other *maotas*? I will highlight this in terms of the friction between "essentialism" and "epochalism," as argued by Geertz.

"Essentialism" is not originally a Geertz term, but it is used often in cultural theory. In fact, essentialism had been a topic of debate in European philosophy for many centuries, with roots perhaps even in the times of Aristotle.[53] However, Geertz uses the term in opposition to "epochalism" in order to understand the tension between tradition and dynamism that exists in a nation state's bid for self-identification.[54]

Peter Sedgwick defines "essentialism" in its basic form, as "the view that there are essential properties which define what something is, and without which it could not be what it is."[55] Essentialism is prominent in various cultures as the traditions and culture of a society become essential characteristics for members of that society, but here we are concerned more specifically with the possibility of a nativist essentialism—a "primordial ethnicity" when it relates to its homeland from afar. Geertz claims that "The pull of indigenous tradition is felt most heavily by its appointed, and these days rather besieged, guardians—monks, mandarins, pandits, chiefs, ulema, and so on;"[56] The tendency then is to return those people to their "natural state" for the "good of society."[57] As such, Geertz argues that essentialism resonates with a "desire for coherence and continuity."[58] But what aspects of ethnic culture are considered essential?

Mark Brett raises an important question from Geertz's argument: who is "deciding what is 'objectively' ethnic identity and what is not?"[59] This is important for Samoans attempting to maintain an ethnic identity in the diaspora. Brett's question could be replicated for diasporic Samoans, in determining which aspects of the *faa-Samoa* should and should not be preserved. It becomes more complicated when considering that the guardians of the *faa-Samoa* differ significantly between the homeland and the host-land. In Samoa, the guardians are the *matai*, who—and it must be emphasised—are in a village setting. Each village has its own understanding and beliefs as to which aspects of the culture should be emphasised and upheld in order to maintain status quo. For diasporic Samoans, the village boundaries obviously do not exist. In fact, throughout the diaspora, each Samoan ethno-community would consist of *matai* from various villages. One can imagine the conflict between *matai* in the diaspora as to which aspects of the *faa-Samoa* are to be preserved, given the differing views between villages. This is the

---

[53] Peter Brooker, *A Glossary of Cultural Theory*, 2nd ed. (London: Arnold, 2003), 89.
[54] Geertz, *Interpretation of Cultures*, 244.
[55] Peter Sedgwick, "Essentialism," in *Cultural Theory: The Key Concepts*, ed. Andrew Edgar and Peter Sedgwick (London: Routledge, 2008), 113.
[56] Geertz, *Interpretation of Cultures*, 244.
[57] Brooker, *Cultural Theory*, 89.
[58] Geertz, *Interpretation of Cultures*, 244.
[59] Mark G. Brett, "Interpreting Ethnicity: Method, Hermeneutics, Ethics," in *Ethnicity and the Bible*, ed. Mark G. Brett (Boston: Brill, 1996), 12.

issue with essentialism and primordial ethnicity as Geertz emphasises the modern state yet pays little attention to transnational contexts where the village structures are absent.

On the other hand, "epochalism" seeks "dynamism and contemporaneity."[60] By this, Geertz stresses that epochalism looks "to the general outlines of the history of our time, and in particular to what one takes to be the overall direction and significance of that history."[61] In relation to essentialism, Geertz implies that it has new challenges in the context of the modern nation state, which is characterised by "self-rule (vs. foreign rule), religious freedom, democracy, egalitarian justice, territorially based citizenship, and ethnic pluralism."[62] In other words, it speaks of a society that relies not on tradition and the past to formulate a new identity, but on human progress and the future.[63]

Geertz's discussion serves well for the modern state, however it must be made clear that Samoa as a modern state is different from the expressions of Samoan identity in diaspora. The question of ethnicity must extend beyond the territories of ethnic homelands, because ethnicity exists also outside of the homeland.[64] Ethnic communities in the diaspora render an intriguing progression from Geertz's discussion on modern state, because we now speak of two states connected through one ethnic identity. In response to Geertz, Brett's discussion of Fredrik Barth highlights the fundamental issue in relation to ethnic identity when encountered with other cultures, discussing the Bible as an analogy:

> This thesis can be well illustrated by the Bible. In this sacred library we find the literary deposits of a people who have been clearly influenced by a range of ancient cultures—to mention a few: Egyptian, Canaanite, Assyrian, Babylonian, Persian, and Hellenistic. Yet we also find attempts to construct a continuity of peoplehood, even through the discontinuities envisaged by prophetic judgments.[65]

Ethnicity does not rest within the boundaries of the modern state but extends beyond. To further this notion, Stuart Hall invites us to think of identity as "a 'production', which is never complete, always in process, and always constituted

---

[60] Geertz, *Interpretation of Cultures*, 244.
[61] Geertz, *Interpretation of Cultures*, 240.
[62] Eloise Hiebert Meneses, "Bearing Witness in Rome with Theology from the Whole Church: Globalization, Theology, and Nationalism," in *Globalizing Theology: Belief and Practice in an Era of World Christianity*, ed. Craig Ott and Harold A. Netland (Grand Rapids MI: Baker Academic, 2006), 238.
[63] Meneses, "Bearing Witness in Rome," 238.
[64] Bryan Cheyette, *Diasporas of the Mind: Jewish and Postcolonial Writing and the Nightmare of History* (New Haven: Yale University Press, 2013), xiii.
[65] Brett, "Interpreting Ethnicity," 14.

within, not outside representation."[66] As peoples cross into other lands, there is a desire for continuity and dynamism, and as a result, ethnic identities evolve. Postcolonial theorist Gayatri Spivak sees the social impact of this process which for the better part, allows for a dialogical process of ethnic development in migration, while new development opportunities emerge for developed nations:

> That it is impossible for the new and developing states, the newly decolonizing or the old decolonizing nations, to escape the orthodox constraints of a 'neoliberal' world economic system which, in the name of Development, and now 'sustainable development', removes all barriers between itself and fragile national economies, so that any possibility of building for social redistribution is severely damaged. In this new transnationality, what is usually meant by 'the new diaspora', the new scattering of the seeds of 'developing' nations, so that they can take root on developed ground?[67]

Spivak's final question alerts us to the possible tension of this transnational process, of having to scatter ethnic "seeds," only for it to be developed on foreign land. The process becomes paradoxical for Samoans who carry their *maota* into new and foreign lands, with a contentious view of where the "seeds" take root. *Who is to benefit from migration? The homeland or the new land?* For *Maota Tau Ave*, the answer surely influences the decisions of which aspects of the *faa-Samoa* are to be maintained, creating somewhat of an archetype village framework for diaspora *matai* to work with.

Maota Tau Ave *as Essentialist*

To understand why Samoans carry their *maota*, we must discuss a basic understanding of the *faa-Samoa*. The *faa-Samoa* is in one aspect the Samoan culture.[68] It is however much broader than being a cultural pattern as it pertains to the Samoan way of life being lived out each day and not restricted to isolated events, such as village customs and important ceremonies. The *faa-Samoa* is culture, and it is also the way of life. Thus, the *faa-Samoa*, with its overwhelming prominence, is an integral part of Samoan society.

How is *faa-Samoa* so prominent? Samoans live according to the most important principle, *fa'aaloalo*. *Fa'aaloalo*, often translated as "respect," is central to the *faa-Samoa*. But *fa'aaloalo* is more than just respect, it is an acknowledgment of space between one and the Other. This space is known as *va*. Airini et. al define *va* as "a spatial way of conceiving the secular and spiritual dimensions of

---

[66] Stuart Hall, "Cultural Identity and Diaspora," in *Colonial Discourse and Post-Colonial Theory: A Reader*, ed. Patrick Williams and Laura Chrisman (London: Harvester Wheatsheaf, 1994), 222.
[67] Gayatri Chakravorty Spivak, "Diasporas Old and New: Women in the Trasnational World," *Textual Practice* 10.2 (1996): 245.
[68] Aumua Mataitusi Simanu, and Luafata Simanu-Klutz, *Sāmoan Word Book* (Honolulu: Bess, 1999), v.

relationships and relational order, that facilitates both personal and collective well-being."[69] This is important to Samoans as they seek to strengthen relationships and ties between families and villages. It is because of *fa'aaloalo* that order in the village is maintained. Theoretically speaking, *Maota Tau Ave*, and the *faa-Samoa*, harbour an "essentialist" position.

To explain the essentialism of the *faa-Samoa*, let me clarify from a sociological standpoint. The *faa-Samoa* maintains social order as village members are expected to live according to it. Each village is largely self-governed by the village council, consisting of chiefs or *matai*. The *matai* are individuals who are elected by each of the families as leaders. Collectively, as representatives of their families, the *matai* meet regularly at the village council to discuss village matters.

The *matai* uphold the *faa-Samoa* through different village laws, and impose sanctions to help regulate those laws. Those who fail to uphold the *faa-Samoa* run the risk of being penalised, and depending on the nature of the transgression, they may also be banished from the village, either indefinitely or permanently. Accordingly, all matters are dealt with by the village council with the exception of homicidal acts which are handled by local police. Even then, offenders of homicidal acts and their families are given additional sanctions by the village council. The principle for any offender therefore is to bear in mind that the consequences of their actions not only affect them but the offender's family.

This prominent nature of the *faa-Samoa* is recognised by all, and as such, the tendency to uphold its values is naturalised. More importantly, the *faa-Samoa* points to the identity of Samoans. Specifically, the *faa-Samoa* denotes a Samoan's dignitaries and their identity. Samoans henceforth, are a proud people, and the connections to the land and to their ancestral roots are of great importance. As a result, when Samoans venture away from their village, they proudly uphold their heritage and identity. They are proud of their identity, and therefore, they *tau ave* their *maota* outside their land, into other lands.

The Samoan diaspora does not consist solely of moving peoples towards the *pull* of the first world, but also includes carrying one's *maota* to inhabit the new world. It becomes a fusion of two worlds and a conversation between two cultures. Such an interaction between the Samoan culture and the culture of the host-land is reminiscent of Bhabha's idea of "hybridity" which refers to

> cultures of a post-colonial *contra-modernity* may be contingent to modernity, discontinuous or in contention with it, resistant to its oppressive, assimilationist technologies; but they also deploy cultural hybridity of their borderline

---

[69] Airini, Melani Anae, and Karlo Mila-Schaaf, *Teu Le Va - Relationships across Research and Policy in Pasifika Education* (Ministry of Education, New Zealand: The University of Auckland, 2010), 10.

conditions to 'translate', and therefore reinscribe, the social imaginary of both metropolis and modernity.[70]

This reflects the dilemma of diaspora communities, as they seek to adopt the best elements from each culture. In this search, there are obviously many questions in relation to one's culture but also that of the host-land. Such questions manifest in dialogue between a critique of the culture of the host-land and self-critical questions of one's own culture.

From a Samoan perspective, carrying the *maota* is not a simple matter of Samoans parking their *maota* in a foreign land. There is internal negotiation involved by way of questioning which elements of the *maota* are actually relevant and applicable in the host-land. Conversely, critiques of the *faa-Samoa* surface, as will the question of whether the *faa-Samoa* is still relevant or perhaps it is a romanticized phenomenon that loses its aura outside of Samoa.

Maota Tau Ave *as Epochalist*

The key element in recognising *Maota Tau Ave* as an epochalist conception is acknowledging the conflict that Geertz speaks about between those with essentialist sentiments and those with epochalist notions. For *Maota Tau Ave*, we must understand the tension that emanates from Samoans who migrate into foreign lands. There is, as Geertz claims, a need for "coherence and continuity" on the one hand, and a desire for "dynamism and contemporaneity" on the other,[71] which is also apparent for Samoan diasporic contexts. But before discussing this tension, let me outline how *Maota Tau Ave* can allow for an epochalist expression.

When carrying one's *maota*, negotiation is allowed because of *fa'aaloalo*. *Fa'aaloalo* is always shown to the other, because of the *va*. The *va* refers to the space between two or more entities and is considered sacred. In any Samoan meeting or gathering, the *va* is acknowledged and kept sacred. This process of keeping the *va* sacred is known as *teu le va*, where *teu* means "keep sacred" or "keep tidy." Airini et. al give a pragmatic understanding of *teu le va* "as the 'valuing', 'nurturing' and 'looking after' of ... relationships to achieve optimal outcomes for all stakeholders."[72] The implication therefore is that while *Maota Tau Ave* carries a strong essentialist mandate to keep the culture and religion, the *va* still holds an important platform for negotiation while upholding the sacredness of the *va*. This allows Samoan diasporic identities to negotiate with the host-land, and to make necessary adjustments to one's *maota*.

Significantly, the words *tau ave* signify the dynamism of the *maota*. Not only does *tau ave* mean "to carry" but *tau ave* also carries the meaning of "evolving" or "developing." The implication is that the *maota* is not absolute but that it will

---

[70] Homi K. Bhabha, *The Location of Culture* (London: Routledge, 1994), 6.
[71] Geertz, *Interpretation of Cultures*, 244.
[72] Airini, Anae, and Mila-Schaaf, *Teu Le Va*, 10.

undergo change. *Tau ave* therefore translates into a process, where certain elements of the *maota* that are deemed relevant will be sustained, while others will be questioned or rejected. It is a tension that is especially evident between Samoans who had migrated from Samoa and second-generation Australian-Samoans. Samoan immigrants, who still hold a strong memory of the homeland, will seek to uphold the culture and religion of their homeland. The second-generation Australian-Samoans will on the other hand find it hard to uphold a culture from a land in which they had never lived.

Maota and Qohelet

The main issue, which Va'a also highlights, "lies at the point of [Samoan] contacts with the larger *palagi* world—the *palagi* community."[73] Va'a continues on to clarify that "the *fa'a-Samoa* emphasizes collective responsibility, the *fa'a-palagi* is most concerned with individual responsibility."[74] These are the two poles which distinguish the tension in *Maota Tau Ave* for Samoan migrants in Australia. To negotiate the position for the Samoan *maota* is to find a balance between the collective responsibility and the ideals of individualism in the new context. As Vaa states: "It is not enough for Samoan migrants to settle themselves within the comforts and other amenities by the Samoan community. They also need to succeed in the life of this larger community."[75]

This is not a simple negotiation. In fact, the ramifications of such deliberation between collective and individual responsibility could be severe from a Samoan perspective. In Samoa, the responsibility to the village was primary and regulated by the village council. Yet as Samoan migrants now away from the village setting, the opportunity to rethink their position becomes a serious consideration. What if the *faa-Samoa* is truly an essentialist phenomenon that Samoans are upholding without critique? What if the Samoan *tautua*[76] is really serving a cultural ideology but does little for their own success in the new land?

As such, attitudes of scepticism and defiance emerge which interestingly resonate with the scepticism of Qohelet. Weeks provides a point for consideration in light of Qohelet's own sceptical attitude as he writes of Qohelet:

> He is, certainly, set apart from tradition, and given distinctive characteristics and experiences: we are supposed to see him as a lone individual, embittered by the realization that all he did for himself proves not to be his at all.[77]

---

[73] Va'a, *Saili Matagi*, 254.
[74] Va'a, *Saili Matagi*, 254.
[75] Va'a, *Saili Matagi*, 254.
[76] *Tautua* can mean "serve," "servant," "service," or "servant." See Vaitusi Nofoaiga, *A Samoan Reading of Discipleship in Matthew*, IVBS 8 (Atlanta: SBL Press, 2017), ix.
[77] Weeks, *Ecclesiastes and Scepticism*, 167.

Perhaps then there is more to Weeks' questioning of Qohelet's scepticism beyond the literary character of Ecclesiastes. It may be that Qohelet is speaking to a diasporic context of fellow Jews who work endlessly (cf. Eccl 2:18–23) only to realise that they are actually upholding a cultural ideology. As such, Qohelet is merely pointing out

> that humans are missing the point, and he presents himself as a man seeking to steer others away from the false expectations and disappointment which he experienced himself, by opening their eyes to the reality of their situation.[78]

I contend that the reality of the migrants' situation relates to the identity of the migrant. If they are missing the point, then it may be that they are struggling with their own cultural and religious identity in a foreign land. I am alerted to Melani Anae's paper which points to the same struggle New Zealand born Samoans have of their identity.[79] Yet in this identity struggle, the Australian Samoan becomes an empiricist, much in the same spirit as Qohelet.[80]

Qohelet's experience is personal which is underscored by the personal pronoun "I." Alicia Ostriker argues that the "I" is "at all times a fiction, a trouble-making construction we are all afflicted with."[81] But what if Qohelet's "I" is representative of an identity? Perhaps the ambiguity, scepticism and pessimism of Qohelet's "I" resonates with someone undergoing an identity crisis. Maybe Qohelet is confused with his own identity, and is using an empirical approach to determine his own diasporic identity, i.e., a sage who upholds traditional Hebrew wisdom, or a sage who must renegotiate the elements of his *maota*.

Conclusion

Maota Tau Ave signifies that maintaining continuance and continuity is not restricted to the homeland, as *ave* signifies that culture and traditions are *carried* beyond the homeland. Yet *tau* with *ave* adds that the *maota* is dynamic and must therefore be renegotiated and repositioned in the new context. The underlying premise then is that *Maota Tau Ave* harbours an essentialist position pertinent for transnational contexts. At the same time, *Maota Tau Ave* does allow for negotiation with the host-land which will impact the makeup of one's *maota*. Therefore, I move from the definition of "the house that is carried" to "the house to carry" to imply the dynamism of the concept for diasporic Samoans. *Maota Tau Ave* in this

---

[78] Weeks, *Ecclesiastes and Scepticism*, 169.
[79] Melani Anae, "Towards a NZ-Born Samoan Identity: Some Reflections on Labels," *Pacific Health Dialog* 4.2 (1997). Although Anae speaks of a New Zealand-born perspective, this also applies to the Australian context.
[80] Alicia Ostriker, "Ecclesiastes as Witness: A Personal Essay," *The American Poetry Review* 34.1 (2005): 8.
[81] Ostriker, "Ecclesiastes as Witness," 8.

sense is not imperative, but indicative. This also reflects a tension that is largely evident in the Samoan diasporic context. It is a tension that is not foreign to Qohelet, who appears conflicted, in some respects, between the two extremes of essentialism and epochalism. Perhaps then, Qohelet may have initiated questions of relevance of upholding Jewish wisdom and culture especially for his foreign context of migration. Intriguingly, this may also raise questions of Qohelet's own identity as a sage. These questions are discussed in the following chapters.

2. Talanoa Intertextually

This work contributes to the growing corpus of literature on intertextuality, but in a very specific way that highlights my location of reading.[1] The questions regarding Ecclesiastes and its possible interactions with the rest of the Hebrew Bible could be answered through a range of biblical reading methods. For this study, my argument will work at the intersections of talanoa, intertextuality and diaspora studies, attending to the ancient context of authorship and a modern context of reading. I will first give a brief background to intertextuality and the use of intertextuality in reading the Hebrew Bible. I will then bring to the fore a Pasifika form of intertextuality known as *talanoa*, which I will utilise in this book, to draw out further implications for a diasporic reading. Such implications will provide methodological and hermeneutical considerations for the ensuing chapters.

INTERTEXTUALITY

The term *intertextuality* was coined by Julia Kristeva,[2] who defines the term in her book *La Révolution du langage poétique* as "the transposition of one or more systems of signs into another, accompanied by a new articulation of the enunciative and denotative position."[3] In simpler terms:

---

[1] A collection of essays that focus on illuminating elements in Ecclesiastes through intertextual readings can be found in: Katharine Dell, and Will Kynes, eds., *Reading Ecclesiastes Intertextually*, LHBOTS 587 (London: Bloomsbury, 2014). Further readings from Asian and Pasifika (Pacific) perspectives can be found in Jione Havea and Peter H.W. Lau, eds., *Reading Ecclesiastes from Asia and Pasifika*, IVBS 10 (Atlanta: SBL Press, 2020).
[2] Julia Kristeva, *Desire in Language: A Semiotic Approach to Literature and Art*, trans. Thomas Gora, Alice Jardine, and Leon S. Roudiez, European Perspectives (New York: Columbia University Press, 1980), 15.
[3] Kristeva, *Desire in Language*, 15. See also: Julia Kristeva, *La Révolution Du Langage Poétique* (Paris: Éditions du Seuil, 1974), 59–60.

> Poststructuralists such as Julia Kristeva … did not search for the meaning of a text by investigating its author's intentions or the text's own structures, but by exploring the many possible dialogues of a text with other texts and contexts.[4]

Barton notes that Kristeva's focus was "not to reconstruct the 'intertexts', except as illustrating the truth of these definitions, but to reflect on what the whole concept implies about human culture in general."[5] Kristeva thus views the text as "a permutation of texts, an intertextuality: in the space of a given text, several utterances, taken from other texts, intersect and neutralize one another."[6]

Yet within biblical studies, intertextuality has been heavily utilised as a method of interpretation, with biblical scholars seeking out allusions and echoes of themes between texts in order to highlight historical and/or hermeneutical insights.[7] Barton explains that

> In biblical studies today the term is widely used to cover all cases of interrelation between texts in the Bible, and hence to include what has more traditionally been referred to as 'Scripture citing Scripture', 'inner-biblical interpretation', and the 'reception' of earlier biblical texts in later ones.[8]

Indeed, it seems that intertextuality as a practice is not a recent phenomenon, but in some respects has been practised for centuries dating back to the times of Origen who in his allegorical interpretation of the Bible effectively used scripture to interpret scripture.[9]

In modern times, the intertextual manner of interpreting the biblical text has consisted largely of two different forms, namely, "diachronic" intertextuality, which is associated with "author-oriented" and "historical" interpretations, and "synchronic" intertextuality, which consists of a "reader-oriented" or "literary" reading of the text.[10] Barton explains that for diachronic interests, "the focus can be on either the historical development of texts, in which a later one draws on an earlier one," while a synchronic approach attempts to locate "a possible interrelation between texts that can be discerned by someone who reads them together,

---

[4] Sébastien Doane and Nathan Robert Mastnjak, "Echoes of Rachel's Weeping: Intertextuality and Trauma in Jer. 31:15," *BibInt* 27 (2019): 415.
[5] Barton, "Déjà Lu," 9.
[6] Kristeva, *Desire in Language*, 38.
[7] Cf. Katharine Dell and Will Kynes, eds., *Reading Job Intertextually*, LHBOTS 574 (New York: Bloomsbury, 2013), xviii.
[8] Barton, "Déjà Lu," 2. Also see Peter D. Miscall, "Isaiah: New Heavens, New Earth, New Book," in *Reading between Texts: Intertextuality and the Hebrew Bible*, ed. Deanna Nolan Fewell (Louisville: Westminster John Knox, 1992), 44.
[9] Anthony C. Thiselton, *New Horizons in Hermeneutics: The Theory and Practice of Transforming Biblical Reading* (Grand Rapids: Zondervan, 1992), 169–71.
[10] Barton, "Déjà Lu," 2.

especially when, as in the case of the Bible, they form part of a defined corpus (or canon)."[11]

Patricia Tull prefers to name the two approaches as "traditionalists" and "radical intertextualists." Like the diachronic version, traditionalists rely on "linear, historicist models of interpretation that seek to identify chronological relationships among texts."[12] On the other hand, Tull argues that radical intertextualists "view texts as being so thoroughly and deeply interwoven that tracing lines among them becomes as meaningless as distinguishing among water drops in the ocean."[13]

Geoffrey Miller argues that intertextuality in the "radical" form

> is a more authentic application of intertextual study than the traditionalist approach. The study of the dialogical nature of language, devoid of any fixation on tracing the influence of one text on another, is precisely the kind of study that Kristeva was advocating when she coined the term 'intertextuality'.[14]

Barton notes that "the absolute polarization of these two approaches is probably exaggerated,"[15] because even though biblical scholars have made use of the two approaches as methods of interpreting texts, it must be remembered that "intertextual theory, however, as it was developed by Kristeva and her fellow poststructuralists, is not an interpretive method but more of a mindset, a way to think about texts."[16] And here lies the new distinction for Barton: this theoretical form of intertextuality as intended by Kristeva is called "hard" intertextuality, and the form that treats intertextuality as an interpretive method he names "soft" intertextuality.[17] To clarify this distinction, Barton refers to the anthropological opposites of "emic" and "etic." Clayton and Rothstein write:

> while influence prefers what the anthropologists call "emic" explanations, those in keeping with patterns of thought that would make sense to the men and women being written about, the critics who practice intertextuality often prefer "etic"

---

[11] Barton, "*Déjà Lu*," 2. Also see Geoffrey D. Miller, "Intertextuality in Old Testament Research," *CurBR* 9.3 (2011): 285.
[12] Miller, "Intertextuality," 286.
[13] Patricia Tull, "Intertextuality and the Hebrew Scriptures," *CurBS* 8 (2000): 62.
[14] Miller, "Intertextuality," 286.
[15] Barton, "*Déjà Lu*," 7.
[16] Katharine Dell and Will Kynes, "Introduction," in *Reading Job Intertextually*, ed. Katharine Dell and Will Kynes (New York: Bloomsbury, 2013), xxii.
[17] Barton, "*Déjà Lu*," 9.

explanations, those geared for the analyst and not for the ideologically blinded analysand.[18]

In other words, hard intertextuality is linked to an etic explanation, as it is "not interested in establishing what are the actual influences on an author" but "seeing the text at the centre of many other texts, many of which the author may well be unaware of."[19] Soft intertextuality on the other hand, resonates with an emic description, where the interest lies with trying to understand those about whom the text is written.

Benjamin Sommers, like Barton, also tries to articulate a simple distinction along similar lines:

> Intertextuality is concerned with the reader or with the text as a thing independent of its author, while influence and allusion are concerned with the author as well as the text and reader. Intertextuality is synchronic in its approach, influence or allusion diachronic or even historicist.[20]

Biblical scholars who use intertextuality to interpret texts are likely to differ on matters of theory, but it may be apt then, as Barton and Sommers argue, to consider the fruits of the intertextual labour. It may be more helpful to distinguish between scholarly goals, whether it is synchronous or diachronic, author-centred or reader-centred, soft or hard intertextuality.

Although we may still be unsure as to an author's intention, even if there is no real doubt about the chronology of the texts, the value of intertextuality as an approach lies in the comparisons between a variety of genres and traditions. In terms of chronology, much of the Hebrew Bible would have been available to such a late text as Ecclesiastes. Katharine Dell and Will Kynes in *Reading Job Intertextually* sum up a view that is shared with the study of Qohelet in this book:

> in thoroughly investigating the question of intertextuality in Job, this volume unearths both historical and hermeneutical insight, addresses texts across the canon and beyond, and attends to the roles of both the author and the reader as it examines not merely formal similarities but connections between specific texts, demonstrating how Job breaks the bounds of the "Wisdom Literature" category, its meaning shaped by the diverse texts to which it alludes and illuminated by the intertextual dialogue initiated by texts that refer to or resonate with it.[21]

---

[18] Jay Clayton and Eric Rothstein, "Figures in the Corpus: Theories of Influence and Intertextuality," in *Influence and Intertextuality in Literary History*, ed. Jay Clayton and Eric Rothstein (Madison, Wisconsin: The University of Wisconsin Press, 1991), 17, as cited in Barton, in "*Déjà Lu*," 10.
[19] Barton, "*Déjà Lu*," 10.
[20] Benjamin D. Sommer, *A Prophet Reads Scripture: Allusion in Isaiah 40–66*, Contraversions: Jews and Other Differences (Stanford: Stanford University Press, 1998), 8.
[21] Dell and Kynes, "Introduction," xviii.

For the purposes of this study, my reading will focus on the relationships between texts—in Qohelet as well other parts of the Hebrew Bible and non-biblical texts—specifically as a way of highlighting indicators for a diasporic location for Qohelet. This may also help us to answer questions pertaining to Ecclesiastes as an example of a literary genre, and its position in the canon.

The intertextual enterprise also offers a way for moving beyond the constraints of dominant positions of reading that tend to limit the text's application and restrict its meaning. Mieke Bal argues that much of the dominant position in reading comprises that of "white middle-class, middle-aged men," who in their reading positions, often exclude "what is perceived as other" such as "women—or blacks, or gays, or the young, or the poor."[22] From a feminist perspective, Bal believes that "reflection on that position of dominance, and its influence on the readings which the group produces, is imperative if we wish to understand better what happens in meaning-production."[23] She demonstrates such reflection in an intertextual reading of the story of Jephthah's daughter in the book of Judges—whom she names "Bat"[24]—with philological ideas drawn from Freud.[25] Through her analysis, she proposes a feminist philology as a way of countering the male dominant position which can lead to a "systematic distortion of concepts which have a specific, gender-related meaning. Virginity is such a concept."[26] What emerges from Bal's reading, among other intertextual possibilities, is a rereading of Bat's virgin state from a female conception of virginity, where the focus is not on her sexual activity, but on her transition "from one life-phase to the next."[27] This intertextual analysis not only highlights relationships between the texts, biblical and philological, but points out the reality of texts as "occasion[s] for meaning: signifier, rather than signified."[28]

TALANOA

As an Australian of Samoan heritage, I employ the means my parents and ancestors have used to probe the world around them (cultural and visual texts), and that

---

[22] Mieke Bal, "Introduction," in *Anti-Covenant: Counter-Reading Women's Lives in the Hebrew Bible*, ed. Mieke Bal, Bible and Literature Series 22 (Sheffield: Almond, 1989), 15.
[23] Bal, "Introduction," 15.
[24] Short for "Bath-Jephthah" ("daughter of Jephthah") in order to repel her nameless state in the book. See Mieke Bal, "Between Altar and Wondering Rock: Toward a Feminist Philology," in *Anti-Covenant: Counter-Reading Women's Lives in the Hebrew Bible*, 212.
[25] Bal refers in particular to Freud's 1918 essay "The Taboo of Virginity" to highlight how the virginity of a woman marks her as the exclusive possession of a man. See Bal, "Between Altar," 219.
[26] Bal, "Between Altar," 211.
[27] Bal, "Between Altar," 217.
[28] Bal, "Introduction," 14.

is through *talanoa*.²⁹ Using *talanoa* as a way of examining texts (literary, oral, cultural, visual, etc.) is not a new venture, and it is not confined to a single definition.³⁰ Thus, relative to the various considerations of how *talanoa* takes place, I implement a number of standpoints for my own *talanoa*. Firstly, I want to *talanoa* with Jione Havea's understanding of *talanoa*, who states that *talanoa* is

> the confluence of three things: story, telling and conversation. Talanoa is not story without telling and conversation, telling without story and conversation, or conversation without telling and story. Talanoa is all three—story, telling, conversation—as one.³¹

Havea's explanation elucidates the fluid nature of *talanoa* while also emphasising the essential need for conversation to manifest. In other words: *What is the point of a story if it does not stimulate conversation and dialogue?*

So in *talanoa* with Havea, I utilise my own Samoan understanding which sees *talanoa* as a construct of *tala* and *noa*. Samoan words often materialise from the observatory nature of Samoans through their culture and wisdom.³² In this instance, the word *tala* has many meanings. In its verbal form it can denote "to open," "to unpack," "to untie," or "to extend." In its noun form, *tala* can mean "story," the fin spine of a fish, or the front and back of a Samoan *fale* (house). The word *noa* also has a number of meanings, such as "nothing," "emptiness," "void," or it can also refer to the knot of a rope or fishing net. This latter meaning of *noa* is reminiscent of Samoan fishing and sea-life, which intriguingly is the source of much of Samoa's wisdom. Hence, *talanoa* can refer to metaphorical untying of knots, as envisioned in the untying of knots in an *upega* (fishing net) before being used for fishing.³³

For this study, I aim to *tala* (untie) the *noa* (knots) that exist in the text, by which the *noa* implies ambiguous, awkward and equivocal parts that problematise

---

²⁹ I have provided a similar discussion of *talanoa* elsewhere. See Brian Fiu Kolia, "'Arriving Like a Fish of the Night' (*'Tō'ai faa-I'a a le Pō'*): An Australian-Samoan Diasporic Reading of *Pāsaḥ* in Exod 12:12–13 through a Samoan Fishing Proverb," in *Reading the Bible in Australia*, ed. Barbara Deutschmann, Deborah Storie, and Michelle Eastwood (Eugene: Wipf & Stock, 2024), 102–19.
³⁰ For a thorough discussion on the various meanings and uses of *talanoa* in theorising and analysing texts, see Matt Tomlinson, "Talanoa as Dialogue and PTC's Role in Creating Conversation," Pacific Journal of Theology 2/59 (2020): 35–46.
³¹ Jione Havea, "Bare Feet Welcome: Redeemer Xs Moses @ Enaim," in *Bible, Borders, Belonging(s): Engaging Readings from Oceania*, ed. Jione Havea, David J. Neville and Elaine M. Wainwright, SemeiaSt 75 (Atlanta: Society of Biblical Literature, 2014), 210.
³² Penehuro Fatu Lefale, "*Ua 'Afa Le Aso* Stormy Weather Today: Traditional Ecological Knowledge of Weather and Culture, the Samoa Experience," *ClimC* 100.2 (2010): 323–25.
³³ A similar understanding of *talanoa* (*taranoa* in Solomon Islands) was shared by Robert Fakafu, a Solomon Islands native and PhD candidate at Otago University, during the *Legacies of Slavery and Colonisation in Aotearoa and Pasifika Virtual Conference*, hosted by the Council for World Mission in 2020.

our reading. In this *tala*-ing of the *noa*, I do so from the standpoint of a second-generation Australian-born Samoan, who is aware of the obvious tensions in how I read the text as a child of migrants, and as a settler who is mindful of the colonial propensities of my residence in light of other settlers. This informs my position as a biblical scholar who is intent on decolonial readings and interpretations of the biblical text/s.

Finally, I want to also consider *talanoa* as an extension into the unknown. To *talanoa* in this sense is to *tala* (extend) the conversation into the *noa* (void) of inquisitory reflection. Analogously, the mind is like the oceanic waves of the *moana*: drifting, ebbing and flowing, back and forth to other spaces. Thus, I ask the question: What if we follow the ebbing waves to those *noa* (voids) in order to take the conversation further? Could we push the boundaries in biblical interpretation beyond the traditional western forms, to not only probe the *noa* (knots) in the text but to also challenge us as readers? These may ignite newer interpretations which I will take up at different points in this book, particularly in the final chapter. At this point, it is important that I make mention of this as one of my methodological aims, in order to give rise for decolonial readings of the text. *Talanoa* in this sense allows space for a decolonised reading that frees itself from the colonial legacies of mission-taught biblical reading.

Indeed, this is an alternative (alter-native?)[34] way of interrogating biblical texts which may in turn inform our intertextual efforts. Intertextuality has been practiced for many centuries, yet we are mainly aware of its western renditions. It is thus worthy for us to consider intertextuality from a Pasifika perspective, in light of its own texts and worldviews.

TALANOA AS INTERTEXTUALITY

To consider *talanoa* as intertextuality, how may we come to define texts? Should the focus solely be on the written text? David Penchansky suggests that this may be limiting the application of intertextuality. To increase creativity, it may be more fruitful to expand on the definition of texts to include "texts of culture," including unwritten culture, as well as the interactions between written and unwritten culture.[35] The juxtaposition of these types of texts not only increases the scope of intertextuality as a reading method but allows for more analysis of "how the subtle and not-so-subtle variations indicate the tension or ideological struggle that occurs at the junctures of the juxtaposition" of those texts.[36] Miller reluctantly concedes that scholars "could conceivably include unwritten discourse in their

---

[34] Nāsili Vaka'uta, *Reading Ezra 9–10 Tu'a-Wise: Rethinking Biblical Interpretation in Oceania* (Atlanta: Society of Biblical Literature, 2011), 2 n.5.

[35] David Penchansky, "Staying the Night: Intertextuality in Genesis and Judges," in *Reading between Texts: Intertextuality and the Hebrew Bible*, ed. Danna Nolan Fewell (Louisville: Westminster John Knox, 1992), 78.

[36] Penchansky, "Staying the Night," 79.

purview. The question of how texts are related is more important."[37] In this respect, *talanoa* reflects and promotes the intentions of intertextuality, as Pasifika texts of culture are often in *talanoa* with one another. This is perhaps seen profoundly in Samoan oratory where *matai* (chiefs) who meet in *talanoa* are often engaging in rhetoric that compares stories, and thus fleshing out intertextual connections that seek and promote *faiā* (kinship/relationship) between villages and families. In this sense, the focus of kinship through *talanoa* provides a more fervent nuance to what we might consider as "relationship between texts." Given my reading background as a diasporic Australian-Samoan, some comparison with oral Samoan texts is appropriate.

Talanoa in the Hebrew Bible

To consider *talanoa* as a way of interrogating texts and looking at the relationship between texts, let us consider intertextuality and some of its application in research on the Hebrew Bible. As mentioned, the aims and foci vary between intertextual critics, but the idea of analysing the relationship(s) between texts remains the same. For the purposes of this study, I want to contribute to the corpus of intertextuality by highlighting *talanoa*. In intertextual readings of the Hebrew Bible, there are some noted motifs for reading in this manner. To clarify, I will discuss some intertextual readings which highlight thematic and social justice concerns, to show how intertextuality is utilised in biblical studies. This will also give insight into how I will use *talanoa* as a reading tool in this work. I will also discuss some examples of how Ecclesiastes is read *talanoa*-wise. This will provide indicators as to how I approach the question of genre for Ecclesiastes later in this book.

Talanoa between Hebrew Bible texts

One way to imagine *talanoa* between texts, is through readings that seek out a common theme. Much like how *talanoa* participants would deliberate over a matter of importance, facing one another and focusing on the *faiā* (kinship, relationship), we could envisage texts as *talanoa* participants, face-to-face, engaging in a relational exchange for *faiā*. For instance, Peter Miscall looks at the biblical theme of creation by analysing "Isaiah and Genesis as intertexts without deciding or arguing for a particular historical priority."[38] Moreover, Miscall reads "Isaiah in light of Genesis, and to assess the impact of some of the associations between them."[39] In his interpretation, he finds intertextual allusions to the creation in Genesis 1 in the latter chapters of Isaiah (65:17; 66:22). By the concluding

---

[37] Miller, "Intertextuality," 288.
[38] Miscall, "Isaiah," 47.
[39] Miscall, "Isaiah," 47.

chapters Isaiah has made his purpose clear: "a new heavens, a new earth and a new book."[40]

This theme of creation is also explored by Hilary Marlow through an intertextual comparison between the books of Job and Amos. Marlow's analysis unearths commonalities that speak to the theme of creation, such as key phrases that appear in both texts, shared vocabularies and themes as well as motifs of the natural world to name a few.[41] For example, Marlow notes the key phrase of "treading on the high places" (דרך על־במתי) which is found in Job 9:5–10 and in the creation hymn in Amos 4:13. In her analysis of the common phrase, Marlow argues that

> These represent the only uses of the construction דרך על־במתי in the Hebrew Bible. Both Job and Amos use the qal participle of דרך with Job favouring the *plene* spelling ... vocabulary, syntax and theme come together to suggest an intentional connection between the two texts.[42]

Marlow also notes the use of the verb הפך as shared vocabulary in Job 9:5; 12:5 and Amos 5:8 "with reference to the created order."[43]

Job 9:5	"mountains are *overthrown* [הפך]"
Job 12:5	"waters that *overwhelm* [הפך] the land"
Amos 5:8	"*turns* [הפך] deeps darkness into dawn"[44]

Further, Marlow considers "motifs of the natural world" which speak to how the created order is ultimately controlled by God. For instance, the understanding that God controls the sun appears in both Job 9:7 and Amos 8:9 but with contrasting motifs. Job 9:7 highlights that "the sun is specifically depicted as under the command of God: 'he speaks to the sun (חרס) and it does not rise.'"[45] However, the same motif is used to emphasise the threat in Amos 8:9 but with different vocabulary "I will make the sun (שמש) go down at noon and darken the earth in broad daylight."[46] We may imagine *talanoa* in this sequence of readings where these different readings are conversation partners sitting around a Samoan *fale* (another Samoan word for house), who engage in *talanoa* around the theme of creation and the natural world, attempting to *tala* (untie) the *noa* (knots) that emerge from their juxtapositions.

---

[40] Miscall, "Isaiah," 48.
[41] Hilary Marlow, "Creation Themes in Job and Amos: An Intertextual Relationship?," in *Reading Job Intertextually*, ed. Katharine Dell and Will Kynes (New York: Bloomsbury, 2013), 147–54.
[42] Marlow, "Creation Themes," 147.
[43] Marlow, "Creation Themes," 148.
[44] For comparison, I have summarised Marlow's analysis in this format. For her detailed discussion, see Marlow, "Creation Themes," 148.
[45] Marlow, "Creation Themes," 151.
[46] Marlow, "Creation Themes," 151.

Another feature of intertextuality in biblical studies is its use to challenge and transform key themes and theologies within the Hebrew Bible canon. The theme of salvation/deliverance comes under scrutiny through L. Daniel Hawk's juxtaposing of Lot's escape from YHWH's destruction of Sodom (Gen 19:1–29) and Rahab's escape from the slaughtering of Jericho by the Israelites (Josh 2:1–24; 6:22–25).[47] In this juxtaposition, we can envision a *talanoa* taking place through these two stories, as Hawk puts forward a challenge to "exclusivistic notions of salvation" and thus "transforms" the ubiquitous theme of deliverance and salvation.[48] However, in order to "transform" an earlier text or idea, it seems necessary to be clear on the chronological order and likely knowledge of the earlier texts.

On the theme of social injustice, we can envision another *talanoa*, as Penchansky analyses three texts (Gen 19, Gen 24, and Judg 19) intertextually in order to highlight, among other issues, the mistreatment of women in these texts.[49] In doing so, Penchansky achieves two ends: on one end he reveals the misogynistic and anti-feminist attitudes in the societies that produced such texts, yet on the other end, the *talanoa* functions "rhetorically to provide a sympathetic point of view from the perspective of the female character."[50]

These injustices are revisited by Hyun Chul Paul Kim, but from a diasporic perspective. His intertextual reading of Ruth vis-à-vis Esther focus on their diasporic identities: "Ruth is the foreigner among Jews and Esther, the Jew among foreigners."[51] Kim notes the use of an intertextual reading in identifying issues faced with diasporic people in the ancient biblical world, "replete with many dimensions of hardship, oppression, threat, survival, and heroics."[52] Indeed, Kim explains that

> both Ruth and Esther endure the harsh ordeals of relocation, following the loss of their loved ones—also their indispensable social guardians. As ethnic minorities and women, both encounter immense social, economic, and political threats. Furthermore, both are restricted within the confines of the androcentric culture.[53]

This reading allows us to consider the complex struggles faced by diasporic people, but also to locate them in "hybrid, liminal spaces, causing them to juggle two

---

[47] L. Daniel Hawk, "Strange Houseguests: Rahab, Lot, and the Dynamics of Deliverance," in *Reading between Texts: Intertextuality and the Hebrew Bible*, ed. Danna Nolan Fewell (Louisville: Westminster John Knox, 1992), 89.
[48] Hawk, "Strange Houseguests," 96.
[49] Penchansky, "Staying the Night," 78.
[50] Penchansky, "Staying the Night," 84.
[51] Hyun Chul Paul Kim, "Ruth Vis-À-Vis Esther: Reading Intertextually Ruth the 'Widow' and Esther the 'Orphan' as Diasporic 'Immigrants'," *The Korean Journal of Old Testament Studies* 74 (2019): 19. Kim quotes this line from Kandy Queen-Sutherland, "Ruth, Qoheleth, and Esther: Counter Voices from the Megilloth," *Perspectives in Religious Studies* 43 (2016): 230.
[52] Kim, "Ruth Vis-À-Vis Esther," 19.
[53] Kim, "Ruth Vis-À-Vis Esther," 30–31.

or more identities and belongingness."[54] Intertextuality helps to reconsider these two biblical figures from a diasporic perspective, but also provides implications for understanding diaspora and its associated social injustices.

Intertextuality can serve also to define diasporic contours and indicate a possible diasporic location.[55] This would constitute a diachronic style of textuality. Gil Rosenberg is among those who argue, more like Sommer, that intentionality is key to establishing intertextual connection. Rosenberg's intertextual analysis of the birth proclamations to Sarah and the wealthy woman of Shunem, highlights that both stories use the phrase כעת חיה, "in due time" (Gen 18:10, 14; 2 Kgs 4:16–17).[56] The occurrence of the phrase takes place in the two stories "in the context of an annunciation 'type-scene.'"[57] As Rosenberg argues, it is likely that the authors "already had other such type-scenes, and their surrounding contexts, in mind."[58] One could thus make connections between these type-scenes with the ideal setting that inspired them.

ECCLESIASTES TALANOA WITH HEBREW BIBLE TEXTS

The quest of this study is grounded methodologically in an intertextual *talanoa* of Ecclesiastes, and while I pursue new insights and discussion points, reading Ecclesiastes intertextually is not new. I draw our attention to a volume of essays edited by Dell and Kynes that has been compiled for the very purpose of bringing Ecclesiastes into intertextual conversations with the Hebrew Bible, and with texts throughout history. The purpose of the collection was to bring Ecclesiastes into a broader conversation, rather than being "read solely in the context of a cordoned-off Wisdom Literature."[59] Seeing this intertextual connection might also allow us to envision a *talanoa* of Ecclesiastes *with* other Hebrew Bible texts, seeking *faiā* with the rest of the Hebrew Bible corpus.

In this volume, we find some intriguing possibilities in reading Ecclesiastes. The opening essay by Dell explores "intertextual links between Ecclesiastes and Genesis 1–11." Following Kynes, she subdivides "the notion of intertextual links into three categories—that of quotation (explicit, intentional reference), allusion (implicit, intentional reference) and echo (implicit, unintentional reference)."[60]

---

[54] Kim, "Ruth Vis-À-Vis Esther," 35.
[55] See Kim, "Ruth Vis-À-Vis Esther," 18–58. Noah Hacham in "3 Maccabees and Esther: Parallels, Intertextuality, and Diaspora Identity," *JBL* 126 (2007): 767, notes that reading Esther alongside 3 Maccabees highlights a diasporic location.
[56] Gil Rosenberg, "כעת חיה: An Allusion Connecting Genesis 18:10, 14 and 2 Kings 4:16–17," *JBL* 139 (2020): 701.
[57] Rosenberg, "כעת חיה," 704.
[58] Rosenberg, "כעת חיה," 705. Also see: Robert Alter, "How Convention Helps Us Read: The Case of the Bible's Annunciation Type-Scene," *Prooftexts* 3.2 (1983): 115–30.
[59] Dell and Kynes, *Reading Ecclesiastes Intertextually*, ix.
[60] Katharine Dell, "Exploring Intertextual Links between Ecclesiastes and Genesis 1–11," in Dell and Kynes, *Reading Ecclesiastes Intertextually*, 5.

Yet, as she discovers, the parallels between Genesis and Ecclesiastes are more implicit than explicit. While there are links that can be established through synchronic intertextual comparison with regards to theological interests between the texts, Dell is reserved "when it comes to strong intentional intertextual allusions."[61] The strongest evidence of an intertextual allusion between the two texts is "found in the link between Eccl 3:20 and 12:7 and Gen 2:7 and 3:19" through the language of "dust," "return," and "spirit."[62] However, for Dell, "Echoes are more prevalent than actual allusions," and this is what makes the reading of Ecclesiastes intertextually an enriching exercise.[63]

Kynes also finds allusions in Ecclesiastes to the Torah, specifically, between Eccl 11:9 and Num 15:39:

> First, Qoheleth's joy declares, "Rejoice, young man, while you are young, and let your heart cheer you in the days of your youth. Follow the inclination of your heart (לבך) and the desire of your eyes (עיניך)" (11:9a). Immediately, Qoheleth's piety responds, "But know that for all these things God will bring you into judgment" (11:9b).[64]

However, Kynes asks: "But is this Qoheleth's voice, or that of a pious redactor? Either way, in the juxtaposition of permissiveness and piety, we hear Qoheleth's pessimism, as well."[65] This range of attitudes—joy, piety, and pessimism—which Qohelet displays in 11:9 seems to contradict the allusion found in Num 15:39: "'You have the fringe [ציצת] so that, when you see it, you will remember all the commandments of the LORD and do them, and not follow after your heart [לבבכם] and your eyes [עיניכם], which you follow after unfaithfully'."[66] In other words, the message in Numbers is one that discourages people from following their heart, while Qohelet encourages his listeners to follow their heart.

In dealing with this dilemma, Kynes concludes that the author of Ecclesiastes does not reject Numbers but reinterprets it. He states: "This reinterpretation suggests he does not see the pursuit of joy and the obedience of God's commandments as in opposition with one another, but that he believes God has in fact commanded his people to pursue joy."[67]

Elsewhere in the Hebrew Bible, Tremper Longman investigates the relationship between Ecclesiastes and 1 Kings, as a way of understanding the common portrayal of Qohelet as King Solomon. In Longman's analysis, there are "no

---

[61] Dell, "Exploring Intertextual Links," 13.
[62] Dell, "Exploring Intertextual Links," 13.
[63] Dell, "Exploring Intertextual Links," 12.
[64] Will Kynes, "Follow Your Heart and Do Not Say It Was a Mistake: Qoheleth's Allusions to Numbers 15 and the Story of the Spies," in Dell and Kynes, *Reading Ecclesiastes Intertextually*, 15.
[65] Kynes, "Follow Your Heart," 15.
[66] Kynes, "Follow Your Heart," 15.
[67] Kynes, "Follow Your Heart," 25.

obvious linguistic links between Ecclesiastes and 1 Kings."[68] However, the name "Qoheleth" itself may provide a clue. Longman points to the fact that the name Qohelet is "an obvious nickname or pseudonym, not a real name."[69] This anonymity allows for Longman to consider who Qohelet may be portraying, and in doing so, he revisits the root קהל of the name Qohelet which means "to gather together, assemble."[70] The translation of the name Qohelet therefore provides an interesting intertextual reference to 1 Kings, as he argues:

> The translations "Preacher" and "Teacher" give no obvious connection to the figure of Solomon in 1Kings, but the rendition "Assembler" may well hint at an association with that king since the root *qhl* in various forms occurs a number of times in relationship to Solomon while he dedicates the newly built Temple (1 Kgs 8:1, 2, 14, 22, 55, 65). Thus, it appears that "Assembler" (Qoheleth) may be an intertextual reference to 1 Kgs 8 and a subtle hint that Solomon is the referent.[71]

The intertextual connection does not aim to solve the question of authorship for Ecclesiastes, but to provide additional hermeneutical insights into understanding Qohelet's message. As Longman contends, Qohelet was constructed in the image of Solomon as found in 1 Kings 8, to foreground the author's message that "because of death, injustice, and the inability to discern the proper time, life lacks meaning if one tries to find it in wealth, work, wisdom, pleasure, or anything other than God."[72]

Intertextual connections are also to be made between Ecclesiastes and the prophets. Mary Mills engages with Ecclesiastes and Jonah using Mikhail Bakhtin's theories regarding polyphonic narration. According to Mills, the focus on conversational narrative in Bakhtin's critical method can be used as a "tool for the dialogical development of individual and corporate self knowledge."[73] When applied, the narrative voices in Eccl 2–6 and Jonah can be "fleshed out through conversations inside and between characters concerning the problems of everyday life."[74] By focusing on the conversational aspects and polyphonic narration of Ecclesiastes and Jonah, Mills argues that links in the line of thought between the two books can be established: "If Jonah struggles with his very nature as prophet, Qoheleth struggles with the uselessness of the human intellect as a medium for

---

[68] Tremper Longman, "Qoheleth as Solomon: 'For What Can Anyone Who Comes after the King Do?' (Ecclesiastes 2:12)," in Dell and Kynes, *Reading Ecclesiastes Intertextually*, 48.
[69] Longman, "Qoheleth as Solomon," 48.
[70] Longman, "Qoheleth as Solomon," 48.
[71] Longman, "Qoheleth as Solomon," 48.
[72] Longman, "Qoheleth as Solomon," 55.
[73] Mary Mills, "Polyphonic Narration in Ecclesiastes and Jonah," in Dell and Kynes, *Reading Ecclesiastes Intertextually*, 74.
[74] Mills, "Polyphonic Narration," 74.

producing wisdom since it does not enable enhancement of life."[75] From a stylistic point of view, the intertextuality between the two books "validates the view that an individual voice can be radically internally discrepant while remaining coherent (Ecclesiastes), and queries the value of radically self-sustaining belief (Jonah)."[76]

HEBREW BIBLE TALANOA WITH EXTRA- AND NONBIBLICAL TEXTS

Let us consider *talanoa* of the Hebrew Bible with extra- and nonbiblical texts. To help us envision *talanoa* further, I note that intertextuality not only consists of analysis of Hebrew Bible texts but it also allows for examining the relationship between the biblical text and other types of intertexts, such as extrabiblical texts, ancient literature and oral cultural "texts." Barton writes:

> Reading intertextually has nothing to do with the religious authority of the texts, and there is no assumption that the 'best' or 'correct' intertext will be another book in the canon. One can perfectly well read Genesis and the Epic of Gilgamesh as intertexts, or indeed Genesis and Darwin's *Origin of Species*—which would be an interesting experiment![77]

With this in mind, *talanoa*, when read along with these other intertexts, allows us to focus on the task of hermeneutical illumination as opposed to upholding religious authority.

Noah Hacham conducts an intertextual reading between both Hebrew and Greek versions of Esther and 3 Maccabees. While he acknowledges that comparing similar story lines and themes can be "striking," Hacham argues that a look at "the unique linguistic, as opposed to the thematic-structural, parallels between the texts allow determination, in [his] opinion, of direct literary dependence."[78] Intriguingly, Hacham looks at the Greek versions of the two texts and notices a total of nine Greek words that are unique to both 3 Maccabees and Esther.[79] He also finds that "the most significant parallel between Greek Esther and 3 Maccabees relates to a phrase found in ancient Greek literature only in these two works ... 'spear and fire' (δόρατι χαί πυρί)."[80] In this instance, Hacham establishes intertextual connections outside the biblical corpus as he finds resonance with ancient Greek literature.

The intertextual net can be cast even further, as resonances with the arts are deemed to be an important way of reconfiguring ideas of the biblical narrative. Sebastian Selvén reimagines the binding of Isaac in Gen 22, using Stephen King's

---

[75] Mills, "Polyphonic Narration," 81.
[76] Mills, "Polyphonic Narration," 82.
[77] Barton, "*Déjà Lu*," 6.
[78] Hacham, "3 Maccabees," 767.
[79] Hacham, "3 Maccabees," 773.
[80] Hacham, "3 Maccabees," 772.

"The Gunslinger" and J. R. R. Tolkien's epic "The Return of the King" as intertexts.[81] Of the intertexts of King and Tolkien, Selvén claims that

> both King and especially Tolkien can be useful for thinking about Abraham here; Roland has his own personal motives that trump his care for Jake when this love gets put to the test, and Denethor has a trauma lingering from the sending out of his first son, Boromir, the death of whom he has recently been informed about.[82]

These two events in the story make for interesting intertextuality, which Selvén believes can lead to the reader questioning Abraham's motives. Using this as a framework, Selvén invites the reader to reconsider the phrase "after these things" in Gen 22:1, in light of sending Ishmael "to what he must think is his death, as a prologue or preparation for Genesis 22."[83] When read this way, Selvén reasons

> we might imagine an Abraham much less balanced than we may have thought of before, and one who might react quite differently to such a command than he might otherwise have done. If we imagine Abraham as more guilt-ridden and less rational than usual, we may even ask whether the command might have been quite welcome.[84]

To think of Abraham this way may seem radical, but the use of intertexts in this way certainly opens up new ways of understanding the text, while also alerting us to some of the obvious horror that traditional readings make obscure.

Intertextuality also allows for the reader to consider a diversity of cultural forms and practices as intertexts that could enhance biblical interpretation. Jione Havea in "Bare Feet Welcome: Redeemer Xs Moses @ Enaim," invites readers into the world of Pasifika culture, to consider Pasifika intertexts as a way of reimagining the biblical world and biblical characters.[85] Using this culture as an intertext, Havea notes that in the story of Moses's death,

> what the people do is dishonoring. This is, of course, suggestive of how they feel about their leader. They could carry his remains for proper burial with the ancestors in Canaan, but they leave him as if he belongs nowhere. In spite of how biblical theologians read the story of Moses, i give more weight to the action of the people. They must know that it is disrespectful to walk away from his dead

---

[81] Sebastian Selvén, "The Binding of Isaac in J.R.R. Tolkien and Stephen King," *BibInt* 28 (2020): 150–74.
[82] Selvén, "Binding of Isaac," 169.
[83] Selvén, "Binding of Isaac," 169.
[84] Selvén, "Binding of Isaac," 169.
[85] Jione Havea, "Bare Feet Welcome," 209–22.

body, seeing that they are carrying the remains of Joseph for burial in Canaan, but they are not troubled.[86]

Havea also uses "cultures where people remove their shoes or sandals when they enter homes" as an intertext to read the burning bush story in Exod 3.[87] As such, the cultural practice insinuates to the reader that "the command to Moses suggests that he has arrived and is welcomed."[88] The "holy ground" therefore is considered holy because it is hospitable and welcoming, so from a Pasifika point of view, failure to remove one's shoes in such holy places is a sign of disrespect.[89]

Further to cultural practices as intertexts, engagement with cultural wisdom and language can also be fruitful. Levesi Afutiti claims that as with other languages, "Samoans regard their language, with reference to its wisdom sayings, as a repository that contains their cultural and traditional values. Samoan cultures and traditions are embedded in proverbial and wisdom sayings, making those a Samoan text."[90] However, in terms of biblical exegesis, the connection between Samoan wisdom sayings and the biblical text has been restricted, due in part to the reluctance of interpreters to stray from traditional exegetical methods. Afutiti argues that this prohibits any reader from discerning how the text reveals itself "in the reader's world, in which one learns from his or her language and traditional teachings."[91]

Afutiti proposes an intertextual connection be made, to demonstrate how the text could be illumined from a Samoan worldview. To do so, Afutiti utilises Samoan wisdom sayings (*muagagana*) and proverbial expressions (*alagaupu*) to point out allusions in the biblical text. For example, the *muagagana*, "*E sau a le fuauli ma le palusami e iloga a ona toa le moa*" translated as "*Fuauli* [taro] and *palusami* have completely filled and satisfied the desire of hunger"[92] alludes intertextually to Ps 63:1, 3. While the saying denotes how taro and *palusami* fulfil the Samoan desire for food, Afutiti argues that the saying "could also reflect a longing for God as we find in Ps 63:1, 3."[93] Further, the satisfaction the Samoan experiences after receiving their favourite food of taro and *palusami* is implied to be indicative of the satisfaction the Psalmist obtains from God's steadfast love.

---

[86] Havea, "Bare Feet Welcome," 215. Note: Havea prefers to use lowercase "i" as he does "not see the point in capitalizing the first person when s/he *is* in relation to everyone/everything else." See Havea, "Bare Feet Welcome," 209 n.2.
[87] Havea, "Bare Feet Welcome," 216.
[88] Havea, "Bare Feet Welcome," 216.
[89] Havea, "Bare Feet Welcome," 216–17.
[90] Levesi Laumau Afutiti, "Native Texts: Samoan Proverbial and Wisdom Sayings," in *Sea of Readings: The Bible in the South Pacific*, ed. Jione Havea, SemeiaS 90 (Atlanta: SBL Press, 2018), 53.
[91] Afutiti, "Native Texts," 60.
[92] Afutiti, "Native Texts," 63. *Palusami* is a Samoan delicacy made from young taro leaves and salted coconut cream. The combination of *palusami* and taro is a staple food for Samoans.
[93] Afutiti, "Native Texts," 63.

In addition to cultural practices and language, the use of one's cultural identity as a cultural intertext to read alongside the biblical text could highlight identity issues. For example, Inise Foi'akau uses her identity as *Marama iTaukei* (indigenous Fijian woman) to highlight the significance of Zipporah in the male-dominant book of Exodus. She also acknowledges that despite being a *Marama iTaukei*, her migration to Australia consequently identifies her as a *yalewa tani* (a foreign woman) and a *yalewa bokala* (a woman living on the fringes) while on foreign land.[94] As an initial step, Foi'akau names Zipporah by her Fijianised name "Sipora" "in honor of the many *yalewa bokala* (wo-man commoner) and *yalewa tani* (foreign wo-man) who are nameless in *iTaukei* (indigenous Fijian) circles. In this way, Sipora becomes a naming of the nameless and a voicing of the voiceless."[95] By naming Sipora, she is identified with the *marama iTaukei*, however, as Exod 18:1–6 suggests in a number of translations, she moves outside of her homeland. In doing so, she transitions from *marama iTaukei* to *yalewa bokala* and *yalewa tani*. From Foi'akau's Fijian perspective, she finds that while the *yalewa bokala* and *yalewa tani* are normally unnamed in *iTaukei* circles, the text actually names this *yalewa bokala* Zipporah/Sipora. Accordingly, "she is Sipora, and she responds to an act of YHWH. She is an agent on the move."[96]

Another example of where identity is used as an intertext emerges from the experience of a diasporic Samoan in New Zealand. Martin Mariota utilises his Samoan *Palagi*[97] identity to reread Moses in Exod 2–3. In clarifying his Samoan *Palagi* identity, Mariota explains his two worlds:

> the world of the palagi discourse, as reflected through my birthplace and upbringing in Aotearoa New Zealand; as well as the world of the Samoan discourse, as reflected through my ethnicity and theological training in Samoa. As an ethnic minority in Aotearoa New Zealand, I was able to mimic the New Zealand lifestyle and values and progress through the palagi education system. Through my theological training in Samoa, I have been enriched with a renewed understanding of Samoan discourse, a voice to speak in *fono* (meetings), and credibility with the elders.[98]

In these worlds, or spaces, Mariota argues that they can be spaces for empowerment. Moses, in similar fashion, moves between spaces and as such, "the naïve

---

[94] Inise Vakabua Foi'akau, "Sipora (Zipporah), Both Native and Foreigner: A *Marama Itaukei* Reading of Exodus 4:24–26," in Havea, *Sea of Readings*, 118. Foi'akau defines these native words as such in her chapter.
[95] Foi'akau, "Sipora (Zipporah)," 118.
[96] Foi'akau, "Sipora (Zipporah)," 128.
[97] Martin Wilson Mariota, "Moses, Both Hebrew and Egyptian: A Samoan *Palagi* Reading of Exodus 2–3," in Havea, *Sea of Readings*, 103 n1, explains that "Palagi used to be in reference to white Europeans (who first arrived on ships with masts that were seen to "burst the sky") but nowadays also refers to natives who behave as if they are white Europeans."
[98] Mariota, "Moses, Both Hebrew and Egyptian," 105.

assumption that Moses was only Hebrew, only Egyptian, or only Midianite" is problematic for Mariota.[99] Rather, using his polycultural background as an intertext, Mariota conducts a Samoan *Palagi* reading to highlight that Moses was a fusion of various cultures, empowering him "with the necessary polycultural capital to push the boundaries of the Hebrew discourse (of slavery and oppression under the Egyptian rule) and negotiate an alternative discourse based on hope and promises."[100]

ECCLESIASTES TALANOA WITH EXTRA- AND NONBIBLICAL TEXTS

Having considered intertextuality between Hebrew Bible and nonbiblical texts, let us turn to the relationship between Ecclesiastes and nonbiblical texts as intertexts. For instance, Thomas Esposito examines echoes of Ecclesiastes in the works of T. S. Eliot. His analysis reveals "some startling parallels between the two writers, the most notable being the acute awareness of their time-bound quest for the union of the timeless and the temporal."[101] The issue at hand, according to Esposito, is that "what Qoheleth calls *hā'ōlām* (Ecclesiastes 3:11), the desire for a divine perception of time and the meaning of life, has been placed by God in the human heart but nevertheless remains unfulfilled."[102]

In trying to solve this dilemma for Qohelet, Esposito details some of the echoes of Ecclesiastes in Eliot's work, in order to draw hermeneutical insights for understanding Qohelet's "futile pursuit of *hā'ōlām*."[103] As a starting point, a common connection between the two writers can be drawn from echoes of הבל through "images of smoke, fog, and wind [that] recur frequently in Eliot's work as symbols of the fleeting nature of time and the mortal end of human life."[104]

Delving through Eliot's works, Esposito refers to certain examples that reflect a connection between the English author and Ecclesiastes. For instance, in Eliot's poem *Choruses from the Rock*, Esposito argues that the line "'O world of spring and autumn, birth and dying! / The endless cycle of idea and action' seems to be a summary of Ecclesiastes 1."[105] In another one of Eliot's poem titled *Burnt Norton*, there is an allusion to the recurring wind in Ecclesiastes 1:6, through the "monotonous cycle of nature and the frivolous inert boredom of his contemporaries" as communicated in the poem.[106] An interesting reflection on earth in Eliot's poem *East Coker*, reads like Eccl 3:

---

[99] Mariota, "Moses, Both Hebrew and Egyptian," 105.
[100] Mariota, "Moses, Both Hebrew and Egyptian," 114.
[101] Thomas Esposito, "Echoes of Ecclesiastes in the Poetry and Plays of T.S. Eliot," *Logos* 24.2 (2021): 98.
[102] Esposito, "Echoes of Ecclesiastes," 99.
[103] Esposito, "Echoes of Ecclesiastes," 99.
[104] Esposito, "Echoes of Ecclesiastes," 107.
[105] Esposito, "Echoes of Ecclesiastes," 107.
[106] Esposito, "Echoes of Ecclesiastes," 107.

Houses live and die: there is a time for building
And a time for living and for generation
And a time for the wind to break the loosened pane
And to shake the wainscot where the field-mouse trots
And to shake the tattered arras woven with a silent motto. (1.123)[107]

In addition to his poetry, there are also allusions to Ecclesiastes in Eliot's plays, for example, "In the *Family Reunion*, the troubled Harry comes across as a young Qoheleth in outlook, musing darkly on his past with lines reminiscent of *hebel* and the course of motion in Ecclesiastes 1."[108]

The intertextual analysis of allusions and echoes of Ecclesiastes in Eliot's works invite the reader of Ecclesiastes to consider an alternative understanding of *hā'olām*. Qohelet struggles with *hā'olām* and even admits to the idea being elusive to human understanding (3:11), but when read along with Eliot, it may be "that in the rush of twirling and whirling wind, *hā'olām* is truly experienced, not merely perceived as frustrated desire."[109]

Another example of intertextuality between Ecclesiastes and non-biblical texts is seen through John Jarick's reading of Ecclesiastes alongside ancient Greek comic plays. Jarick does not make suggestions that Qohelet was familiar with Greek theatre in order to posit hermeneutical significance, but a synchronic intertextual interrogation "may encourage readers to hear Ecclesiastes' pessimistic ponderings differently, as the similarities in theme, imagery and language with the Greek comedians cause that ancient laughter to echo in our ears."[110]

For example, the topsy-turvy world of Qohelet, as reflected in Eccl 10:8 "Whoever digs a pit will fall into it; and whoever breaks through a wall will be bitten by a snake" can be heard in the Greek play, *Acharnians*, where "Aristophanes' protagonists are also alert to the vicissitudes of life, but they rather relish the likelihood of such mishaps occurring in the lives of their antagonists (and furnishing the audience with some laughter)."[111]

The theme of enjoyment in Ecclesiastes, reflected through Qohelet's recommendation "to eat, and drink, and enjoy themselves" (8:15) (Gk: τοῦ φαγεῖν καὶ τοῦ εὐφρανθῆναι) is echoed through a similar statement uttered by a number of Aristophanes' protagonists. The Chorus Leader in the *Acharnians*, for example, says: "The more I kept inviting him 'do drink, recline, take this cup of fellowship' (πινε, κατάκεισο, λαβε τήνδε φιλοτησίαν), the more he kept setting our vine props afire and violently spilling the wine from our vines."[112]

---

[107] Esposito, "Echoes of Ecclesiastes," 110.
[108] Esposito, "Echoes of Ecclesiastes," 108.
[109] Esposito, "Echoes of Ecclesiastes," 119.
[110] John Jarick, "Ecclesiastes among the Comedians," in Dell and Kynes, *Reading Ecclesiastes Intertextually*, 177.
[111] Jarick, "Ecclesiastes among the Comedians," 178.
[112] Jarick, "Ecclesiastes among the Comedians," 179.

Moreover, Qohelet's vexation over the wicked receiving divine blessings which belong to the righteous, and the righteous suffering the fate that should be granted to the wicked (e.g., 7:15, 8:14) seems to resonate with this reflection in the Aristophanean world:

> Just consider the current state of our human existence; who wouldn't think it's madness, or even divine malevolence? It's a fact that many people are wealthy despite being scoundrels who've amassed it unjustly, while a good many worthy people fare badly and go hungry, and spend most of their time in *your* company. (*Wealth*, ll. 500–504)[113]

This reflection of the comedies of Aristophanes is done through a philosophical lens, which for the reader of Ecclesiastes, provides an alternative way of answering the question of moral chaos.

Reading Ecclesiastes alongside Greek comedians provides a perspective that sheds light on Qohelet's pessimism, particularly from a philosophical standpoint. As Jarick concludes: "The quest to cope with life is arguably what drives all great literature, and so to find Ecclesiastes among the comedians may be no strange thing at all."[114]

Perhaps what might seem strange, on surface level, is using the ocean as a cultural text to read Ecclesiastes intertextually. Mariana Waqa uses the ocean to read Ecclesiastes intertextually, along with the wisdom of Sirach. For Pasifika, the ocean is known as *Moana*, as Waqa explains:

> For Micronesian, Polynesian, and coastal Melanesian Islanders, Moana is like a mother who provides food for her children—she embraces and sustains their livelihood, but she also has the power to teach and discipline from her recondite (a subject that is little known) depths. Moana is alive, her tides ebb and flow, and her waves surge and break. She is fluid and rhythmic, with the ability to swell beautifully or crash with torrential rapidity. Moana envelops; she overlaps and crosses boundaries.[115]

Waqa uses the *Moana* as a framework for reading, and claims "that the biblical text, much like the Moana, is both fluid and wild; it is also life-sustaining; its words have the power to teach and discipline from the depths of its flow."[116] Intriguingly, the *Moana*, with its wisdom-like qualities, is analogous to Sophia, the female personification of Wisdom in Sir 24.

---

[113] Jarick, "Ecclesiastes among the Comedians," 180.
[114] Jarick, "Ecclesiastes among the Comedians," 187.
[115] Mariana Waqa, "Sophia, Untameable Like Moana: An Oceanic Reading of Sirach 24 with Ecclesiastes 7:10–12," in Havea and Lau, *Reading Ecclesiastes from Asia and Pasifika*, 86.
[116] Waqa, "Sophia," 86.

Waqa's oceanic reading "dives deep into the textual abyss" to highlight the enigmatic characteristic of Sophia in Sir 24:2–3, by including Qohelet in the intertextual dialogue.[117] Waqa brings to focus Qohelet's claim in Eccl 1:2 that "all is הבל." Beneath the surface, Waqa acknowledges the multivalence of הבל but prefers to translate הבל as "breath" as "this rendering anticipates the *chasing after the wind* that Qoheleth references as a meaningless and ineffectual activity in Eccl 1:14."[118] This translation of הבל as "breath" highlights the enigma of Sophia because

> as *breath*, she cannot be fully grasped and therefore controlled by sage, priest, or prophet; so Qoheleth cautions that to pursue her is a 'chasing of the wind', a quest that 'increases sorrow' (Eccl 1:18) for men like him who desire and attempt to possess her.[119]

As a result, Waqa suggests that Qohelet's claim of הבל is more than just a show of his frustration, but a "warning of Sophia's volatile nature—she stations herself for no one and moves according to her own ways," much like the *Moana*.[120]

SUMMARY

The use of talanoa with intertextuality in interpreting the biblical text has a number of important benefits. The analysis of the relationships between texts have prompted some scholars to adapt a diachronic form of intertextuality to argue the possibility of later texts using or being influenced by earlier texts, while others have utilised a synchronic form of intertextuality that is not interested in authorial intention but how one text may illuminate hermeneutical insights in another and vice versa. For this book, talanoa might resemble this western approach, but it has its own integrity as it encourages fluidity in approach when looking at the relationships between texts.

In my view, we need not provide general arguments for or against intentionality, as long as we remain clear as to our objectives.[121] What I intend to do is to juxtapose Qohelet alongside other Hebrew Bible texts in the style of talanoa, but in this study, for the purpose of considering an alternative location for Qohelet's voice of scepticism. At the same time, I also want to challenge from my own cultural perspective the notion of Qohelet as a book from a separate tradition called wisdom. As a diasporic Samoan in Australia, I read Qohelet intertextually with my own cultural texts, in particular, that of the Samoan migration mandate of *Maota Tau Ave* (which I discuss in the next chapter). Such interrelations may

---

[117] Waqa, "Sophia," 86.
[118] Waqa, "Sophia," 88.
[119] Waqa, "Sophia," 88.
[120] Waqa, "Sophia," 88.
[121] Cf. Russell L. Meek, "Intertextuality, Inner-Biblical Exegesis, and Inner-Biblical Allusion: The Ethics of a Methodology," *Bib* 95 (2014): 284.

indeed be "spatial" as opposed to temporal, but as Miscall argues, "No text is an island."[122]

WHERE QOHELET FITS

Contrary to the classification of wisdom literature, recent commentary seems to question the validity of wisdom as a literary genre in the Hebrew Bible, reflected sharply by the querying title of Sneed's edited volume: *Was There a Wisdom Tradition?*[123] Sneed's volume consists of essays which ask this question of wisdom's place in the canon, ranging from one side of the spectrum that advocates the maintaining of wisdom as a category, to others which radically question the notion of biblical wisdom. Through intertextual analyses in later chapters, I will show that this latter position gives rise to further questions that will be discussed in the final chapter.

At this point, we affirm the general direction taken by Kynes. Kynes believes that "biblical scholarship is currently suffering from a Wisdom Literature category that is plagued by definitional deficiency, amorphous social location, and hemorrhaging 'influence', among other maladies."[124] This may be the case, and indeed, the resonances between Ecclesiastes and the rest of the Hebrew Bible need further probing.

The classification of wisdom literature may not be as assured as earlier scholars have claimed and so trying to understand scepticism in Ecclesiastes may require a different approach. Indeed, perceiving links between Ecclesiastes and the rest of the Hebrew Bible may also provide indicators of a diasporic location beyond "the broad interconnectedness of biblical literature."[125] An approach that reflects such connections, as Kynes promotes, would be to (re)read Ecclesiastes intertextually. The implications drawn from the contexts of reading in the ensuing chapters may push us to reconsider how Ecclesiastes fits into the canon.

In addition to Kynes and others,[126] I propose *Maota Tau Ave* "The House to carry" as an talanoa/intertextual framework to reread Ecclesiastes; to reimagine

---

[122] Miscall, "Isaiah," 45.
[123] Sneed, *Was There a Wisdom Tradition?*
[124] Will Kynes, *An Obituary for "Wisdom Literature": The Birth, Death, and Intertextual Reintegration of a Biblical Corpus* (Oxford: Oxford University Press, 2019), 25.
[125] Stuart Weeks, *An Introduction to the Study of Wisdom Literature* (New York: T&T Clark, 2010), 140.
[126] See: Hubert Tita, "Ist Die Thematische Einheit Koh 4,17–5,6 Eine Anspielung Auf Die Salomoerzählung? Aporien Der Religionskritischen Interpretation," *BN* 84 (1996): 87–102; Anton Schoors, „(Mis)Use of Intertextuality in Qoheleth Exegesis," in *Congress Volume: Oslo 1998*, ed. A. Lemaire and M. Sæbø, VTSup 80 (Leiden: Brill, 2000), 45–49; Ruth Fidler, "Qoheleth in "the House of God" Text and Intertext in Qoh 4:17–5:6 (Eng. 5:1–7)," *HS* 47 (2006): 7–21; Jennifer Barbour, *The Story of Israel in the Book of Qohelet: Ecclesiastes as Cultural Memory*, OTM (Oxford: Oxford

Qohelet's space of interrogation as the *maota* which he carries and the *maota* from which he critically engages with his reality. I will be utilising this framework from an alternative or alter-native space, and as such, this exercise would constitute a type of "synchronic intertextuality" or a "reader-centred intertextuality"[127] as I read from my position as a diasporic Australian Samoan. The hermeneutical insights gleaned from this reading might also generate an alternative way to understand the place of Ecclesiastes in the canon.

CONCLUSION

This *talanoa* entails a conversation between Qohelet and intertexts of my diasporic background as a way of highlighting the diasporic tendencies in the text. After all, in spite of a Deuteronomic theology that promotes the teaching that righteous behaviour equates to blessing while wicked actions lead to curse, we hear the voices of dissonance from Qohelet (as well as Job).

In the next chapter, I continue the *talanoa* by thinking more intently around the concept of *maota* and its diasporic nuance through the Hebrew equivalent of בית and its cognate forms. The analysis of texts that dialogically inform each other, as proposed in this work, will expand our horizons of reading, both in the present and in the past.

University Press, 2012); Bernard M. Levinson, ""Better That You Should Not Vow Than That You Vow and Not Fulfull": Qoheleth's Use of Textual Allusion and the Transformation of Deuteronomy's Law of Vows," in Dell and Kynes, *Reading Ecclesiastes Intertextually*, 28–41, Kynes, "Follow Your Heart," 15–27.

[127] Kynes, "Follow Your Heart," 16.

3. House: From Homeland to Diaspora

Maota Tau Ave, introduced in chapter 1, signifies *maota* (house) as a key analogy for understanding kinship and social institutions. It also presents the dynamism of the Samoan *maota* when shifted from the homeland to a transnational context. An interesting parallel exists in the biblical Hebrew context, with the Hebrew word for "house": בית.

Preexilic *Bêt 'Āb*[3]

Cynthia M. Baker states that בית is "a multipurpose word with dozens of connotations and many forms" and signifies "both a domicile and the range of meanings encompassed by the terms 'household' and 'home.'"[1] The word בית is used in a variety of ways—in biblical but also post-biblical circles—and commonly in combination with other words which designate everything from nation or *ethnos* (as in *bet Yisrael*, the "house" or "people" of Israel), to discipleship circles (as in *bet* Shammai and *bet* Hillel), to institutions and their places of meeting (as in *bet din*, law court; *bet ha-midrash*, study house; and *bet ha-knesset*, house of assembly or synagogue), to categories of legal principles (*bet av*), to every manner of place or container (as in *bet yad*, sleeve; or *bet ha-sater*, the "secluded place."[2] In sum, בית "denotes a discursive space within which subjects or persons, cultural institutions, and sociospatial location are inextricable from each other."[3]

Among the familial connotations, בית also carries another key meaning. It is often used in the Hebrew Bible to refer to the temple or the house of the LORD. Within the same semantic field is בית אל or "house of god/God," which Jules Francis Gomes suggests fits better with the term "sanctuary" as an overarching

---

[1] Cynthia M. Baker, *Rebuilding the House of Israel: Architectures of Gender in Jewish Antiquity*, Divinations: Rereading Late Ancient Religion, ed. Daniel Boyarin et al. (Stanford: Stanford University Press, 2002), 55; Chapman, *The House of the Mother*, 25; Shunya Bendor, *The Social Structure of Ancient Israel: The Institution of the Family (Beit 'Ab) from the Settlement to the End of the Monarchy*, ed. Emunah Katzenstein, Jerusalem Biblical Studies 7 (Jerusalem: Simor, 1996), 54.
[2] Baker, *Rebuilding the House of Israel*, 55–56.
[3] Baker, *Rebuilding the House of Israel*, 56.

term as opposed to a fixed building.[4] The building of YHWH's בית is a place of divine "rest," as developed by Deuteronomy and the Chronicler.[5] It is during a period of rest from warfare granted by YHWH that David sees as an opportunity to put a positive mark on his dynasty.[6] Ironically, בית in the Hebrew Bible also carries the meaning of "dynasty" which points to the Davidic dynasty.[7]

The correlation with the Samoan concept of *maota* is uncanny, particularly the way בית can be adapted to any use or space. From a diasporic perspective of *Maota Tau Ave*, the adaptive nature of בית is significant because the dynamic nature of *maota* means that *maota* must also be adaptive. How is בית able to adapt to various uses and spaces? A starting point would be to view one of the earlier and most common usages of בית in the biblical text, through the form בת אב (*bêt 'āb*), "house of the father."

Bêt 'Āb (House of the Father)

Having acknowledged the various nuances above, it is important that we begin with a basic use of בית in order to examine combinations with other lexical items. Perhaps the most common form of בית is when it is used as a construct with אב *'āb* (father) which becomes *bêt 'āb* (house of the father).[8] The patrilineal contours of the biblical narrative are further emphasised by this construct, and as a result, much of the kinship and lineage conversations are located within the father or the husband's house. Scholars have long held *bêt 'āb* as "the basic building block of the tribal structure."[9] For instance, Shunya Bendor explains how *bêt 'āb* fits within larger kinship structures:

> The theoretical sequence was *šebeṭ* (שבט = tribe) / *mišpaḥa* (משפחה = clan) / *bêit 'ab* (בית אב = family). *bêit 'ab*, the smallest unit in the sequence *beit 'ab* /

---

[4] Jules Francis Gomes, *The Sanctuary of Bethel and the Configuration of Israelite Identity* (Berlin: de Gruyter, 2006), 1.
[5] Victor (Avigdor) Hurowitz, *I Have Built You an Exhalted House: Temple Building in the Bible in Light of Mesopotamin and Northeast Semitic Writings*, ed. David J. A. Clines and Philip R. Davies, JSOTSup 115 (Sheffield: JSOT Press, 1992), 330.
[6] Tomoo Ishida, *History and Historical Writing in Ancient Israel: Studies in Biblical Historiography* (Leiden: Brill, 1999), 149; Hurowitz, 330; Simon Goldhill, *The Temple of Jerusalem* (Cambridge: Harvard University Press, 2005), 22.
[7] Ishida, *History and Historical Writing*, 149; Goldhill, *Temple of Jerusalem*, 22; Also see Wolfgang Oswald, *Staatstheorie Im Alten Israel: Der Politische Diskurs Im Pentateuch Und in Den Geschichtsbüchern Des Alten Testaments* (Stuttgart: Kohlhammer, 2009), 63.
[8] The Hebrew אב בית (*bêt 'āb*) is transliterated in various forms by different scholars. For the purpose of consistency in this book and in accordance with my own opinion of the correct transliteration, I will follow Chapman's transliteration (*bêt 'āb*), unless quoting a different form by a different author.
[9] Chapman, *House of the Mother*, 20.

3. House: From Homeland to Diaspora

mišpaḥa / šebeṭ, is common in biblical literature, and numerous passages attest to its importance.[10]

As Bendor implies, *bêt 'āb* is the basic unit of a family, and at the same time points to the father as the point of reference for family groups in biblical literature. The term *bêt 'āb* occurs frequently in the ancestral narratives.[11] It is important to note that in the biblical narrative, *bêt 'āb* often overlaps with the term *mišpaḥa*.[12] The fundamental difference, as pointed out by Baruch A. Levine, is ownership of land and property: *mišpaḥa* does not imply ownership of land and property, but *bêt 'āb* does.[13] The socioeconomic connotations of *bêt 'āb* are quite clear with the patriarchal narratives as well as "the Gideon and Abimelek narratives (Judg 6:27, 9:18), in the Samson cycle (Judg 14:15, 19, 16:31), and frequently in the David stories (1 Sam 17:25, 22:1)."[14] Bendor points to other nuances of *bêt 'āb* in Deut 14:22–26, which "reflects the place of the *beit 'ab* in ritual" while texts such as Isa 3:6; Judg 11:2–11 and 1 Sam 2:27–33 "reflect the importance of the *beit 'ab* in everyday life, in inheritance and in continuity through generations."[15]

On the other hand, an understanding of *bêt 'āb* as the basic unit of a family obscures the vantage point of mother units. Scholars such as Carol Meyers, Cynthia Chapman and Sarah Shectman point to this very problem[16] with biblical evidence which I will discuss later. At this stage, it is important to acknowledge the existence of other vantage points of kinship groups because they allow us to venture outside the traditional patrilocal confines of the *bayit* into other gender-inclusive "territories" and permutations, but also to other lands in a diasporic and transnational context.

FUNCTION OF *BÊT 'ĀB* IN THE BIBLICAL NARRATIVE

Aside from the kinship structures that *bêt 'āb* denotes, scholars argue various interpretations as to the function of *bêt 'āb* in the biblical narrative. John Rogerson and Philip R. Davies speak of two specific functions of *bêt 'āb* in the Hebrew Bible. First, *bêt 'āb* denoted a family living together, as in Gen 7:1 and 50:8

---

[10] Bendor, *Social Structure*, 45; see also Norman K. Gottwald, *The Tribes of Yahweh: A Sociology of the Religion of Liberated Israel 1250–1050 B.C.E* (Maryknoll: Orbis 1979), 237–337.
[11] Baruch A. Levine, *Numbers 21–36: A New Translation with Introduction and Commentary*, AB 4A (New York: Doubleday, 2000), 334.
[12] Paula M. McNutt, *Reconstructing the Society of Ancient Israel*, ed. Douglas A. Knight, LAI (Louisville: Westminster John Knox, 1999), 88.
[13] Levine, *Numbers 21–36*, 334.
[14] Levine, *Numbers 21–36*, 334.
[15] Bendor, *Social Structure*, 45–46.
[16] Carol Meyers, *Discovering Eve: Ancient Israelite Women in Context* (New York: Oxford University Press, 1988), 39. Also see Chapman, 51–74; Sarah Shectman, "Israel's Matriarchs: Political Pawns or Powerbrokers?," in *The Politics of the Ancestors: Exegetical and Historical Perspectives on Genesis 12–36*, ed. Mark G. Brett, Jakob Wöhrle, and Friederike Neumann, FAT 124 (Tübingen: Mohr Siebeck, 2018), 151–65.

whereby "the *bet av* of an unmarried man or woman would be that of their father, and in this case the term would refer to a nuclear family."[17] Another function that Rogerson and Davies explain "is to denote descent."[18] This second use provides a connection between *bêt 'āb* and lineage, as Rogerson and Davies continue:

> A good example is Genesis 24:38, where Abraham's servant is instructed to travel to Mesopotamia to Abraham's 'father's house' to seek a wife for Isaac. Obviously *bet av* here refers not to a residential group but to a descent group. It is probably best understood as a lineage, from which Abraham had separated but within which he wished his son to marry.[19]

Yet lineage is not just restricted to patriarchal setting, because *bêt 'ēm* ("house of the mother") in the stories of Rebecca (Gen 24:28) and Ruth (Ruth 1:8) highlight the significance of maternal descent.[20] The question of lineage is therefore an important characteristic of kinship structures.[21] The importance of lineage is especially evident in the biblical text through the many genealogies, that point to beneficiaries of a promise, or to individuals who are eligible in royal succession.

However, as with many of the genealogies, there are sometimes women included and foreigners, who may not be as prominent as their male counterparts. Chapman and Meyers emphasise these different vantage points, particularly the perspective of the mother. The androcentric nature of the biblical text does not entirely suppress the voice of the mother, as "the term *bêt 'ēm*, translated literally as "house of the mother," appears four times in the Bible (Gen 24:28; Ruth 1:8; Song 3:4; 8:2)."[22] This distances *bêt* from its patrilocal lineage undertones and calls for greater scrutiny, which I will discuss later.

The importance of lineage foregrounds the function of *bêt 'āb* in a political sense—*bêt 'āb* provides a negotiation point for political succession. Political rulers are succeeded within the predecessor's house in the biblical narrative. Such narratives are referred to as "succession narratives," a term coined by Leonhard Rost (in 1929) whose "hypothesis revolved around the identification of a 'succession' theme in the text."[23] It is in this political sense that *bêt 'āb* can mean "royal household" or "dynasty."[24] Apart from Solomon, another example is the

---

[17] John Rogerson, and Philip R. Davies, *The Old Testament World* (New York: T&T Clark International, 2005), 32.
[18] Rogerson, and Davies, *Old Testament World*, 32.
[19] Rogerson, and Davies, *Old Testament World*, 32.
[20] Thalia Gur-Klein, *Sexual Hospitality in the Hebrew Bible: Patronymic, Metronymic, Legitimate and Illegitimate Relations, Gender, Theology and Spirituality*, ed. Lisa Isherwood (London: Routledge, 2014), 285.
[21] Lawrence E. Stager, "The Archaeology of the Family in Ancient Israel," *BASOR* 260 (1985): 22.
[22] Chapman, *House of the Mother*, 51. Also see Meyers *Discovering Eve*, 179.
[23] Gillian Keys, *The Wages of Sin: A Reappraisal of the 'Succession Narrative*, ed. David J.A. Clines and Philip R. Davies, JSOTSup 221 (Sheffield: Sheffield Academic, 1996), 14.
[24] Levine, *Numbers 21–36*, 334.

3. House: From Homeland to Diaspora

successor of Gideon in Judg 9. Upon Gideon's death, Abimelech succeeded Gideon as the ruling judge over Shechem, but only after Abimelech had murdered his half-brothers with the youngest, Jotham the only survivor. Yet in this story, even though Abimelech was acknowledged as the son of Gideon's slave woman (Judg 9:18), he was a son nevertheless.[25] Even though they were from the same household, the political conflicts of *bêt 'āb* may eventuate if there are different motherly kinfolk.

EFFECTS OF MIGRATION

There is general consensus among scholars that *bêt 'āb* began in preexilic times.[26] During these times, the use of *bêt 'āb* was carried from the household into larger contexts. In Joel Weinberg's assessment of the cognate term *bêt 'ābôt* (or *'ābot*) "house of the fathers," he finds that

> A further investigation of the use and distribution of this term in the different levels of the Old Testament reveals that *bêt 'ābôt* or *'ābôt* is dominant in the postexilic parts of the Old Testament, while in the pre-exilic parts, the term *bêt 'āb* is characteristic.[27]

Over time, *bêt 'āb* had experienced a shift in meaning which coincided with the change in context. The meaning of *bêt 'āb* evolved from its singular household meaning in the preexilic Jewish context to the monarchial setting, into the plural postexilic form *bêt 'ābôt* (house of the fathers). Weinberg confirms the necessity of this postexilic form because "consolidation among the exiles and returnees furthered the formation of a new social construction from the pieces of pre-exilic institutions—the *bāttê 'ābôt* of the sixth to fourth centuries BCE."[28]

The need for consolidation among the exiles and returnees became the fundamental framework for reinstitution of the kinship structures which the Israelites were used to. Outside of the Pentateuch and Joshua, the significance of this is largely apparent in Ezra-Nehemiah and Chronicles.[29] Levine explains that

> In this light, it is reasonable to suggest that the term *bêt 'ābôt* was introduced by postexilic writers to designate the ancestral clans of the returning Judeans, now repossessing the lands they had owned before the Exile.[30]

---

[25] David Janzen, "Gideon's House as the אטד: A Proposal for Reading Jotham's Fable," *CBQ* 74 (2012): 474.
[26] Joel Weinberg, *The Citizen-Temple Community*, trans. Daniel L. Smith-Christopher, JSOTSup 151 (Sheffield: JSOT Press, 1992), 60.
[27] Weinberg, *Citizen-Temple Community*, 49.
[28] Weinberg, *Citizen-Temple Community*, 61.
[29] Levine, *Numbers 21–36*, 335.
[30] Levine, *Numbers 21–36*, 335.

It could also be argued that while they were in exile, kinship language was a "mechanism for survival" for the Jewish diaspora.[31]

Daniel Smith-Christopher outlines two aspects of the Hebrew diaspora communities that highlight the persistent character of diasporic communities:

> (1) a strong sense of identity that is separate from those traditions and cultures that surround them, and (2) the necessity to "maintain their social boundaries," that is, to protect this unique identity through a strong emphasis on internal solidarity and consistency.[32]

The new context, through migration, called for the need for solidarity by maintaining an identity in new ways, in spite of the new diasporic setting, so that the Israelite community does not lose their identity due to outside influence. It is apparent that due to the new context, the *bêt 'ābôt* acquired a shift in meaning, and shift in application of kinship terminology for the exiled community.

In summary, the *bêt 'āb* reflect the shifts from the early tribal household into the greater context of Israel's nationhood as a monarchy, to the postexilic *bêt 'ābôt* as a community seeking consolidation amidst the chaos in the exile but also seeking ancestral ties as they return to their ancestral lands. Anne-Mareike Wetter states that "The meaning of this term fluctuates between the semi-literal meaning of an individual household and a more metaphorical entity (Israel)."[33] The ambiguities continue into the uses of the *bêt 'ābôt* and *bet 'ēm* terminology.

BÊT 'ĒM (HOUSE OF THE MOTHER)

The term *bêt 'āb* has received significant scholarly attention, given its importance in identifying kinship structures in the Hebrew Bible, but also as a metaphor for the greater house of Israel. Yet, somewhat obscure in the conversation is the alternative to *bêt 'āb*, which is "house of the mother." However, Shectman explains that despite the limited mention of the term itself, the function of *bêt 'ēm* is rather significant in Genesis.[34] I will survey the work of three scholars—Meyers, Chapman, and Shectman—to further gauge the shifts in *bayit* through *bêt 'ēm*. The discussion will suggest that the topic of social liminality is common in these texts, and in ways that are especially relevant for diaspora readers.

---

[31] Daniel L. Smith, *The Religion of the Landless: The Social Context of the Babylonian Exile* (Bloomington: Meyer-Stone Books, 1989), 63.
[32] Smith-Christopher, *Biblical Theology of Exile*, 138.
[33] Anne-Mareike Wetter, *"On Her Account": Reconfiguring Israel in Ruth, Esther, and Judith* (London: Bloomsbury, 2015), 51.
[34] Shectman, "Israel's Matriarchs," 153.

3. House: From Homeland to Diaspora

CAROL MEYERS

Meyers outlines her concerns with *bêt 'āb* stating that it is "clearly male oriented and derives from lineage concerns, that is, from the way descent and property were reckoned along patrilineal lines."[35] It is therefore important when she mentions the appearance of *bêt 'ēm* in Song of Songs, as an alternative vantage point. As a result, she continues:

> But here in the Song we encounter a situation devoid of such concerns. Rather, the situation is one of relationships, and the primary orientation lies with the female of the pair. Without the matter of lineage reckoning as part of the dynamics of the Song ... the internal functional and relational aspect of household activity, in which females played a strong if not dominant role, is appropriately expressed by "mother's house" and not "father's house."[36]

By this, Meyers pays closer attention to the internal workings within the household, which are often lost amidst the concerns for lineage. More importantly, it introduces a vantage point that is more interested in maintaining internal relationships as opposed to trying to establish external links.

CYNTHIA R. CHAPMAN

Continuing on from Meyers, Chapman extends the discussion of kinship relations in her important work *The House of the Mother: The Social Roles of Maternal Kin in Biblical Hebrew Narrative and Poetry*. Chapman's discussion enters deeper into the vantage point of mothers which Meyers promoted:

> This book demonstrates that when we take into account the associated maternal kinship designations that emerge in house-of-the-mother texts, we can build a case for understanding the term *bêt 'ēm* or "house of the mother" as an indigenous Hebrew kinship designation for the "uterine family."[37]

The concept of "uterine family" presents a more intimate look at relationships in the house, particularly those of uterine connections, although nested within the house of the father. Chapman writes:

> Comprising a mother and her biological and adopted children, the house of the mother is distinct within yet supportive of the house of the father upon which it depends. In its most basic form, a *bêt 'ēm* represents a social and spatial subunit nested within the larger house of the father.[38]

---

[35] Meyers, *Discovering Eve*, 180.
[36] Meyers, *Discovering Eve*, 180.
[37] Chapman, *House of the Mother*, 51.
[38] Chapman, *House of the Mother*, 51.

Genesis 24:28—Rebekah

For Chapman, *bêt 'ēm* proves to be a viable alternative to *bêt 'āb* "as an indigenous, Hebrew designation for what anthropologists term "the uterine family.""[39] First, is the *bêt 'ēm* in Gen 24, the story of Rebekah's betrothal to Isaac. According to Chapman, the Rebekah story in Gen 24 seems to fit a postexilic dating despite traditional source critical analysis attributing the chapter to a Yahwistic source.[40] Chapman surveys the various reasons argued by scholars, such as Alexander Rofé, for this dating, such as the existence of Aramaic language and features[41] and the theology and literary style, which point to the Rebekah story as "a late addition to an existing Abraham cycle."[42]

The late addition of the Rebekah story disrupts the narrative from Sarah's death in Gen 23 to Abraham's death and Isaac's marriage notification.[43] Yet at the same time, it is strategically placed as Chapman makes note that "chapter 24 is also in conversation with existing Abrahamic genealogies in its repeated identification of Rebekah as 'the daughter of Bethuel, son of Milcah whom she bore to Nahor' (Gen 24:15, 24, 47)."[44]

Rebekah's lineage obviously raises questions, as Chapman probes into why her paternal grandmother is mentioned and not her own mother?[45] Chapman contends: "I would argue that the author of Gen 24 knew of the tradition of Nahor having both a wife, Milcah, and a concubine, Reumah (Gen 22:20–24), and he wanted to specify that Rebekah was born into the line that extended through a wife."[46] By instituting the *bêt 'ēm* entity, the author gives Rebekah more favourable origins.

We also learn of the relationships inside the *bêt 'ēm* as Rebekah runs to her mother's house to tell them of the visitor, and in the *bêt 'ēm* we are introduced to

> Rebekah's brother in a direct, unmediated way ... Laban is not identified as "Bethuel's son," and he is not located with reference to the house of his father.

---

[39] Chapman, *House of the Mother*, 74.
[40] Chapman, *House of the Mother*, 51–52.
[41] Alexander Rofé, "An Enquiry into the Betrothal of Rebekah," in *Die Hebräische Bibel Und Ihre Zweifache Nachgeschichte: Festschrift Für Rolf Rendtorff*, ed. Erhard Blum, Christian Macholz, and Ekkehard W. Stegemann (Neukirchen-Vluyn: Neukirchener Verlag, 1990), 27–39. Also see Mark G. Brett, "Yhwh among the Nations: The Politics of the Divine Names in Genesis 15 and 24," in *The Politics of the Ancestors: Exegetical and Historical Perspectives on Genesis 12–36*, ed. Mark G. Brett, Jakob Wöhrle, and Friederike Neumann (Tübingen: Mohr Siebeck, 2018), 115.
[42] Chapman, *House of the Mother*, 52. See Rofé, "An Enquiry into the Betrothal of Rebekah," 27–39. Also see: David Carr, *The Formation of the Hebrew Bible: A New Reconstruction* (Oxford: Oxford University Press, 2011), 280–81.
[43] Chapman, *House of the Mother*, 52.
[44] Chapman, *House of the Mother*, 52.
[45] Chapman, *House of the Mother*, 52.
[46] Chapman, *House of the Mother*, 52.

Instead, he is named, tied directly to Rebekah as "her brother," and located in the "house of her mother." All of these details suggest that the shift to the mother's house entails a shift in the key relationships; we are now focusing on Rebekah, her mother, and her brother.[47]

This is a significant shift in the common *bêt 'āb* understanding that usually focuses on paternal lineage and succession, but here, we are introduced to uterine relationships that present the vantage point of the mother and other non-father members in a household. In fact, Chapman states that "The 'house of the mother' is introduced from the vantage point of a young, marriageable daughter." At the same time,

> The dominant figure with Rebekah's *bêt 'ēm* is her brother Laban. He is party to every action that occurs within the *bêt 'ēm:* he opens the house to the stranger, hosts the dinner, accepts the marriage proposal, receives gifts, and pronounces the marriage blessing.[48]

Although Rebekah is mentioned as the daughter of Bethuel in the narrative, Chapman correctly points out that while Bethuel has authority, he is "clearly ancillary to that of Laban."[49] Laban is perhaps dominant in the narrative due to other interests as the brother-sister relationship between Rebekah and Laban hints at "economic underpinnings."[50] As Chapman argues: "The linking of the jewelry to Laban's haste suggest that the economic value of the jewelry precipitates Laban's hospitality."[51] Kinship is apparently up for negotiations that can be influenced by "money."

Ruth 1:8—Orpah and Ruth

The dating of Ruth is difficult to determine. One explanation for a possible dating is through the argument that the function of the book of Ruth was "to acknowledge, address, and attempt to ameliorate the problem of David's Moabite roots."[52] However, Katherine E. Southwood would argue that Ruth's Moabite heritage was of little significance for most of the book of Ruth, as she assimilated into the Israelite way.[53] Her marriage to Boaz and birth of their son seem to accentuate her assimilation.[54] As a result, this means that "its historical context, therefore, has to be a

---

[47] Chapman, *House of the Mother*, 54.
[48] Chapman, *House of the Mother*, 58.
[49] Chapman, *House of the Mother*, 58.
[50] Chapman, *House of the Mother*, 54.
[51] Chapman, *House of the Mother*, 54.
[52] Chapman, *House of the Mother*, 59. Also see Kristin Nielsen, *Ruth: A Commentary*, OTL (Louisville: Westminster John Knox, 1997).
[53] Katherine E. Southwood, "Will Naomi's Nation Be Ruth's Nation? Ethnic Translation as a Metaphor for Ruth's Assimilation within Judah," *Humanities* 3 (2014): 120.
[54] Southwood, "Will Naomi's Nation," 119.

time period when the Davidic dynasty was under threat. Unfortunately, this could be any time from the actual reign of David through the postexilic effort to reinstate the monarchy under Zerubbabel."[55] Chapman therefore concludes that while we cannot be precise as to the dating, "if the book of Ruth is in conversation with an existing David narrative," then the late seventh-century may possibly be the earliest date.[56]

The house into which Naomi has married "has ceased to exist" due to the death of her husband Elimelech, and his two sons who had taken Moabite wives, Ruth and Orpah.[57] The vantage point therefore, like Gen 24, according to Chapman, is "once again that of a marriageable woman. Neither Ruth nor Orpah had children from their first husbands, so now widowed, Naomi hopes each can remarry."[58]

What we see here as we did in Gen 24, is that the *bêt 'ēm* is a space for negotiating marriage. The hope was that each of Ruth and Orpah would return to their own *bêt 'ēm* in order to negotiate new marriages so that "they could leave again to live in their new husbands' houses."[59] But as the story goes, we only see Orpah return to her mother's house while Ruth follows Naomi. The lack of details regarding Orpah's return denies us valuable information of Orpah's *bêt 'ēm* and it would be an interesting vantage point to consider.

Song of Songs

The dating of Song of Songs and therefore the *bêt 'ēm* is most likely postexilic, as Chapman notes that although the poetry may come from an earlier date, "the current collection is considered one of the latest books of the Bible."[60] The "house of the mother" occurs twice in the Song while *bêt 'āb* does not occur at all.[61] The female protagonist in the Song is "part of a family that consists of her mother and uterine brothers, whom she refers to as "my mother's sons" (Song 1:6)."[62]

The household described here points to an understanding of *bêt 'ēm* in the Song as a physical space, while the second reference suggests that it is also the space where she envisions "finding her uterine brother (Song 3:4; 8:1–2)."[63] Yet it is clear that the book is not at all focused on marriage as in Gen 24 and Ruth. There are allusions to marriage, for instance, when the woman is called by her lover "my sister, my bride" or "my bride."[64] But as Chapman points out, the nature

---

[55] Chapman, *House of the Mother*, 59.
[56] Chapman, *House of the Mother*, 59.
[57] Chapman, *House of the Mother*, 60.
[58] Chapman, *House of the Mother*, 60.
[59] Chapman, *House of the Mother*, 61.
[60] Chapman, *House of the Mother*, 61.
[61] Chapman, *House of the Mother*, 61.
[62] Chapman, *House of the Mother*, 61–62.
[63] Chapman, *House of the Mother*, 62.
[64] Chapman, *House of the Mother*, 62.

of the love poems points more to a longing between two lovers, as the woman speaks of her *bêt 'ēm* as a private place where she and her lover can "engage in sexual activity."[65] Despite that, Chapman is adamant that despite the sexual focus of the poems, the *bêt 'ēm* is still spoken from the vantage point of a marriageable woman.[66]

More importantly, Chapman illumines the fact that the "speaker's father is absent from the book."[67] It is a rare moment where the father has no authority, and I wonder whether this reflects a context where the father indeed had no influence. In trying to comprehend the shifts in understanding *bayit*, the fact that the father is absent may point to a context that is father-less, or tradition-less! In the spirit of *talanoa*, perhaps the *bêt 'ēm* in the Song points to the operation of *bayit* outside of Israel, and in the diaspora.

Allow me to clarify or to *tala* (extend) into the *noa* (void): *bêt 'ēm* in the Song is a private place because the woman desires for her lover to be alone there with her. This concern with the private life suggests "that the Song was composed in a Hellenized atmosphere."[68] In the Hellenistic context, women were relieved from their traditional legal and social restrictions.[69] *Bêt 'ēm* in the Song therefore seems to include notions of freedom and autonomy, and a desire for the private life away from the public eye. While the context of Palestine itself was Hellenized during the late Second Temple period, we could also argue that the context was diasporic geographically, or at least sociologically through transnational influences.

Dinah: Daughter of Leah

Chapman's query continues onto the story of Dinah in Gen 34, which does not mention *bêt 'ēm* explicitly, but "provides several clues that we are dealing with issues understood to fall within the purview of the *bêt 'ēm*."[70] The first clue is the unusual description of Dinah as the daughter of Leah:

> It is unusual to identify a person through her mother, so the fact that this narrative opens with a maternal genealogy suggests that we are dealing with an event where the house of Leah will prove central, just as in the story of Joseph, the

---

[65] Chapman, *House of the Mother*, 63.
[66] Chapman, *House of the Mother*, 63.
[67] Chapman, *House of the Mother*, 64.
[68] Ariel Bloch and Chana Bloch, *The Song of Songs: A New Translation with an Introduction and Commentary* (Berkeley: University of California Press, 1995), 27.
[69] Joan B. Burton, "Themes of Female Desire and Self-Assertion in the Song of Songs and Hellenistic Poetry," in *Perspectives on the Song of Songs/ Perspektiven Der Hoheliedauslegung*, ed. Anselm C. Hagedorn (Berlin: de Gruyter, 2005), 182.
[70] Chapman, *House of the Mother*, 64.

house of Rachel was central. It is also significant that Dinah's pathway to her father in this opening verse is mediated through her mother.[71]

The other significant aspect of identifying Dinah as the daughter of Leah is the allusion to the controversial role her uterine brothers Simeon and Levi play in the narrative. Jacob and his house are approached by Hamor and Shechem for the marriage proposal, in spite of the horrendous rape of Dinah which angers her uterine brothers.[72] But while it is Jacob and his house that he addressed, it is Simeon and Levi "that answer the request, deal deceitfully, and demand circumcision on a prerequisite to a broader marriage treaty."[73] Their authority over Dinah is made clear when she is referred to as "daughter" (Gen 34:17).[74]

What ensues is conflict between Jacob and his sons over the mass killing of the Shechemites, as Jacob is concerned over his *bayit*. Simeon and Levi, the uterine brothers of Dinah, "seem more concerned with their mother's house, which they feel has suffered an assault. They respond unrepentantly, 'Can he treat our sister as a whore?' (Gen 34:31)."[75] While we do not see the *bêt 'ēm* as a physical space in this story, we still see the social functions in action. As such, Chapman concludes that "This text would then be an example of the *bêt 'ēm* as a kinship group with specific social functions acting outside of the physical space of the *bêt 'ēm*."[76]

Summary

Chapman draws a host of conclusions. In all the texts she analyses, the view of *bêt 'ēm* is from the vantage point of marriageable daughter. The daughter is also "expected to leave her natal home and marry into the house of her husband."[77] In these examples we also see the emphasis on uterine connections in the *bêt 'ēm* such as those of the mother and the uterine brothers. These uterine brothers also act as guardians and authority over their uterine sister.[78]

Furthermore, Chapman finds that although it is difficult to date the texts that contain the term *bêt 'ēm*, they each seem "to postdate and amplify the genealogy and epic story of a foundational male figure—Abraham, Jacob, David, or Solomon."[79] Most likely it is later writers reflecting back on these foundational characters.

---

[71] Chapman, *House of the Mother*, 65.
[72] The view that Dinah was raped is disputed by some scholars. For instance, see Eve Levavi Feinstein, *Sexual Pollution in the Hebrew Bible* (Oxford: Oxford University Press, 2014), 77.
[73] Chapman, *House of the Mother*, 65.
[74] Chapman, *House of the Mother*, 65.
[75] Chapman, *House of the Mother*, 66.
[76] Chapman, *House of the Mother*, 67.
[77] Chapman, *House of the Mother*, 67.
[78] Chapman, *House of the Mother*, 67.
[79] Chapman, *House of the Mother*, 67.

3. House: From Homeland to Diaspora

Chapman also highlights that each text seems to have a concern with intermarriage with foreigners. In the examples, Chapman explains that Abraham sends his servant to Aram so that Isaac does not marry a Canaanite, while Rebekah's Terahite genealogy is given emphasis in the narrative. Ruth is presented as a devoted daughter-in-law who chooses to remain with Naomi despite Naomi telling her to return back to her home. As a result, the portrayal of Ruth "clarifies and cleanses King David's genealogical association with Moab."[80] The acts of Hamor and Shechem with the rape of Dinah put an end to Dinah's marriage negotiations as Shechem and Hamor are massacred "because Shechem was a foreigner, an uncircumcised Hivite, who had 'defiled her'."[81] In the case of the female protagonist in the Song, while her being called a Shulammite in Song 7:1 may point her to being from Jerusalem, one may conclude that "the tense and at times adversarial relationship that she has with the 'Daughters of Jerusalem' suggests that she might be an outsider to this group."[82]

Chapman draws additional conclusions, however, from a diasporic perspective, and these have significant implications for a cross-cultural dialogue with the Samoan *maota*. For example, suggestion of the protagonist in the Song as an "outsider" is significant because Samoans in the diaspora are always seen as "outsiders" by those in the homeland. As in Gen 24, Samoan kinship in the diaspora is often linked in some way to traditional family groups in the homeland. For Samoans in the diaspora, the longing may be to stay connected with the *fanua* (land) and the *'āiga* (family), by carrying the *maota* (or *bayit*) into foreign lands. To be an outsider, therefore, is to not to disconnect, but to remain connected.

SARAH SHECTMAN

Shectman approaches the question of Israel's matriarchs in two ways: fictional politics of the characters in the narrative (literary), and the real politics of the historical background of the narrative (historical).[83]

Fictional Politics (Literary Level)

Shectman notes that the stories in Genesis are mostly personal and family-centred. They show ethnonational concerns as the patriarchs are "literary stand-ins for the groups that emerge in the course of the narrative."[84]

Shectman's focus then moves to the function of the matriarchs in these narratives, particularly in Gen 12, 20 and 26. In Gen 12, Sarai is used by Abram for economic gain. Gen 20 focuses on Abimelekh's relationship to Abraham and God. Gen 26, consisting of a promise to the patriarch, neglects the political marriage-

---

[80] Chapman, *House of the Mother*, 68.
[81] Chapman, *House of the Mother*, 68.
[82] Chapman, *House of the Mother*, 68.
[83] Shectman, "Israel's Matriarchs," 151.
[84] Shectman, "Israel's Matriarchs," 152.

alliance and economic gain completely.⁸⁵ The roles of the matriarchs start off insignificantly and may be seen as mere "pawns" in the stories, but as the narrative progresses, their roles increase.⁸⁶

Shectman then argues that they are not pawns, but powerbrokers. After Isaac's birth, Sarah moves to drive Hagar and Ishmael away to nullify the threat to Isaac of Ishmael's existence. Significantly, YHWH is Sarah's ally in this ploy who orders Abraham to adhere to Sarah's demands. In similar fashion, Rebekah intervenes between two sons, as she plays a critical role in Jacob's inheritance and birthright, although this time, the cunning of the "queen mother" figure is more profound given that Esau and Jacob are both her sons! Rachel and Leah also play critical roles in securing Jacob's departure from Laban's household to establish his own: a household that will become the nation of Israel.⁸⁷ Further, Rachel and Leah were able to break ties between Israel and Aram that had been a significant aspect of Abraham's descendants. This break enabled Jacob and his family to return to Canaan and establish the nation of Israel.⁸⁸

Hagar is also a powerbroker in the narrative because despite being cast out, she receives a blessing from YHWH in that she would become the progenitor to a nation that rivals Abraham's descendants in numbers.⁸⁹ Perhaps less glorious is the episode of Lot's daughters who, while not powerbrokers in the strict sense of the word, do exercise a plan in having sex with their drunken father.⁹⁰ Their descendants become the nations Moab and Ammon. The story of Dinah in Genesis 34 provides a final point of reflection for Shectman, that while Dinah may be a pawn in this episode, the case of her rape "appears at a crucial juncture where the Israelites end up differentiating themselves from another people (or rather, maintain differentiation when faced with the option of assimilation)."⁹¹

Real Politics (Historical Level)

In trying to ascertain the politics from an historical point of view, Shectman argues that "There is strikingly little in the Pentateuch—not only in Genesis but elsewhere as well—forbidding foreign marriages unilaterally."⁹² In conversation with Albert de Pury, it seems that the Priestly writer is actually concerned with Abraham's "multinational offspring" despite narrowing down the inheritor of the covenant to Isaac. P therefore sees all the different people of Abraham's lineage as "heirs to the land (though not the covenant)" and who "rightfully live in the

---

⁸⁵ Shectman, "Israel's Matriarchs," 152.
⁸⁶ Shectman, "Israel's Matriarchs," 153.
⁸⁷ Shectman, "Israel's Matriarchs," 154.
⁸⁸ Shectman, "Israel's Matriarchs," 155.
⁸⁹ Shectman, "Israel's Matriarchs," 155.
⁹⁰ Shectman, "Israel's Matriarchs," 155–56.
⁹¹ Shectman, "Israel's Matriarchs," 156.
⁹² Shectman, "Israel's Matriarchs," 156.

3. House: From Homeland to Diaspora

land together."[93] This then correlates to a Persian-period setting for de Pury, as the narrative does not just focus on the Canannites but also the Edomites and Arabs who were living as neighbours with Israel under Persian rule.[94]

Shectman makes a telling observation that although these various groups may all trace their roots back to Abraham, they are differentiated through their mothers! While the politics of the Genesis men revolve around land and water rights negotiations, the politics of the women on the other hand deal with the birth of children, which relates to the politics of the men. Shectman notes that "the matriarchs often take an active and important role in ensuring the progress of the lineage."[95] Their roles redefine the purpose of marriage in the Genesis narrative as the marriages are not only endogamous and serve to solidify alliances, but they also differentiate Israelites from other cultural groups. Similarly, Lot's daughters create "new non-Israelite lineages" while Rachel and Leah sever all endogamous possibilities between Jacob and Laban through a treaty in Gen 31.[96] The patriarchs, particularly Abraham, extend their borders with a multinational focus, but the matriarchs "pull in the opposite direction—to make sure that the particularism of Israel is ensured despite their husbands' prolific begettings."[97] Shectman concludes that the matriarchs "complicate our understanding of Israel as a purely patrilineal society, demonstrating as they do that simple patrilineality is not enough to determine lines of succession."[98]

SAMOAN ANALOGIES

There are areas in the discussions above that give rise to analogies in my own context that suggest further implications as to the effect of migration on understanding *bayit*. More importantly, I suggest that migration yields new complexities for, and even scepticism towards, traditional kinship structures.

UTERINE CONNECTIONS

The discussions above raise a key question: How do "uterine" subunits function in the diaspora among Samoan communities? This is significant for migrant Samoan families, because the uterine connection does not just emphasise connections between uterine family members, but it is what connects Samoans back to the homeland or the *fanua* (land). As Tui Atua Tupua Tamasese Efi explains: "*Fanua* is also the word for placenta. *Fanua* meaning land and *fanua*

---

[93] Shectman, "Israel's Matriarchs," 157.
[94] Shectman, "Israel's Matriarchs," 157.
[95] Shectman, "Israel's Matriarchs," 158.
[96] Shectman, "Israel's Matriarchs," 160.
[97] Shectman, "Israel's Matriarchs," 161.
[98] Shectman, "Israel's Matriarchs," 163.

meaning placenta frame and define Samoan rights and access to land."[99] While a uterine connection with land is not evident in the biblical texts under discussion, Samoan analogies may provide some implications for further interpretations of *bêt 'ēm*. We see in Gen 24 and Ruth that the *bêt 'ēm* terminology comes into play particularly in exchanges between homeland and diaspora.

Despite the opportunities available in *Maota Tau Ave*, complexities arise in diaspora, and also sceptical responses, as some Samoans no longer see the relevance of land ties. Indeed, in my own experience, the voices heard are of second-generation Australian Samoans, as well as oppressed migrants who no longer see a future in the Samoan *matai* system.

MARRIAGE

Marriage negotiations between Samoans who live on opposite sides of the Pacific Ocean are common, which brings our attention to some details in Gen 24 that are potentially relevant.

The mission of Abraham's servant alludes to a migration issue which puts Abraham's contract with YHWH at risk.[100] YHWH had instructed Abraham in Gen 12 to leave the land of his father and migrate to a land that he will reveal. In searching for Isaac's wife, Abraham is reluctant for Isaac to marry the Canaanite women and sends his servant on a mission back to the land of his father, to find his son Isaac a wife. A dilemma arises for Abraham as the narrative reaches a situation where Isaac cannot remigrate back to the old country, and Rebekah needs to migrate to Abraham's household.[101] This foreshadows potential movements and migrations[102] in the narrative for the purpose of avoiding intermarriage with the Canaanites—a sentiment analogous to Ezra-Nehemiah[103]—but only through the manipulative rhetoric of the servant.[104]

To my mind, the servant's rhetoric resonates with the voices of change and manipulation of Samoans in the diaspora. Cultural traditions and practices are often manipulated to fit the diasporic context, but they also serve an agenda that can be sceptical of the traditions of the homeland. Could such insights inform Qohelet's own position of scepticism?

---

[99] Tui Atua Tupua Tamasese Ta'isi Efi, *Su'esu'e Manogi: In Search of Fragrance*, ed. Tamasailau M. Suaalii-Sauni et al., 2nd ed. (Wellington: Huia, 2018), 205.
[100] Brett, "Yhwh among the Nations," 123.
[101] Brett, "Yhwh among the Nations," 123; cf. David Frankel, *The Land of Canaan and the Destiny of Israel: Theologies of Territory in the Hebrew Bible*, Siphrut 4 (Winona Lake: Eisenbrauns, 2011), 246–47.
[102] Chapman, *House of the Mother*, 59. I say "movements" and "migrations" in reference to Rebekah's prospective migration, as Chapman states that Rebekah "will ultimately marry out of her natal home and reside with her husband."
[103] Brett, "Yhwh among the Nations," 121–22.
[104] Brett, "Yhwh among the Nations," 125.

Cultural

In the Samoan analogy, the economic and social benefits of migration are obvious. But when marriage fails, uterine connections are reestablished for Samoan women. For instance, while Ruth is idealised in the narrative, Samoan norms would favour Orpah as she returns to her original *maota*, to her original *'āiga*. These women in the Samoan context are known as *nofotane* (lit. living with male spouse). But when the spouse dies, the *nofotane* must return back to her father's household, or face contempt and ridicule in her deceased husband's village. We do not hear Orpah's story, but it would be intriguing to see how Ruth would be perceived in the Samoan context. If Ruth had a Samoan story, it would most likely be appreciated by Samoans in the diaspora because, in their view, Ruth would be the outcast, and outcasts have a better standing in the diaspora.

Conclusion: The Diasporic *Bayit*

As the Samoan diasporic context shows, such attitudes of scepticism and resistance would not just be against external forces. There is every likelihood that scepticism and resistance were channelled towards internal processes, or cultural practices and traditional wisdom that perhaps held little to no value in the diaspora. This brings me to the discussion on *bêt 'ēm*.

Meyers, Chapman and Shectman provide an important alternative to understanding kinship structures under the traditional *bêt 'āb* entity. Specifically, we became alerted to the significance of household structures where the mother, the daughter and the sons of the mothers played social responsibilities, both inside and outside the *bêt 'ēm*. Negotiations for marriage became a key feature of the *bêt 'ēm* which saw the uterine brothers of the daughter rise to authority, especially in place of the absent father. We also saw the roles of the matriarchs emerge as critical people, especially in the Genesis narrative, who were able to negotiate for their sons in light of their husbands' agendas. Consequently, households were perceived through the vantage points of mothers, brothers and marriageable daughters. *Bêt 'ēm* therefore enables the *bayit* to become a space for resistance and scepticism. It allows the other vantage points or the other voices, to question the wisdom of the father.

Furthermore, the shift in understanding *bayit* from these different vantage points also opened up the possibility for viewing the *bayit* from afar. In each of the examples that Chapman discussed, there was physical distance between the *bayit* of the negotiator and the *bayit* of the marriageable woman. Vantage points emerge when one is destined to move and migrate. Migration then may be the key factor in the mutations of the older *bêt 'āb* structure. The *bêt 'ēm* texts are indicative of the effects of migration that put into question the issue of patriarchal lineage. I conclude that the evidence of kinship mutations in postexilic and diaspora contexts opens up more space for skeptical wisdom. Chapman already points out that those in these marginalised vantage points are deemed "outsiders."[105] Perhaps Qohelet too was an "outsider."[106]

---

[105] Chapman, *House of the Mother*, 68.
[106] Cf. Smith-Christopher, *A Biblical Theology of Exile*, 173.

4. Qohelet and Diaspora Studies

Ecclesiastes has an unorthodox approach to the questions of life, making it seemingly out of place in the Hebrew Bible. The heterogenous nature of the debate regarding the date and setting of Qohelet further highlights the difficulties in reading Ecclesiastes. Doug Ingram maintains that the text of Ecclesiastes is deliberately ambiguous.[1] Ingram's position is suggestive for our purposes, because such ambiguity creates a platform which allows for more voices to enter the inner-biblical debate, while at the same time opening up possibilities for further perspectives in contemporary reading—including our diasporic perspective.

The text itself contains a great deal of evidence not only of unorthodox philosophical musings, but also of an unconventional context. But which context? A host of modern scholars have voiced their opinion on the matter, and a majority of them can only collectively agree that it is not preexilic. It may be as late as the Hellenistic period, but modern scholars are unable to find consensus in their reasoning. One of the difficulties here is that ideas about "context" have focused on dating rather than social context.

Some locate Ecclesiastes in the Persian period. Seow and Fox base their arguments on linguistic evidence in the text, noting in particular the Persian loan words and Aramaisms.[2] Additionally, Seow believes that the economic interests shown in the text are a Persian influence.[3] On the other hand, scholars such as Crenshaw are unconvinced by Seow, preferring a Hellenistic date.[4] Supporters of a Hellenistic date highlight philosophical elements consistent with Hellenistic and Greek thought and culture. Craig Bartholomew also disagrees with Seow, noting that while Seow is correct in drawing attention to economic elements, this does not necessarily have to suggest Persian influence. Rather, Bartholomew believes

---

[1] Doug Ingram, "The Riddle of Qohelet and Qohelet the Riddler," *JSOT* 37 (2013): 485. Also see Doug Ingram, *Ambiguity in Ecclesiastes*, LHBOTS 431 (London: Bloomsbury, 2006).
[2] Seow, *Ecclesiastes*, 20; Fox, *Qohelet and His Contradictions*, 151.
[3] Seow, *Ecclesiastes*, 21.
[4] James L. Crenshaw, *Qoheleth: The Ironic Wink* (Columbia: University of South Carolina Press, 2013), 58.

that there is much evidence of Greek thought and culture consistent with a Hellenistic date.[5]

In these arguments, it is obvious that there were external influences upon Qohelet. The book's content is inconsistent with conventional Jewish wisdom and tradition, as well as with the Deuteronomic formula of deeds and consequences. The difficulty with dating reflects this, and there is an array of possible influences that may have shaped Qohelet's unorthodox position.

Yet if there is evidence of external influence, then this is also reason to argue for a diasporic setting. Smith-Christopher believes that the wisdom of Ecclesiastes and Proverbs promote ethics in a diasporic setting, citing the cynicism of Qohelet as a reflection of people trying to survive in a dehumanising context.[6] He further adds that Ecclesiastes makes the most sense when read in the context of diaspora.[7] Fox also considers a diasporic setting as he finds that in 5:7 *medinah* (province) is indicative of Jews living in the empire, either Persian or Hellenistic.[8] Weeks also contends that the possibility of a diasporic setting cannot be ignored.[9] It is my hope also that this study paves the way for current diasporic perspectives to engage with biblical questions from the diasporic space.

A CASE FOR A DIASPORIC CONTEXT

While Qohelet is critical of certain aspects of Jewish wisdom and Jewish life, Qohelet's critique of the temple in chapter 5 is perhaps the most suggestive of a diasporic perspective. The negative judgement on temple practice, including the suggestion that God lives in heaven, demotes the temple in Qohelet's imagination. Norbert Lohfink believes that 5:1–6 is the final part of Qohelet's "religious critique" which begins from 4:17.[10] The suggestion that God lives in heaven and that the people are on earth for Lohfink then is a sign of divine withdrawal.[11] I contend that this "distance" is more profound than just a spiritual withdrawal, but fits with an exilic setting, of a people removed from their land, who no longer worship in the temple of YHWH.

The several references to Jerusalem also provoke an obvious question: Why is there no reference to YHWH, or YHWH's temple? Why is there no "fear of YHWH"? The name YHWH is the personal name of God for Israel, yet there is no mention of YHWH anywhere in Eccl 5 and in the rest of the book; instead, the

---

[5] Craig G. Bartholomew, *Ecclesiastes* (Grand Rapids, MI: Baker Academic, 2009), 57.
[6] Smith-Christopher, *Biblical Theology of Exile*, 168–73.
[7] Smith-Christopher, *Biblical Theology of Exile*, 168.
[8] Fox, *Ecclesiastes*, xiv.
[9] Weeks, *Ecclesiastes and Scepticism*, 7.
[10] Norbert Lohfink, *Qoheleth: A Continental Commentary*, trans. Sean McEvenue (Minneapolis: Fortress, 2003), 3.
[11] Lohfink, *Qoheleth*, 75.

name "Elohim" is employed. This coheres with Job's preference for Elohim and Eloah. So is there a question about whether someone away from YHWH's jurisdiction might reflect on a (foreign) temple? Could this be termed a "temple of Elohim," rather than a temple of YHWH? These questions fit also with a diasporic context, and it is these implications for a diasporic reading that I wish to pursue.

LOCATING A MOTIVATED READING

I confess that a motivation for testing this diasporic reading arises from the experience of Samoans living in the Australian diaspora. The details of this location are set out in chapter 2, so only a brief summary is necessary at this point. The rest of the chapter will engage the theoretical perspectives that come from diaspora studies as a field. I belong to the diaspora who, as Segovia writes, are a "growing segment of people from the Third World who are forced to live—for whatever reason, though usually involving a combination of sociopolitical and socioeconomic factors—in the First World."[12] For years, Samoans have left their homeland in search of better opportunities for work and education in New Zealand. From there, they dispersed into Australia, from suburb to suburb, state to state, in search of a better life. With the better lifestyle came a completely different experience—one where the values and insights of that different lifestyle came into conflict with the ethno-cultural values of the homeland.

The question that continues to hamper Samoans in the diaspora is whether or not they should maintain the culture and customs of the homeland, including religious practices. As Samoans continue to exist as an ethnic group in a multi-ethnic society like Australia, the relevance of the Samoan culture comes into question. Should they still uphold the *faa-Samoa*?

With this perspective, I enter the scholarly debate surrounding Qohelet's voice as resonant with a people detached from their homeland, dispersed into a foreign land away from their old religious institutions. A key question within the inquiry is whether or not the pessimistic and defiant tone of Qohelet arises not just from frustration with Israelite Wisdom and Deuteronomic formulae, but also from an ambivalent acceptance of the wisdom of the new land. Before setting out the details of my hypothesis, however, it will be necessary to provide a general introduction to diaspora studies.

EMERGENCE OF DIASPORIC STUDIES

Diasporic studies was a significant development out of postcolonial studies, as focus shifted towards transnational communities. This focus on the transnational space was prominent in the theoretical groundwork of diasporic studies, as laid by scholars such as Edward Said, Homi Bhabha, Frantz Fanon, Stuart Hall, Paul

---

[12] Segovia, "Hermeneutics of the Diaspora," 60.

Gilroy, James Clifford and others.[13] As Mark Shackleton argues, these authors and others "vitalized postcolonial and diaspora studies, challenging ways in which we understand 'culture' and developing new ways of thinking beyond the confines of the nation state."[14] I have chosen such authors because their insights help define the emphasis of my approach. While a diasporic perspective is postcolonial, I do not emphasise the resistance to colonial power typical of postcolonial thought, but will rather investigate the thought worlds of diasporic identities regardless of whether there is resistance towards the colonial power (host nation) or not.

EDWARD SAID

For this talanoa of diasporic theorists, I begin with Edward Said, a prominent voice in postcolonial theory whose work navigates the complexities of the diasporic space/s from an American-Palestinian perspective. For instance, in his classic work *Orientalism*, Said highlighted the experiences of Arab and Islamic identities. Astonishingly, the problems that he wrote about in 1977 are still relevant, as he argues that the notion of the Orient in Britain, France and America, correspond not to a "stable reality" but to "the impulse not simply to describe, but also to dominate and somehow defend against it."[15] What Said suggests is that the experience of the Orient, especially in the West, is a struggle, and that the

> task for the critical scholar is not to separate one struggle from another, but to connect them, despite the contrast between the overpowering materiality of the former [West] and the apparent other-worldly refinements of the latter [Orient].[16]

As often acknowledged today, the struggle of the Orient is frequently obscured by propaganda promoting Western interests. But what Said highlights is not an "aggressive, race-oriented nationalism" but a consideration of the Other by providing an opportunity for dialogue. Said's claims reflect the need for dialogue with the Other, that is, the West but also Jewish identities in hostile relations with Palestinians. Nor does he avoid a self-critical understanding of Arab and Islamic identities. The description of postcolonial conditions then informed Said's own experience of living in diaspora, as he "entered into the life of the West, and yet retained some organic connection with the place [he] originally came from."[17] The retention of connection with the homeland is a crucial element of the diasporic experience because it places the diasporic identity in a mode where one culture crosses over into another, or of one world into another.

---

[13] Mark Shackleton, "Introduction," in *Diasporic Literature and Theory—Where Now?*, ed. Mark Shackleton (Newcastle UK: Cambridge Scholars, 2008), xl.
[14] Shackleton, "Introduction," xl.
[15] Edward Said, *Orientalism* (London: Penguin, 2003), 331.
[16] Said, *Orientalism*, 332.
[17] Said, *Orientalism*, 336.

Stuart Hall

Continuing the conversation, I cross over to cultural theorist Stuart Hall, a Jamaican native who migrated to London in the 1950s for his education and eventually to live. Hall argues that the native identity should not be viewed as an "accomplished fact," instead "as a 'production', which is never complete, always in process, and always constituted within, not outside, representation."[18] This understanding of cultural identity provides the fabric of diasporic identities, which have traditionally been thought of as "scattered tribes" who exist with a longing for the homeland. Hall's understanding of diasporic identities goes beyond this, as he writes:

> The diaspora experience as I intend it here is defined, not by essence or purity, but by the recognition of a necessary heterogeneity and diversity; by a conception of 'identity' which lives with and through, not despite, difference; by *hybridity*. Diaspora identities are those which are constantly producing and reproducing themselves anew, through transformation and difference.[19]

In Hall's book *Journey to Illusion*, he describes his experiences and the anxieties of first arriving in London, and the eerie similarity of his own struggles as a native in Jamaica, to his experience in London. Hall's recollection of his first impressions upon arriving are striking:

> the difficulties my family background had bequeathed to me of neither wanting any identification with my own social stratum, nor being able to feel present in my own homeland, conscious of the chasm that separated me from the multitude—had turned up to meet me on the other side of the Atlantic. This made me feel like I was travelling forwards towards the past![20]

Yet despite these early encounters, Hall found that his own hybridity had evolved, which is typical of the diasporic experience. His emotional and political ties to Jamaica had strengthened in some instances, while they had diminished in other respects.[21] Significantly, what emerged was a new vantage point that was not transfixed to one position, but from more than one.[22] Hybridity was not merely a creole zone, or a "problem space" but was considered to be an opportunity "to change not the answers but the questions. It provided not only a home from home, but a new site of knowledge."[23] For Hall, being in a

---

[18] Hall, "Cultural Identity," 222.
[19] Hall, "Cultural Identity," 235.
[20] Stuart Hall, *Familiar Stranger: A Life between Two Islands* (Durham: Duke University Press, 2017), 153.
[21] Hall, *Familiar Stranger*, 169.
[22] Hall, *Familiar Stranger*, 172.
[23] Hall, *Familiar Stranger*, 172.

diasporic position evidently harboured a new perspective and a new way of understanding one's cultural identity.

Homi Bhabha

This experience of multiple worlds providing new perspectives gives rise to what Indian-British critical theorist Homi Bhabha terms "hybridity." Bhabha's definition of hybridity is quite sophisticated and requires unpacking. In his essay "Signs Taken for Wonders," Bhabha speaks of "hybridity" as

> the sign of the productivity of colonial power, its shifting forces and fixities; it is the name for the strategic reversal of the process of domination through disavowal (that is, the production of discriminatory identities that secure the "pure" and original identity of authority).[24]

Disavowal is where hybridity is claimed. The hybrid identity ceases from a simple mimicry of ways of life being enforced by colonial powers. Consequently, a new hybrid identity emerges where discrimination and domination of the colonial powers are replaced with "strategies of subversion that turn the gaze of the discriminated back upon the eye of power."[25] The emergence of the hybrid identity occurs in the "Third Space," which Bhabha believes is necessary for production of meaning, in communication between two cultures.[26] In this Third Space there is no fixed interpretation of cultural symbols, rather, such symbols can be "appropriated, translated, rehistoricized and read anew."[27] This gives rise to a "split-space of enunciation" which paves the way for an "*inter*national culture" that is not a romanticisation of multicultural diversity, but a recognition of the hybridity of culture.[28] Bhabha's hybridity concept is somewhat of a crossing between borders, as hybridity does allow for cultures to step beyond boundaries. This is a significant point for diasporic theory as hybridity can occur at home but also in the diaspora where physical boundaries are being crossed as well as cultural. Bhabha realises that hybrid identities are usually subordinated identities due to the fact that they are trying to uphold their indigenous cultural traditions. This is a view that is articulated in dialogue with the Algerian critic Frantz Fanon. Bhabha elaborates:

> Fanon's desire for the recognition of cultural presence as 'negating activity' resonates with my breaking of the time-barrier of a culturally collusive 'present'. … The negating activity is, indeed, the intervention of the 'beyond' that establishes

---

[24] Homi K. Bhabha, "Signs Taken for Wonders: Questions of Ambivalence and Authority under a Tree Outside Delhi, May 1817," *Critical Inquiry* 12.1 (1985): 154.
[25] Bhabha, "Signs Taken for Wonders." 154.
[26] Bhabha, *Location of Culture*, 36.
[27] Bhabha, *Location of Culture*, 37.
[28] Bhabha, *Location of Culture*, 38.

a boundary: a bridge, where 'presencing' begins because it captures something of the estranging sense of the relocation of the home and the world—the unhomeliness—that is the condition of extra-territorial and cross-cultural initiations.[29]

While Fanon does not specifically write about the diasporic experience, I contend that the experience of diasporic identities equates to the desire for recognition of cultural presence as Fanon argues. In particular, first-generation migrants who seek to maintain cultural and ancestral links with the homeland, with subsequent perpetuation of those links mandated to second- and later generations.

FRANTZ FANON

Fanon was a pioneer of postcolonial studies. I include him in my argument as his work is influential in diasporic theory, particularly the idea of negating colonial influence that hinders the native experience. When the native migrates to a foreign land, the colonial experience is reiterated in the encounter with a dominant majority.

In his classic work *The Wretched of the Earth*, Fanon spoke of the Algerian experience against the French colonisers and emphasised the need for decolonisation. The negative treatment of colonised natives justifies the need for decolonisation, as the natives are often dehumanised and spoken of in "zoological terms."[30] Yet not all natives succumb voicelessly to such negative treatment, as they become aware and cause anxiety to the colonisers.[31] The attitude of the natives that emerges begins the process of decolonisation.

In the process of decolonisation, the natives begin to reject Western values even as they are being taught of its "wealth," but the dehumanising attitude is difficult to ignore as "the colonized masses mock at these very [white] values, insult them, and vomit them up."[32] What occurs here is the emergence of the "beyond" where colonial boundaries are crossed, and new spaces are created.[33] Fanon prescribes here, the power of the "native intellectual" as he writes:

> The native intellectual takes part, in a sort of auto-da-fé, in the destruction of all his idols: egoism, recrimination that springs from pride, and the childish stupidity of those who always want to have the last word. Such a colonized intellectual, dusted over by colonial culture, will in the same way discover the substance of

---

[29] Bhabha, *Location of Culture*, 9.
[30] Frantz Fanon, *The Wretched of the Earth*, trans. Constance Farrington (repr. New York: Grove Weidenfield, 1991), 42.
[31] Fanon, *Wretched of the Earth*, 43.
[32] Fanon, *Wretched of the Earth*, 43.
[33] Cf. Bhabha, *Location of Culture*, 9.

village assemblies, the cohesion of people's committees, and the extraordinary fruitfulness of local meetings and groupments.[34]

Native intellectuals ostensibly take a path from a native who was considered a "lost soul" to a native intellectual who was considered by the colonisers to be a "saved soul." Yet, Fanon pointed out that the native intellectual condemned the very Western values of the colonisers that they had embraced, and as such "the whole system totters."[35] What is crucial here is the "turning of the tables" that sees the native intellectual become aware of the experience of being colonised, and then (re)negotiating with his or her native background in order to decolonise their colonised mind. It is a struggle, and one which Fanon believes if violent, then so be it, because the colonisers' own act of colonisation had attempted to distort, disfigure and destroy the oppressed people.[36]

I contend that Fanon's argument would also apply to natives who migrate, whether to the "centres of population" or to other lands, because they may still defend native traditions, as opposed to neglecting them.[37] It is in this complex account of resistance that Fanon's argument crosses over to diasporic theory. As Hall argued, natives are far from a final product, they are constantly evolving.

PAUL GILROY

A new understanding of cultural identity from a diasporic perspective is a disruption of "the cultural and historical mechanics of belonging" according to Guyanese-English scholar in cultural studies, Paul Gilroy.[38] Gilroy, in his book *The Black Atlantic Modernity and Double Consciousness*, speaks about the need to reread the ordeal of blacks in the west, acknowledging that the experience of blacks in modern times had gone through an emancipation from their slave history. In light of their bondage past, the blacks' "progress from the status of slaves to the status of citizens led them to enquire into what best possible forms of social and political existence might be."[39] In his book *Against Race: Imagining Political Culture Beyond the Color Line*, Gilroy states: "it disrupts the fundamental power of territory to determine identity by breaking the simple sequence of explanatory links between place, location, and consciousness."[40] In fact, Gilroy argues that the term "diaspora," since its ancient usage, needed new meaning that resonated with modern times as opposed to the "nationalisms" and "subaltern imperialisms" that

---

[34] Fanon, *Wretched of the Earth*, 47.
[35] Fanon, *Wretched of the Earth*, 221.
[36] Fanon, *Wretched of the Earth*, 170.
[37] Fanon, *Wretched of the Earth*, 111.
[38] Paul Gilroy, *Against Race: Imagining Political Culture Beyond the Color Line* (Cambridge, MA: Harvard University Press, 2000), 123.
[39] Paul Gilroy, *The Black Atlantic: Modernity and Double Consciousness* (London: Verson, 1993), 39.
[40] Gilroy, *Against Race*, 123.

was characteristic of late nineteenth century Britain.[41] Part of that new meaning, Gilroy contends, is a need for these characteristics to be stripped away from the term so that diaspora

> might offer seeds capable of bearing fruit in struggles to comprehend the sociality of a new phase in which displacement, flight, exile, and forced migration are likely to be familiar and recurrent phenomena that transform the terms in which identity needs to be understood.[42]

Another factor of this struggle to comprehend the new phase, is to understand that diaspora is more than just movement, but what *causes* these movements. Gilroy reasons that "push factors are a dominant influence"[43] because the desperation in movement is crucial to diaspora. More than just being a long and meandering journey, diaspora has the sense of urgency, because violence at home threatens life, and therefore *pushing* these movements to occur.[44]

As a result, a discrepancy between "locations of residence" and "locations of belonging" eventuates.[45] This comes with the 'push' that causes migrants to leave their homelands and find refuge in a new land. But while they find a *new home*, they long for their *old home* which means that the diasporic identities become conscious of their diasporic state, which is significant because it provides opposition. Specifically, "Consciousness of diaspora affiliation stands opposed to the distinctively modern structures and modes of power orchestrated by the institutional complexity of nation-states."[46] Such a realisation gives rise to creativity in thinking that encourages conversation and interaction and even synchronises significant parts of their social and cultural identities.[47]

JAMES CLIFFORD

Amercian Anthropologist James Clifford, whose work focuses on the influence of contemporary society on Indigenous peoples, contends that "indigenous attachments to place are complexly mediated and do not necessarily entail continuous residence" because a number of native people have migrated from ancestral lands to urban centres.[48] As such, Clifford talks of relocated native communities as "indigenous diasporas." This is the modern day reality.[49] The problem, as Clifford

---

[41] Gilroy, *Against Race*, 123.
[42] Gilroy, *Against Race*, 123.
[43] Gilroy, *Against Race*, 123.
[44] Gilroy, *Against Race*, 123.
[45] Gilroy, *Against Race*, 124.
[46] Gilroy, *Against Race*, 124.
[47] Gilroy, *Against Race*, 129.
[48] James Clifford, *Returns: Becoming Indigenous in the Twenty-First Century* (Cambridge: Harvard University Press, 2013), 70.
[49] Clifford, *Returns*, 71.

points out, is that in the contemporary world, migration and displacement are considered normal for the diasporic experience, yet there is a focus to downgrade indigenous people to their histories of marginalisation.[50] There is an obvious need for refocusing to reconcile the "diasporic *dimensions* or *conjunctures* in contemporary native lives."[51] Such is the changing character of native lives, as their existence in modern times becomes a lot more complex. To this, Clifford states:

> The language of diaspora can be useful in bringing something of this complexity into view. It cannot transcend the tension between the material interests and normative visions of natives and newcomers, particularly in structurally unequal settler-colonial situations.... But when diasporic displacements, memories, networks, and reidentifications are recognized as integral to tribal, aboriginal, native survival and dynamism, a lived, historical landscape of ruptures and affiliations becomes more visible.[52]

Such ruptures and affiliations are what Clifford seeks to unravel in his work *Returns*, and he does so by analysing a number of diasporic communities around the world including Indian, Chinese, and Pacific diaspora communities. In these diasporas, Clifford finds that there are certain dialectical instabilities. Borrowing key terms from Vijay Mishra, Clifford distinguishes between diasporas that are focused on returning to the homeland, which Mishra calls diasporas of "exclusivism," to diasporas that are more interested in interaction and crossover, which Mishra has termed diasporas of "the border."[53] The complexity of diasporic identification can never be limited to two classifications, particularly in the modern era, nevertheless, they possess an "analytic strength" which we can theorise.[54]

GAYATRI CHAKRAVORTY SPIVAK

Another element of diversity of diasporic classification is brought forward by Spivak in her essay "Diasporas Old and New: Women in the Transnational World." Spivak urges us to consider the contemporary notions of diaspora in contrast to the old. She states that the old diasporas resulted from "religious oppression and war, of slavery and indenturing, trade and conquest, and intra-European economic migration which, since the nineteenth century, took the form of migration and immigration into the United States."[55] The new diasporas on the other hand, are

---

[50] Clifford, *Returns*, 71.
[51] Clifford, *Returns*, 71.
[52] Clifford, *Returns*, 71–72.
[53] Clifford, *Returns*, 72. Also see Vijay Mishra, *The Literature of Indian Diaspora: Theorizing the Diasporic Imaginary* (London: Routledge, 2007), 104.
[54] Clifford, *Returns*, 72.
[55] Spivak, "Diasporas," 245. In the discussion, Spivak focuses on her own identity and context of "South Asia, the place of my citizenship, the United States, the source of my income, and Northwestern Europe, the object of my limited expertise" ("Diasporas," 261).

grounded in transnationality and the migrancy of labour. Precisely, the new diaspora according to Spivak entails "Eurocentric migration, labour export both male and female, border crossings, the seeking of political asylum, and the haunting in-place uprooting of 'comfort women' in Asia and Africa."[56]

While there is a clear changing in trends from the old to the new, it is significant to consider Spivak's conjecture that "woman's relationship to each of these phenomena is oblique, ex-orbitant to the general story."[57] In light of the previous theorists who are all male, it is significant to hear the voice of women in the conversation (much as we have considered the implications of the "house of the mother" in the Hebrew Bible), in particular, "in untangling the relationship between gender and the subjectivity of the Other."[58] In making her point, Spivak articulates factors which represent this neglect of "women in the transnational world," listing them as "(1) homeworking, (2) population control, (3) groups that cannot become diasporic, and (4) indigenous women outside of the Americas."[59]

So firstly, in a transnational setting, homeworking deals with the roles women play at home which Spivak considers as a division of class that is grossly manipulative within society. In these roles, women

> do piece-work at home with no control over wages; and thus absorb the cost of health care, day care, work place safety, maintenance, management; through manipulation of the notion that feminine ethics is unpaid domestic labour ('nurturing') into the meretricious position that paid domestic labour is munificent or feminist, as the case may be.... The women stay at home, often impervious to organizational attempts through internalized gendering as a survival technique.[60]

The stereotype associated with what women do at home might be largely ignored in contemporary economic models, but Spivak highlights these gendered roles in a bid to reveal the systemic oppression in the new diasporas.

Secondly, the issue of population control is claimed by Spivak to be detrimental to women, stating that there is an "obvious blackmailing potential in the connection between aid packages and population control."[61] Aid packages might seek to serve the financial imbalance of "the appalling disequilibrium between people and Earth's resources" which those in the North might view as caused by

---

[56] Spivak, "Diasporas," 245.
[57] Spivak, "Diasporas," 246.
[58] Harry Blagg, and Thalia Anthony, *Decolonising Criminology: Imagining Justice in a Postcolonial World*, Critical Criminological Perspectives (London: Palgrave Macmillan, 2019), 207.
[59] Spivak, "Diasporas," 246.
[60] Spivak, "Diasporas," 246.
[61] Gayatri Chakravorty Spivak, "They the People: Problems of Alter-Globalization," *Radical Philosophy* 157 (2009): 33.

overpopulation mainly by the "poor" South.[62] However, Spivak argues that the effect of aid packages "stands in the way of feminist theory because it identifies women with their reproductive apparatus and grants them no other subjectship."[63] For instance, internationally aided education programmes are "tailor fit for the dominant forces in the global economy,"[64] where:

> The control, either of the bodies of women through coercive population policy, or of their minds through an 'education' that propagates the 'values' underlying the financialization of the globe, is too often celebrated as free choice and 'women in development.'[65]

Spivak contends that a more constructive approach to aid packages in a transnational setting would be to empower women so that they can "resist the crimes committed in the name of population control."[66]

Thirdly, Spivak maintains that women in the new diasporas may be classed within "groups that cannot become diasporic." She defines these groups as "those who have stayed in place for more than thirty thousand years"[67] which by implication refers to subaltern groups as opposed to elite groups in society. The point behind this distinction is that diasporic people through their mobility are privileged like the elite. For instance, diasporic people are able to acquire properties in the host land which may reverse their loss of land and achieve a similar position to the elite. The subaltern groups who have stayed in place might not acquire such privilege. The implication therefore is that women cannot become diasporic, not due to a lack of mobility, but because their experience resonates with the underprivileged state of subaltern groups.

This space of difference—between the elite and subaltern, or those who cannot become diasporic—links to the final list that Spivak identifies as "indigenous women outside of the Americas." Spivak states that large groups which fall into "this space of difference subsist in transnationality without escaping into diaspora. And indeed they would include most indigenous groups outside Euramerica."[68] The issue here for Spivak, is that indigenous women are being exploited, for "in the context of colonial production, the subaltern has no history and cannot speak,

---

[62] Spivak, "They the People," 33.
[63] Spivak, "Diasporas," 246.
[64] Spivak, "They the People," 33. Spivak quotes from Amaryllis Tiglao Torres, "Women's Education as an Instrument for Change: The Case of the Philippines," in *The Politics of Women's Education: Perspectives from Asia, Africa, and Latin America*, ed. Jill Ker Conway and Susan C. Bourque (Ann Arbor: The University of Michigan Press, 1995), 117.
[65] Spivak, "They the People," 33.
[66] Spivak, "They the People," 34.
[67] Spivak, "Diasporas," 247.
[68] Spivak, "Diasporas," 247.

the subaltern as female is even more deeply in shadow."[69] In other words, these depictions of indigenous women "reflect patterns of colonial epistemic subjugation. Indigenous women are stripped of their agency and subjectivity; they are objectified as empty sites on which the masculinities of the coloniser and the colonised compete."[70]

Within the diasporic experience, there must be recognition of the subjugation and colonisation of women. Their experience is one that reveals the colonial and oppressive nature of the transnationality of labour and economic models, but also how the transnational world has been dependent on their exploitation. Spivak's critique of transnational labour has significant implications for understanding the manipulative tendencies of diaspora towards women and other disenfranchised groups. Conversely, this is also important for diasporic studies to consider ways of empowering women and liberating the manipulated Other.

SUMMARY

The theoretical scope provided by these scholars is fundamental for this study. Not only do the arguments and theoretical insights provide key questions in my study of Qohelet, but more importantly, they reveal the changing nature of the study of diaspora, from forced dispersion of natives to other lands, to the complexity and dynamism of new diasporas that seek to *cross* borders and interact. From a modern diasporic perspective, border-crossing transcends hybridity, as the hybrid identity seeks to interact and adapt, but also maintains elements of their indigenous identity necessary for existence. Also, as one recognises their own vulnerability in diaspora, one must also come to terms with the endangerment of women and other disenfranchised groups, whose experiences have been ignored to the benefit of transnational economies. The implications raised from this provide an opportunity for inquiry into Qohelet's distinct perspective, especially as I attempt to offer my contribution to the discussion of the voice of Qohelet.

DIASPORIC STUDIES AND BIBLICAL STUDIES

Biblical Scholars specialising in diasporic perspectives such as Daniel Smith-Christopher, Fernando Segovia, and Gale A. Yee, among others, have provided different perspectives on exiles and other geographic movements of peoples in the Bible. Accordingly, I will analyse the works of Smith-Christopher, Segovia, and Yee in order to explore the implementation of diasporic conjunctures and dimensions in biblical analysis. I have chosen these authors, firstly, as they have written extensively on the need for diasporic perspectives in biblical interpretation, and secondly, because of the diversity of their experiences as diasporic identities. In

---

[69] Gayatri Chakravorty Spivak, "Can the Subaltern Speak?," in *Colonial Discourse and Post-Colonial Theory: A Reader*, ed. Patrick Williams and Laura Chrisman (London: Routledge, 2013), 83.

[70] Blagg and Anthony, *Decolonising Criminology*, 207; Spivak, "Can the Subaltern Speak?," 83.

reading Qohelet, I aim to utilise such diasporic perspectives to unravel the possibility of a diasporic setting for Ecclesiastes.

DANIEL L. SMITH-CHRISTOPHER

Smith-Christopher is a pioneer of diasporic perspectives in reading the biblical text. In his classic work, *The Religion of the Landless: The Social Context of the Babylonian Exile*, Smith-Christopher revisits the Babylonian exile through the lens of the diaspora, which he refers to as the "Fourth World."[71] This perspective administers a theology, which Smith-Christopher describes,

> is the theology of those "migrants" and "refugees" who choose to live without power, yet as a people. The paradigms for Fourth World theology contrast sharply with theologies of liberation (with their focus on the biblical events of Exodus) that have either made their peace with power or seek to restore power.[72]

Smith-Christopher makes a key distinction here: while Bhabha makes a case for disavowal of colonial power, Smith-Christopher focuses on the idea of surviving amidst the reality that diasporic identities inhabit. Such a reality, as expressed in the case studies that he explains, is centred on diasporic communities being dominated by a majority power. This formulates Smith-Christopher's perspective for rereading the Babylonian exile, as he writes:

> By identifying the sociological mechanisms of minorities who are confronted with the culture of power, the behavior and theology of the Babylonian Exile can be illuminated as a *creative response* to social realities, and not merely the desperate struggle of a culture in decline.[73]

The foundation of Smith-Christopher's argument lies in the ability of diasporic minorities to survive in the world of the dominating majority. Consequently, he explicates "mechanisms for survival"[74] which emerge as a result of this diasporic reality. These "mechanisms of survival" also describe in additional detail the reality of the diasporic minority. In light of diasporic theory, these "mechanisms for survival" have significant implications for reading the biblical exile, and related biblical texts. My analysis will therefore seek to underscore those implications.

MECHANISMS OF SURVIVAL

Smith-Christopher conceives four behaviour patterns which he terms "mechanisms for survival" that formulate diasporic perspectives in biblical interpretation. It is a significant study in his major work *The Religion of the Landless* that has

---

[71] Smith, *Religion of the Landless*, 8.
[72] Smith, *Religion of the Landless*, 9.
[73] Smith, *Religion of the Landless*, 10.
[74] Smith, *Religion of the Landless*, 11.

major implications for the link between diasporic theory and biblical studies. We may note that Smith-Christopher focuses mainly on Priestly literature and post-exilic stories in *Religion of the Landless*, and how certain events in modern history of diasporic significance resonate with such exilic stories from the Bible. I contend that it is necessary to address his "mechanisms of survival" as it possesses implications pertinent to the methodological framework of this research.

These "mechanisms of survival" have been utilised by social groups to "maintain their identity, social structure, and religious/cultural life under stress."[75] The four that Smith-Christopher chooses provide "striking biblical analogies,"[76] not in the sense that they are exactly the same, "but only that they illustrate patterns of behavior that may contribute to developing hypotheses to direct biblical study."[77]

The first mechanism involves "structural adaptation" which entails changes in leadership and authority patterns. It could also see changes in the basic social units of the society, which is often a deliberate strategy.[78] In their indigenous element, minority groups have already set their leadership and patterns of authority, but when such leadership becomes undermined as a result of the new social context, adaptation becomes necessary for survival.[79]

Smith-Christopher explains the second mechanism for survival as "the split in leadership between new leaders who arise to replace the old, defeated leaders who are usually unable to rule the minority group directly."[80] The split articulates two contrasting positions as a result of domination: between leaders who advise a strong, and often violent, position of resistance to the ruling group or population, and leaders who advocate a position of *social* resistance,[81] as Smith-Christopher adds: "Both can be seen in roles of symbiotic relation to the dominant interests; *both can also be forms of resistance.*"[82]

Smith-Christopher's third mechanism for survival involves the establishment of ritual or ritual patterns, that accentuate resistance against foreign influence, often with a concern over purity and pollution from such foreign influence.[83] To provide emphasis to his argument, he uses the insights of Mary Douglas, in her work *Purity and Danger*, as a reference point. According to Douglas, rituals are associated with a fear of pollution and hence a desire to uphold purity. Such fear of pollution is considered to be a "stress point" of a society.[84] For example,

---

[75] Smith, *Religion of the Landless*, 10–11.
[76] Smith, *Religion of the Landless*, 10–11.
[77] Smith, *Religion of the Landless*, 69.
[78] Smith, *Religion of the Landless*, 10–11.
[79] Smith, *Religion of the Landless*, 74.
[80] Smith, *Religion of the Landless*, 10–11.
[81] Smith, *Religion of the Landless*, 10–11.
[82] Smith, *Religion of the Landless*, 79.
[83] Smith, *Religion of the Landless*, 79.
[84] Smith, *Religion of the Landless*, 80.

Douglas points to the Philistine practise of raising pigs which may have contributed to the detestation of pork in the book of Leviticus.[85]

The fourth mechanism is the formation of new folk literature or folklore patterns, which reflect the social experiences of minority groups living in exile.[86] The stimulus for such folklore is the relationship between the minority and those in majority power, and as such, what is usually prominent in folklore is the "hero story" with the emergence of a hero as a new role model for the minority.[87]

As Smith-Christopher points out, there are obvious biblical analogies with these "mechanisms for survival" and together they lay a platform for rereading the Babylonian exile.

Case Studies for Mechanisms of Survival

Smith-Christopher visits four case studies to elucidate these mechanisms, the "Religious Responses to Apartheid in South African Bantustans," "African-American Slavery," "Japanese-American Internment during World War II," and "The Bikini Islanders."[88] It was not Smith-Christopher's intention to make a simple "this is like that" argument, but rather to draw out the experiences of the people in these examples with a view to asking new questions of the biblical texts.[89] Smith-Christopher visits all four cases in his analysis of the four mechanisms, but due to constraints in space, I will highlight one case per mechanism.

In the first mechanism, structural adaptation can be seen in the case of Japanese-American internment in the western United States, during the second World War. The United States produced the Orientation Exclusion Act in 1924, "which prevented immigrants from becoming U.S. citizens and halted any further immigration to the country on the overtly stated basis that Asians could not be assimilated into American life."[90] In light of the Japanese bombing of Pearl Harbor in 1941, the Orientation Exclusion Act was enforced upon Japanese-Americans. As such, Japanese-Americans were sent in trains to internment camps, inland from the U.S. coastal states. They were taken on the grounds that they were cooperating with the enemy, which was based on the pure fact that they had Japanese heritage.

This led to the formation of small Japanese-American societies consisting of first-generation Japanese-Americans known as "Issei" and second-generation Japanese-Americans known as "Nissei."[91] The experiences of these communities

---

[85] Smith, *Religion of the Landless*, 80. See Mary Douglas, *Purity and Danger: An Anlysis of Concept of Pollution and Taboo*, Routledge Classics Edition (repr. New York: Routledge, 2002), 38.
[86] Smith, *Religion of the Landless*, 84.
[87] Smith, *Religion of the Landless*, 10–11.
[88] Smith, *Religion of the Landless*, 70–73.
[89] Daniel L. Smith-Christopher, "Introduction," in *Text and Experience: Towards a Cultural Exegesis of the Bible*, ed. Daniel Smith-Christopher (Sheffield: Sheffield Academic, 1995), 13–14.
[90] Smith, *Religion of the Landless*, 71.
[91] Smith, *Religion of the Landless*, 71–72.

are significant for our analysis of this first mechanism. The Kitano cities in particular were noted for resistance within, such as "work slowdowns, alcoholism (as escapism), humor, and ritualism."[92] Traditionally, the Issei held authority in the Japanese community; but due to the new context, the Issei lost their power. They were no longer the filial authority in Japanese families and neighbourhood. What was telling was the emergence of the Issei women from their state of subjugation, to being able to take classes in Japanese music to floral arrangements. The Issei men on the other hand were deprived of their authority, and were forbidden from political activity. What resulted was a new democracy, as power and influence shifted away from the Issei onto the Nissei, who were known to have strong pro-American feelings.[93]

In the second mechanism which looks at the rise of new leadership, the case study of African-American slavery and the responses from religious circles in pre-Civil War United States, provides an intriguing outlook. As Smith-Christopher notes, "individual slave communities, stories, and cultural studies of small units are more interesting than discussions of the historical details of slavery in the New World."[94] So specifically, the role of African-American preachers during the period of Afro-American slavery, was pivotal as they became "cultural intermediaries" between the African-American slaves and white society.[95] As such, they illustrated examples of the rise of new leadership amidst domination.

Smith-Christopher notes that the slave community were somewhat divided on how they perceived these new black leaders. Some saw them as agents of the white society and accused the black preachers of preaching "pie in the sky" religion,[96] promoting a sense of false hope for the black slave community in light of their oppression. On the other hand, African-American religious scholar Albert J. Raboteau insists that the black preachers were actually creative, as they promoted resistance strategies through biblical interpretation in sermons, hidden social meanings of the spirituals and the social significance of their meetings.[97]

For the third mechanism which entails the establishment of ritual patterns, the example of religious responses to Apartheid in Bantustan communities in South Africa provides an example of resistance in the face of domination and segregation. In particular, a certain ritual by the Zionist Bantu churches is rather significant. To provide context, a Zionist band in the African township of Kwa Mashu felt the need to protect itself from the township by drawing boundaries and setting themselves apart from the rest of the population.[98] Consequently, they

---

[92] Smith, *Religion of the Landless*, 72.
[93] Smith, *Religion of the Landless*, 72.
[94] Smith, *Religion of the Landless*, 71.
[95] Smith, *Religion of the Landless*, 79.
[96] Smith, *Religion of the Landless*, 79.
[97] Smith, *Religion of the Landless*, 79.
[98] Smith, *Religion of the Landless*, 83.

developed a ritual of portraying such separation through vivid dramatisation each Sunday, that in spite of the humidity and heat which would fill a crowded room, the band would shut the doors and windows at certain points of the service.[99] The ritual may seem bizarre, but it communicated a "statement of exclusiveness."[100]

Another ritual that made this same statement was the compulsory removal of footwear in the Zionist Bantu churches. Smith-Christopher refers to a study by South African anthropologist J. P. Kiernan who claims it is insufficient to say that the removal of footwear was biblical but argued that it had a contemporary meaning. Kiernan suggests that it is not the removal of footwear that is of the utmost importance, "but the fact that they are left outside."[101] This is because the shoes and footwear carry the dust of the township, which represents township life, and "is [thus] withheld from crossing the threshold of the meeting-room."[102] Furthermore, Kiernan adds:

> Uncontaminated by alien dust, and with his workday clothes completely concealed under a laundered white robe, the Zionist makes the transition from one social universe to another.[103]

For the fourth mechanism of survival, where types of folklore and literature emerge that reflect the sociological experiences of minorities in exile in relation to a dominant power, Smith-Christopher speaks of a number of cases, but I would like to revisit the example of African-American slavery, where folklore of heroes and laments had emerged, with a heavy biblical influence, and therefore representing a "hermeneutic of the poor."[104] Smith-Christopher brings Albert Raboteau into the discussion, who notes that the context of Israel's exodus from Egypt resonated with a message of a future hope, that was completely different to what African-American slaves were experiencing.[105] Raboteau also points to the Prophetic and apocalyptic books from which slaves drew confidence and assurance that they too would be delivered from their bondage.[106]

Smith-Christopher notes also the situation of the Bikini Islanders, who were forcibly removed from their island homes by the US government, and relocated en masse to other lands, so that the US government could conduct nuclear

---

[99] Smith, *Religion of the Landless*, 83.
[100] Smith, *Religion of the Landless*, 83.
[101] J.P. Kiernan, "Where Zionists Draw the Line: A Study of Religious Exclusiveness in an African Township," *Africa Studies* 33.2 (1974): 83.
[102] Kiernan, "Where Zionists," 83; Smith, *Religion of the Landless*, 83.
[103] Kiernan, "Where Zionists," 83; Smith, *Religion of the Landless*, 83.
[104] Smith, *The Religion of the Landless*, 86.
[105] Albert J. Raboteau, *Slave Religion: The "Invisible Institution" in the Antebellum South*, updated ed. (Oxford: Oxford University Press, 2004), 312; Smith, *Religion of the Landless*, 87.
[106] Raboteau, *Slave Religion*, 312; Smith, *Religion of the Landless*, 87.

weapons testing on the Bikini Atoll of the Marshall Islands.[107] The effects were devastating. From these experiences, Robert C. Kiste points out the emergence of "new histories" of the Bikini natives that sought to reclaim a new sense of continuity and resolve while in their exilic state.[108]

Biblical Applications of Mechanisms of Survival

It is important to note at the outset Smith-Christopher's qualification:

> It may be objected that we are focusing only on *successful* resistance in these case studies. It is true, for example, that many Japanese-Americans fully co-operated with American authorities or went back to Japan; many slaves did not resist or revolt in the Southern states and the Caribbean; and many blacks in South Africa appear to accept the Bantustan arrangement. But we are interested in resistance because it is the Judeans *who successfully maintained their identity that were responsible for the biblical texts we are concerned with. This is therefore not the only social reality, but it is the social reality reflected in the texts*.[109]

The *social reality* is prevalent in his reading of the biblical exile, and it would be helpful to have a look through the four "mechanism of survival" again.

In the first mechanism, Smith-Christopher declares that structural adaptation is perceivable in the exilic society. Evidently, the old structures were violated and new settings must be adapted.[110] It is evident that, when referring to evidence in the books of Ezekiel and Jeremiah, elders were in the Exilic community. Smith-Christopher argues that it showed that "groups of exiles were able to organize themselves into a form of self-government."[111] The old structures, namely the *Bēt 'Āb*,[112] were reshaped as *Bēt 'Āvot* in a situation of crisis (as we saw in chapter 3). Thus, the exile was perceived as the experience of a dominated minority, whose old structures had reformed in response, and in survival, to such dominance "by pulling together into tightly knit groups."[113]

As an example of the second kind of mechanism, Smith-Christopher sees the rise of new leadership in the exile community in the debate between the prophets Jeremiah and Hananiah in Jer 27–28.[114] In the debate, Hananiah opposed Jeremiah's advised submission to Babylon. Smith-Christopher had noted that some scholars had seen Jeremiah's position as "unpatriotic," "unfaithful," or

---

[107] Smith, *Religion of the Landless*, 73.
[108] Smith, *Religion of the Landless*, 86.
[109] Smith, *Religion of the Landless*, 73.
[110] Smith, *Religion of the Landless*, 93.
[111] Smith, *Religion of the Landless*, 93–94.
[112] Smith, *Religion of the Landless*, 116.
[113] Smith, *Religion of the Landless*, 120.
[114] Smith, *Religion of the Landless*, 127.

"ineffective."[115] In fact, John Bright tried to argue Jeremiah's case against claims of "pacifism" and "cowardice" to determine that such claims were doing Jeremiah's character a "grave injustice" and were "unfair."[116] However, Smith-Christopher argues that Jeremiah's strategy of nonviolent social resistance was an alternative means of survival in the exile, to ensure that the Jewish community was to multiply and not decrease.[117]

Smith-Christopher identifies the third mechanism of survival, that is, establishment of ritual patterns, in the Priestly redactors.[118] As Smith-Christopher had brought forward the case of the black preachers during the time of African-American slavery, who had devised resistance strategies through biblical interpretation and carefully crafted sermons, he contends that so too did Israel produce

> creative rituals of survival and resistance reflected in the carefully elaborated laws of the "pure" and "impure," and especially in the concern about the transfer of impurity through contact with the impure, whether animals or people. It was not the *formulation* of laws of purity that represented the most creative response to Exile by the priestly writer, for we have seen that form-critical analysis reveals many of these laws to rest on older traditions. It was rather the *elaboration* of these laws to emphasize *transfer* of pollution and the association of holiness with *separation*.[119]

Smith-Christopher maintains that the context for such elaborations most probably came about during the exile, when the Jewish minority was most likely to have been threatened by majority cultures who had little care for the desires of minorities to uphold their cultural identity.[120]

In the final mechanism of survival which explains the emergence of folklore literature, Smith-Christopher notes the emergence of resistance literature during the Babylonian exile. One literature genre that dominates Smith-Christopher's discussion is the "diaspora novella," a type of literature that is noticed in books such as Esther, Daniel, and the late version of the Joseph story.[121] In these stories, the experience of a hero/heroine is expressed in novella form, where a hero/heroine champions the cause for the dominated minority. Those stories have many similarities which focus on the experience of such heroes/heroines in the diaspora, and how their lives reflect mechanisms for survival. Survival is especially prevalent in these stories during instances in which the protagonist becomes imprisoned. Smith-Christopher contends that the social existence of the Jews in the diaspora

---

[115] Smith, *Religion of the Landless*, 137.
[116] Smith, *Religion of the Landless*, 136–37.
[117] Smith, *Religion of the Landless*, 137.
[118] Smith, *Religion of the Landless*, 139.
[119] Smith, *Religion of the Landless*, 149.
[120] Smith, *Religion of the Landless*, 149.
[121] Smith, *Religion of the Landless*, 153.

resonate with imprisonment. As such, these diaspora hero stories are maintained by the diasporic Jews, as "it is only in the context of this symbolism that the function of the diaspora hero stories as resistance literature of a deported, landless minority make sense."[122]

Rereading the Exile

Since his *The Religion of the Landless*, Smith-Christopher has continued his research with other diasporic identities in relation to the biblical text, such as the Lakota tribe in dialogue with the book of Daniel, as well as conversations with Chinese biblical scholars and students on other questions relating to the biblical texts.[123] These conversations led to a collaboration with other authors in *Text and Experience: Towards a Cultural Exegesis of the Bible*, which Smith-Christopher edited. The questions behind refugee identities, hybridity and exilic existence are serious issues in this work, which lead to a reconstitution in thinking. Take for instance what Smith-Christopher says on the Jewish experience under Persia:

> That a diasporic Judean community, or a quasi-political minority under Persian hegemony, may have carefully constructed a militarist and nationalist story only to savagely criticize it as idolatrous and ultimately disastrous (as the Deuteronomistic Historian clearly does) is an idea that would not spell the end of biblical historiography and most certainly not the end of biblical theology. Rather, it could well be read as a brilliant first move toward the articulation of a community that consists mainly of faithful commitment rather than defined by worldly power.[124]

The resistance behind the new narrative is evident when we reread the exilic experience. That is, the folklore that emerges tells of a greater power (YHWH) to whom the Judean community must be loyal, in defiance of the Persian hegemony.

This raises an interesting question for the study of Ecclesiastes, because Qohelet's critical tone actually reflects a critique of this model of faithful commitment. For example, having read Jeremiah from a diasporic perspective, the questioning of YHWH's jurisdiction may also lead to Qohelet's own questioning of YHWH's authority away from Judah, that is, where is YHWH in the diaspora? Indeed, Qohelet's questioning here is a questioning of conventional wisdom, so to highlight this, the link between YHWH's jurisdiction and conventional wisdom must be understood. As Horst Preuss rightly suggests:

> in the understanding of the "wise" who stand behind this proverbial wisdom YHWH himself has set up this connection between deed and consequence, or act and result, and he watches over this reality. He "recompenses" (שלם = *šillēm*)

---

[122] Smith, *Religion of the Landless*, 174.
[123] Smith-Christopher, "Introduction," 14.
[124] Smith-Christopher, "Introduction," 26.

according to this process and thus people according to their deeds (Prov. 11:31; 13:21; 19:17; 25:21f.), and he brings to completion the act and the consequence that belong to human action. If the wrongdoing of the godless shall "fall" upon them (10:6), then YHWH is the one who stands behind the connection between this act and its consequence. He is the one who returns the consequences of a person's action upon him (השיב = hēšîb, "returns," 24:12). YHWH has established this order, undergirds and maintains it with divine power, operates in and through it, and is its guarantor (12:2; 16:5; 18:10; 20:22; 24:12). That there also are problems associated with such a worldview, including when and precisely why it continues to be related to the life of the individual, is not expressly stated as a theme in these sayings. YHWH functions as the one who originates this order and as the one who continues to oversee it in the present.[125]

That Qohelet questions the validity of conventional wisdom[126] implies that YHWH's functionality may be limited, or that YHWH's jurisdiction is in question, because it is outside of the realms in which the national deity normally functions, that is, outside of Judah. This is not to say that YHWH cannot exist outside Judah, but as exiles, the situation will change for Israel when they become dispersed as highlighted in Deut 4:27–28:

> [27] The LORD will scatter you among the peoples; only a few of you will be left among the nations where the LORD will lead you. [28] There you will serve other gods made by human hands, objects of wood and stone that neither see, nor hear, nor eat, nor smell. (NRSV)

The expectation in Deuteronomy's curses is that as the exiles would be worshipping "wood and stone," and the implication would therefore be that YHWH's jurisdiction is limited. It gives rise to a social perspective where being out of YHWH's jurisdiction translates to being a community away from home, settling in a foreign land. This takes us back to Smith-Christopher's reading of Jeremiah, the prophet to the exiles, and to his reading of Daniel.

Smith-Christopher believes that Fanon's work is critical for a diasporic re-reading of the biblical text:

> Fanon's observations of the symbolic meaning of colonized people's constantly having to live with the statues of the conquerors in their city streets, of being daily reminded of the generals and presidents of some far-away country, were observations that radically transformed my own reading of the book of Daniel, especially regarding the meaning of the story of the three Jews refusing to bow

---

[125] Horst Dietrich Preuss, *Old Testament Theology*, trans. Leo G. Perdue, vol. 1 (Lousiville, KY: Westminster John Knox, 1995), 185–86.
[126] Cf. Lester L. Grabbe, "Intertextual Connections between the Wisdom of Solomon and Qoheleth," in Dell and Kynes, *Reading Ecclesiastes Intertextually*, 211.

to Nebuchadnezzar's statue and the account of Daniel refusing to honor Darius in his prayers.[127]

In his reading of Jeremiah, Smith-Christopher questions Jeremiah's motives as a prophet, and how Jeremiah perceives the exilic community. The prophet poses the question whether Israel, in hindsight, was in need of a radical transformation.

But this line of reasoning might also lead to an understanding of the exilic Jews as victims of an oppressive regime, as opposed to being convicts sentenced for punishment. This is especially the case if responsibility for the exile falls not on the shoulders of the people but on their rulers. In short, the majority of the population may have suffered unjustly.

For such an understanding to hold in Jeremiah, we must consider an alternative argument to the Deuteronomistic theodicy prominent in many parts of the text, where the people are to blame. One might launch a theodicy of the exile where the fault lies on the sins of Manasseh.[128] Bernard Levinson identifies the responsibility of the Deuteronomistic Historian in promoting this theodicy:

> The Deuteronomistic Historian ... assigns primary responsibility for national apostasy to the monarch: it was the pivotal actions of Jeroboam (2 Kgs. xvii 21–23) and of Manasseh (2 Kgs. xxi 1–17) in introducing syncretistic worship that brought about the destruction of Israel and the exile of Judah.[129]

By understanding the exile as attributed to the actions of the monarch, it leaves us with the opportunity to think again about the exilic experience and to perceive alternative interpretations. Smith-Christopher provides one alternative interpretation when he identifies Jer 29:4–7 as alluding to Israel's exile a "diaspora as planned by God."[130] Here, Israel is not just a people in exile, but resemble a community in diaspora, as they are sent into exile to "Build houses ... plant gardens ... take wives and have sons and daughters."[131] As a result, the understanding of intergenerational punishment shifts focus away from the exilic generation as being culprits, towards an innocent community of refugees who are now trying to reestablish themselves in the diaspora.

---

[127] Daniel L. Smith-Christopher, "Reading Jeremiah as Frantz Fanon," in *Jeremiah (Dis)Placed: New Directions in Writing/Reading Jeremiah*, ed. A. R. Pete Diamond and Louis Stulman, LHBOTS 529 (New York: T&T Clark, 2011), 121.

[128] Marvin A. Sweeney, *I and II Kings: A Commentary*, OTL (Louisville: Westminster John Knox, 2007), 432.

[129] Bernard M. Levinson, "The Reconceptualization of Kingship in Deuteronomy and the Deuteronomistic History's Transformation of Torah," *VT* 51.4 (2001): 530.

[130] Smith-Christopher, "Reading Jeremiah as Frantz Fanon," 118.

[131] Smith-Christopher, "Reading Jeremiah as Frantz Fanon," 118.

The ramifications for this are rather significant for Qohelet, who instead of accepting a Deuteronomistic theodicy is provoked to ask new questions—perhaps even accepting Deuteronomy's own limits for YHWH's jurisdiction.

The deed-consequence framework is called into question which means ethics (wisdom) become a matter of debate also. The old ethics are questioned as the new community needs to survive in the midst of a dominating majority, and as Smith-Christopher's "mechanisms for survival" show, critique of the old ways is not only natural but also ambiguous. At best, it is transitional.

I stress that Qohelet's critical tone was resonant with the voice of one trying to survive in the diaspora, as Smith-Christopher suggests.[132] Yet the radical moves in Qohelet go beyond Smith-Christopher's four mechanisms of survival, since the critical wisdom moves away from "Yahwistic" proposals for life in exile.

FERNANDO SEGOVIA

Segovia's hermeneutical inquiry begins by affirming that for a "real reader" or a "flesh and blood reader" the context of the reader is unavoidable and must be taken into account in reading.[133] Segovia argues that reading from this standpoint does not harbour "anarchy and tribalism" as perceived by those obsessed with objectivity,

> but rather of continued decolonization and liberation, of resistance and struggle against a subtle authoritarianism and covert tribalism of its own, in a discipline that has been, from beginning to end and top to bottom, thoroughly Eurocentric despite its assumed scientific persona of neutrality and universality.[134]

He therefore proposes a hermeneutic based on the premise of "the richness and fullness of diversity," that promotes an acceptance of the other, not defined and imposed but as "independent and self-defining."[135] As such, Segovia speaks of his own experience as a Cuban American who represents natives of Latin America and the Caribbean who migrate north to the United States for a variety of reasons. Yet in his experience, he realises on the one hand the importance of acknowledging the Other as Hispanic Americans exist in a multicultural society, and the other hand, Segovia is emphatic about the importance of self-defining rather than being overwhelmed by Otherness imposed upon them.[136] The significance of this for my study lies in the self-defining nature of migrant communities without being preoccupied with trying to change the dominant culture. As in the Samoan diaspora

---

[132] Smith-Christopher, *Biblical Theology of Exile*, 168.
[133] Segovia, "Hermeneutics of the Diaspora," 57.
[134] Segovia, "Hermeneutics of the Diaspora," 57.
[135] Segovia, "Hermeneutics of the Diaspora," 57.
[136] Segovia, "Hermeneutics of the Diaspora," 64.

experience, the choice to migrate to the United States in Segovia's case was his, and not an invitation by the United States.

In reading the biblical text, Segovia argues that the text should be treated as the independent Other just like any other social group, recognising that the text comes from a different historical and cultural context.[137] Segovia also argues that the reader must also see him/herself as a "socially and culturally conditioned" other to the text and other readers, and that the reader's culture, experience and location may impact on their strategy of reading the text. Rather than being concerned with objectivity, Segovia contends that it is more about the reader being self-conscious about his/her strategy for reading.[138]

UNDERSTANDING DIASPORA

Segovia takes a minimalist approach to understanding diaspora, focusing on the simple idea of geographical dispersion of people from their own land to a foreign land.[139] It is migration that Segovia establishes as "the common denominator of the diaspora experience."[140] Furthermore, the geographic movements provide perspective as Segovia writes:

> From this perspective, therefore, Diasporic Studies would be concerned with the analysis of geographic translations of peoples in general, whether in the present or in the past, whether in the West or outside the West. Such breadth of application, I would argue, should be seen not as rendering the term devoid of content, a meaningless signifier, but rather as charging it with an abundance of content, a multifarious signifier. In other words, the common geographical denominator—what I have referred to above as the phenomenon of un-settlement, travel, re-settlement—admits of countless variations, which allow in turn for countless exercises in comparison.[141]

These numerous variations encompass three major phases. First, Segovia notes that in the period of Western imperialism over the non-Western world, there was a huge dispersion of Europeans into the rest of the world. As such, there were numerous consequences for the non-Western peoples including social, cultural, economic, political, religious and educational burdens.[142]

Second, Segovia explains that colonisation led to a great dispersion of non-Western peoples from their homelands, mainly through slavery and indenture, as

---

[137] Segovia, "Hermeneutics of the Diaspora," 68.
[138] Segovia, "Hermeneutics of the Diaspora," 69.
[139] Fernando F. Segovia, "Interpreting Beyond Borders: Postcolonial Studies and Diasporic Studies in Biblical Criticism," in *Interpreting Beyond Borders*, ed. Fernando F. Segovia, The Bible and Postcolonialism 3 (Sheffield: Sheffield Academic, 2000), 17.
[140] Segovia, "Interpreting beyond Borders," 17.
[141] Segovia, "Interpreting beyond Borders," 17–18.
[142] Segovia, "Interpreting beyond Borders," 18.

they were taken as cheap labour for the benefit of systems of production banked on capitalism. As a result, a "new world" emerged as societies took on a more mixed characteristic.[143]

And third, the process of colonisation filtered through to modern times in patterns of migration. Today we see huge numbers of migrants moving legally and illegally, from the non-West to the West, due to the economic pressures created by late capitalism.[144] Segovia sums up:

> Thus, just as the West succeeded in establishing itself quite prominently in the non-West over the greater part of the last five hundred years, so has the non-West begun to establish itself quite firmly in the West in the course of the last few decades.[145]

Segovia contends that "the angle of vision afforded by such a web of diasporic experiences will be increasingly applied"[146] in biblical studies.

GALE A. YEE

Continuing this discussion of ethnicity and diaspora, I turn to Chinese-American biblical scholar Gale A. Yee. Yee reveals that as people of Chinese heritage in America, they are casted as "perpetual foreigners" and the "model minority."[147] So what do these classifications mean? Despite being born in Ohio, and having lived in the United States and Canada, Yee is still met with the question: "Where are you from?"[148] This is the essence of being a perpetual foreigner, that based on her Asian appearance, she will always be deemed a foreigner. Furthermore, Yee's experience as the Other is determined on a different axis to African-Americans. For African-Americans, the axis is colour, that is, black and white. For Chinese-Americans, the axis is citizenship, that is, American vs Foreigner.[149] Ultimately for Yee, her definition as a perpetual foreigner makes her feel that she does not belong in America. At the same time, given her experience teaching in Hong Kong, she feels she does not relate to China either.[150]

Yee indicates that depicting Asians as model minorities in American society is a rather gross generalisation of various Asian immigrant communities, which differ in language, education and economic class.[151] On the one hand, they are

---

[143] Segovia, "Interpreting beyond Borders," 18.
[144] Segovia, "Interpreting beyond Borders," 18–19.
[145] Segovia, "Interpreting beyond Borders," 19.
[146] Segovia, "Interpreting beyond Borders," 23.
[147] Gale A. Yee, "'She Stood in Tears Amid the Alien Corn': Ruth, the Perpetual Minority and Model Minority," in *They Were All Together in One Place? Toward Minority Biblical Criticism*, ed. Randall C. Bailey, Tat-siong Benny Liew, and Fernando F. Segovia (Leiden: Brill, 2009), 120.
[148] Yee, "She Stood in Tears," 120.
[149] Yee, "She Stood in Tears," 121.
[150] Yee, "She Stood in Tears," 123–24.
[151] Yee, "She Stood in Tears," 125.

seen as exemplary yet still inferior to white Americans, while on the other hand, their classification as the model minority means that other racial groups should take after them. The classification as model minority acts more as a critique of other racial groups than an accolade to Asian-Americans.[152]

RUTH: PERPETUAL FOREIGNER AND MODEL MINORITY

Yee suggests that the Book of Ruth is favoured among scholars around the globe given the many international perspectives that are utilised in (re)reading Ruth. In the debate regarding Ruth's identity, Katherine Southwood provides a rigorous analysis of Ruth's integration into the Judahite society, defining Ruth's assimilation as "ethnic translation."[153] Southwood comments that Ruth's crossing from Moab to the land of Judah is a successful one, "*despite* her Moabite ethnic identity."[154] The story therefore speaks of her virtuous character which grants her acceptance. Southwood claims that "although for Ruth boundary crossing appears to be possible, there is nothing in the text to suggest that Moabites more generally are accepted within Judah."[155]

Yee maintains that the story of Ruth resonates with her diasporic experience as a Chinese-American, and as such, Ruth maintains a Moabite identity. In fact, Yee contends that Ruth is the model minority or the model emigreé (*ger*). She becomes the model that portrays God's חסד.[156] Yee elaborates: "She is an exemplar of female empowerment, initiative, hard work, family loyalty, and upward mobility. And to top things off, she does get the guy in the end."[157] Ruth is the perpetual foreigner in that her Moabite heritage ensures that like Asian-Americans, she has not truly identified with the Israelite community. And like Chinese American labourers whose labour contribution to the United States has gone unnoticed, Ruth's labour goes largely unnoticed also. Boaz and Naomi, the named Israelites in the story, do not work, but "exploit and live off the surplus labor of the foreign Other."[158] However, Boaz and Naomi are argued by Southwood to be crucial to Ruth's success, as she claims the vitality of family networks contribute to the success of ethnic translation.[159]

Nevertheless, Yee's reading reveals the ugly neglect and the exploitation experienced by diasporic subjects in the face of the dominating majority. Sadly, as the book of Ruth comes to an end, Ruth does not gets mentioned again in the Hebrew Bible after her body had been exhausted in producing the great King

---

[152] Yee, "She Stood in Tears," 125.
[153] Southwood, "Will Naomi's Nation," 102.
[154] Southwood, "Will Naomi's Nation," 114.
[155] Southwood, "Will Naomi's Nation," 114.
[156] Yee, "She Stood in Tears," 133.
[157] Yee, "She Stood in Tears," 134.
[158] Yee, "She Stood in Tears," 134.
[159] Southwood, "Will Naomi's Nation," 117.

David. Ruth's story reminds those living in the First World of the exploitation occurring in the world, where the First World is guilty of exploiting migrants from developing nations and poor immigrants of cheap labour, who leave their homelands for America looking for jobs.[160]

From Yee's diasporic perspective, there is a lack of recognition, and a lack of attention given to migrants. As a result, success comes at a price when migrants are left to decide between maintaining their identity or assimilating. The choice is not definitive as black or white, but Yee does point out an alarming point between the two contexts. In Moab, Ruth and Naomi suffer terrible losses, yet when they return to Judah, they are successful. What does this say? This seems to answer the question of how YHWH's jurisdiction was to be upheld in foreign lands, many miles away from the Deuteronomic schedule of blessings and curses.[161] The simple answer to the question of jurisdiction for Ruth and Naomi was to return to Judah.

Conclusion

I reviewed proposals for a diasporic framework in dialogue with Smith-Christopher, Segovia, and Yee. Smith-Christopher is an American author, yet he has laid solid foundations for diasporic perspectives to read the Bible, particularly the exile. Viewing the exile from a diasporic standpoint opens up an array of insights that highlight in particular the resistance towards the dominating majority. In the case of Segovia, being Cuban-American is a diasporic identity of one who moved away from his homeland to a new land in an "unforced" migration. From this experience, Segovia conveys the importance of acknowledging the Other. Finally, Yee, the Chinese-American feminist scholar, born in Ohio, living in both the United States and Canada, yet struggling to find acceptance in America, but also in China. She lives between spaces, but struggles to find a resting place. As such, she is the perpetual foreigner and the unflattering model minority. Her critique of the Ruth story provokes a sceptical response and illustrates the limits of Yahwistic theodicies.

These experiences and these elements of diasporic identity provide key questions for reading Qohelet. Qohelet in fact is already attempting a more radical release from Deuteronomic reasoning of life with his unorthodox views. Qohelet may have been speaking from outside Jerusalem, questioning the validity of the deed-consequence scheme, but also seeking a release from it, so that one may enjoy one's own portion in life, and drink wine with a merry heart (Eccl 9:7–10). Yet, Qohelet's questioning may also suggest another dynamic, one where the diasporic experience can be felt in intergenerational terms because in one way or

---

[160] Yee, "She Stood in Tears," 134.
[161] Cf. Mein and his discussion of Ezekiel's contrasting moral spheres of in and outside the land. See Andrew Mein, *Ezekiel and the Ethics of Exile* (New York: Oxford University Press, 2001).

another, diasporic people are perpetual foreigners. Like Yee, I am also met with the question: "Where are you from originally?" And by implication, I am constantly having to bring about the movements of my parents from Samoa to Australia, which enabled my birth in Australia. Despite the diversity in diasporic groups and the diversity in language, economic status and education, we all share a similar experience of colonialism, neglect, exploitation, and over-generalisation. Diasporic identities trying to survive between spaces, provide intriguing perspectives for engaging with the biblical text. They will provide the tools for my inquiry into the social location of Qohelet.

5. Kingship

Using the methodological framework of diaspora studies established in the previous chapter, we turn our discussion to Ecclesiastes. I will make a case that certain indicators in Ecclesiastes suggest a diasporic and migrant influence that might point to a diasporic location. This is a conversation that requires diasporic perspectives to be read with these indicators in order to draw out the implications of a diasporic location. For this study, I refer to three indicators in particular: i. kingship, ii. temple, and iii. the doctrine of retribution. I will discuss the topic of kingship in this chapter and show how Qohelet's comments on this subject suggest diasporic motifs and perspectives.

A preliminary question regarding Qohelet's identity as king: Is Qohelet an actual king or is he posing as one? James Kugel observes that apart from the statement "king in Jerusalem" in 1:1, there is no other mention of Israel, nor are there allusions or references to the historical situation of the people of Israel.[1] This observation supports the claim that Qohelet may not have been a king at all but had adopted the persona of king.[2] This claim is also articulated by Thomas Krüger who identifies two personas which Qohelet reflects from: as "king" and as "wise man."[3] These two positions form a dichotomy of two distinct possibilities of judgment on the various discourses throughout the book. For example, Qohelet has two conflicting views on the theme of toil and gain which Krüger suggests could be solved through a realisation of Qohelet's different personas. Krüger writes: "While 'King Qoheleth' regards work and possessions (2:22–23), as well as pleasure and enjoyment (2:24–26), as worthless, for the 'wise man Qoheleth' pleasure and enjoyment represent the highest and only good (3:12–13)."[4] It seems likely that Qohelet needed to take on the role of king in order to argue for the futility of

---

[1] James L. Kugel, "Qohelet and Money," *CBQ* 51.1 (1989): 47.
[2] Michael V. Fox, *A Time to Tear Down and a Time to Build Up: A Rereading of Ecclesiastes* (Grand Rapids: Eerdmans, 1999), 372–73, Peter Enns, *Ecclesiastes*, The Two Horizons Old Testament Commentary (Grand Rapids: Eerdmans, 2011), 17.
[3] Thomas Krüger, *Qoheleth: A Commentary*, trans. O. C. Dean Jr., Hermeneia (Minneapolis: Fortress, 2004), 45.
[4] Krüger, *Qoheleth*, 46.

wealth. The purpose of Qohelet's announcement in 1:1, therefore, is not to identify him as an actual king. Adopting the royal persona serves to bring greater force to his sceptical views.[5]

In this chapter, I will highlight the scepticism that Qohelet addresses regarding kingship before looking for resonances in the rest of the Hebrew Bible. In discussing these resonances, I look to the stories of Moses, Zerubabbel and Jehoiachin. While scepticism towards kings and leaders is known throughout the Hebrew Bible, I use the stories of these leaders as case studies depicting scepticism in a diasporic setting. I find some resonance in the murmurings of the exodus community and the Samarians' complaint against Zerubbabel with a diasporic attitude of scepticism. I will also discuss the Chronicler's portrayal of the Judean kings in 2 Chr 36.

I will highlight these attitudes in a bid to reveal an ability to show resistance towards leaders. We may presume that such scepticism towards leaders would be frowned upon in a traditional monarchic setting—in the case of Moses, a monarch-like setting. Could it be that such attitudes originated in a diasporic context? I aim to answer this question in the ensuing discussion. Finally, I will address the implications of this discussion for a diasporic understanding of Qohelet's own attitude towards kingship.

KINGSHIP IN QOHELET

Kingship is one of the many topics that Qohelet addresses, particularly in 4:13–16. Yet, the absurdity (*hebel*) of kingship in this text is hard to interpret.[6] In 4:13, Qohelet says: "Better is a poor but wise youth than an old but foolish king, who will no longer take advice." Here, Qohelet uses a form of proverb known as the "Better"-proverb, or טוב-*Spruch*.[7]

THE POOR WISE YOUTH AND THE OLD FOOLISH KING

Walther Zimmerli explains that the טוב-*Spruch* is a reflection on the contexts in which choices are limited as opposed to setting out an absolute standard for good behaviour.[8] In the Hebrew Bible, the טוב-*Spruch* is found throughout the wisdom writings, and commonly in Proverbs. It is also found outside Hebrew wisdom in Egyptian instructional literature.[9]

---

[5] Enns, *Ecclesiastes*, 133.
[6] Weeks, *Ecclesiastes and Sceptism*, 115.
[7] Literally, "better-sayings." See Walther Zimmerli, "Zur Struktur der alttestamentlichen Weisheit," *ZAW* 51 (1933): 192.
[8] Walther Zimmerli, "Ort und Grenze der Weisheit im Rahmen der alttestamentlichen Theologie," in *Les Sagesses du Proche-Orient Ancien* (Paris: Presses Universitaires de France, 1963), 129–36.
[9] Bartholomew, *Ecclesiastes*, 186.

5. Kingship

The premise of the saying in Hebrew wisdom is to designate how one thing would be better than another, through the construction טוב ... מן ... .[10] Seow says that such sayings point to "the irony of human existence" and that "what is really better in this regard is not within the grasp of mortals."[11] In the book of Ecclesiastes, Graham Ogden argues that Qohelet has "made personal application [of the T-S tob-spruch] as a medium for his own unique viewpoint."[12] For Qohelet then, the saying accentuates the severity of Qohelet's scepticism.

Qohelet's criticism starts in 4:13, where the טוב-*Spruch* distinguishes the wise youth from the old but foolish king, which as Glendon Bryce argues, seems to separate any association between wisdom and age in kingship.[13] W. Sibley Towner argues:

> The "doubting syndrome" of the Teacher reasserts itself when he points out that even the success of the youth who replaced the king is of limited duration and that hopes for generations yet to come to continue to grant him enduring praise are merely "chasing after wind."[14]

Towner articulates the horror of knowing that kingship is just a meaningless institution because regardless of whether the successor is wise, the successor's time is limited. The young king in chapter 4 is not the traditional type; he emerges from prison (4:14).

To gain a bit more clarity, we need to look at the Hebrew word being associated with kingship. In the first part of 4:14 (כי־מבית הסורים יצא למלך) the implications of the verb מלך translated in the NRSV as "to reign" is contentious. The discussion among scholars centres on whether למלך refers to an actual historical figure. Most scholars do not approach the question of the ruler's identity in 4:14 with much certainty. Crenshaw, in agreement with other scholars, identifies the affinity of the verse with the Joseph narrative, but otherwise it "contains no specific historical references."[15] Seow is not specific either and does not discuss other למלך nuances besides he who "went forth to reign."[16] Rather, he argues that while למלך does have an historical ring as to its origins, the biblical narrative traditions "do not provide a perfect fit" for any theory regarding the identity of the young king (Jehoiachin?).

---

[10] Zimmerli, "Zur Struktur der alttestamentlichen Weisheit," 177–204.
[11] Seow, *Ecclesiastes*, 187.
[12] Graham S. Ogden, "The "Better"-Proverb (Tôb-Spruch), Rhetorical Criticism, and Qoheleth," *JBL* 96 (1977): 504. Note: Ogden abbreviates Tôb-Spruch as "T-S."
[13] Glendon E. Bryce, "Better-Proverbs: An Historical and Structural Study," in *1972 Society of Biblical Literature Seminar Papers*, ed. L. C. McGaughy, SBLSP 108 (Missoula: Scholars Press, 1972). Also see Ogden, "The 'Better,'" 499.
[14] W. Sibley Towner, "Book of Ecclesiastes," in *NIB* 5:316.
[15] Crenshaw, *Ecclesiastes*, 112. Also see Murphy, *Ecclesiastes*, 42; Towner, "Ecclesiastes," 316.
[16] Seow, *Ecclesiastes*, 184. Also see Fox, *Qohelet and His Contradictions*, 206.

What is envisaged is a situation in which the king has been imprisoned, which makes verse 16 a key verse: "Yet those who came later will not rejoice in him. Surely this also is a vanity and a chasing after wind." The pessimistic attitude here is obvious as Murphy states that "it is at least clear that Qoheleth is underscoring that a king falls out of favor with succeeding generations. Such is the fickleness of the populace and the fate of royal power: vanity!"[17] The premise generally accepted is that "the story presents the typical rather than a specific event or historical characters."[18]

The ambiguity of the king's identity provides an opportunity for alternative interpretation. Perhaps Fox grants this opportunity when he writes:

> The elliptical character of the narration does give the impression that Qohelet is relating an event that was actual to his audience (though perhaps dimly remembered), and that he expects them to recognize the event and flesh it out. The audience must be able to grant the plausibility of the event described in vv. 13–14 in order for the twist in vv. 15–16 to be effective.[19]

Fox suggests that we may not need to know who the characters are. Instead, it may be that the outcomes have a kind of philosophical validity, rather than being a commentary on particular members of the house of David who endured imprisonment or returned from exile. Let us consider one option that might have historical resonance: that it represents the "fickleness of a humanity ready to support any young man wishing to aim at the throne, and just as ready to withdraw their support."[20] Qohelet's scepticism therefore extends to the validity of kingship, which I argue further below, is an attitude that can most likely be located in the diaspora.

KINGSHIP IN THE HEBREW BIBLE

To understand the discourse of kingship in Ecclesiastes, it is helpful to review some of the perceptions of the monarchy in the Hebrew Bible. These views are diverse and often contradictory, and they "have fueled scholarly discussion on the texts' historical and diachronic development for well over a century."[21] I will highlight the shifts in leadership from premonarchy to monarchy, to postmonarchy and the views associated with these notions of kingship and bring them into conversation with the attitudes towards kingship in Ecclesiastes. I will pay particular attention to the social conditions of migration and how they may generate

---

[17] Murphy, *Ecclesiastes*, 43.
[18] Murphy, *Ecclesiastes*, 42.
[19] Fox, *Qohelet and His Contradictions*, 206.
[20] Dominic Rudman, "A Contextual Reading of Ecclesiastes 4:13–16," *JBL* 116 (1997): 71.
[21] Ian D. Wilson, *Kingship and Memory in Ancient Judah* (New York: Oxford University Press, 2017), 18.

attitudes of resistance and scepticism. The kings at the beginning and end of the exile are obviously relevant, but we will begin with the king-like Moses, who is first given the law when Israel is wandering in the desert. As many scholars have pointed out, this primordial setting in the desert bears some analogies with the later experience of exile.

MOSES: THE KING AS A LAWGIVER

Notions of kingship in the Hebrew Bible cannot be restricted to the Israelite kings according to Ian Wilson, who argues that the kingship discourse must also include Moses, who takes the law-giving role commonly associated with kings in the surrounding cultures. He writes:

> He, not the Israelite king, is the human mediator who speaks divine Torah into existence, and he appoints for himself a successor—Joshua—who is to carry on Mosaic leadership as Israel makes its way into, conquers, and ultimately settles in the promised land. For the literati, Moses's relationship with Torah was, then, rather like the relationship between ancient Near Eastern kings and their law collections: Moses, like an Egyptian or Mesopotamian ruler, functioned as the giver of his people's divine law.[22]

In short, the relationship between Moses and law suggests an implicit critique of the monarchic performances in Israel and Judah. Moses therefore replaces the normal law-giving role of the king.

We see the response of the nation towards Moses in the wilderness vary from fear and obedience to hostility and resistance, much as we find in Israel's relationship with some of its kings. A question arises here in critical scholarship: Do these desert narratives reflect prevalent attitudes of scepticism towards kingship and monarchy in a post-monarchial period? The murmuring of Israel is prominent throughout the Exodus and Numbers narratives. Their complaints are depicted as opposition to God but also towards their leader Moses.

Where does this scepticism stem from? The profoundly negative outlook is likely a reflection of a prevalent attitude in the social context. In the example of Israel's murmurs in Numbers, for example, 14:1–4, we see Israel challenge Moses's authority, in the course of expressing their frustrations.[23] Their frustration with Moses led them to call for a return to Egypt, and for a new ראש "captain" to take them back there (Num 14:4).

In Israel's frustration, it is important to notice the longing for Egypt. The wilderness represents the new while Egypt represents the old. Yet, despite the oppression and suffering in the old, it is still preferred to the enigmatic new. This comes across as a typical attitude of those in migration, who in their new location

---

[22] Wilson, *Kingship and Memory*, 68.
[23] Frankel, *Land of Canaan*, 317.

long for their old home.[24] Although this attitude causes YHWH to want to "strike them with pestilence and disinherit them" (14:12), Moses intercedes and instead warns YHWH of the consequences of the divine anger against Israel. As a result, the attitude of Israel does not lead to their demise for Israel does not suffer for their complaint.[25]

In the spirit of *talanoa*, let us probe further. One might infer that this protest is legitimate; the pessimistic attitude of Israel may have been warranted, from the narrator's point of view. In this sense, the murmuring of Israel might be reflective of an attitude of pessimism that may be deemed appropriate, if this was built over generations.

Protest continues in Num 16, where Korah, Dathan, Abiram and On, take two hundred and fifty Israelite men to confront Moses and Aaron. The protest reflects an attitude of resentment towards Moses and Aaron for elevating themselves above the congregation.[26] The idea of a community standard not being met by its leaders presents a different redactional layer to the murmuring tradition in Numbers, because now the complaint is "unrelated to the usual problems of thirst or hunger, and deals squarely with the issue of Moses' leadership."[27]

The theme of murmuring in the wilderness presents the first challenge towards kingship, at least in the canonical order, especially if we take Moses's role as implicitly monarchic. Of particular interest to our own investigation, there is a correlation in these narratives between the murmuring and the migrant state of the Israelites. They long to return to Egypt, due to the dissatisfaction of their current location. As a result, they remain sceptical towards Moses's ambition towards the promised land, by seeking to return, and at the same time wanting to change leadership.

As already suggested, it may be that this scepticism expressed by the Israelites is reflective of a diasporic people who remain doubtful about returning to their homeland. The irony of returning to a homeland which is actually "foreign" to them, is a typical diasporic understanding. Their scepticism puts them at odds with those who spearhead the return, as seen with Israel's critique of Moses. Such a clash could reflect a commonly observed tension between first- and second-generation people in a diasporic setting: The first-generation promote and romanticize the homeland and its traditions, while the second-generation struggle to see its relevance.[28] Such an intergenerational tension seems to resonate with the murmuring narratives. In sum, the migrating Israelites who are sceptictical of their

---

[24] Cf. Gilroy, *Black Atlantic*, 124.
[25] David Frankel, *The Murmuring Stories of the Priestly School: A Retrieval of Ancient Sacerdotal Lore* (Leiden: Brill, 2002), 317.
[26] Phillip J. Budd, *Numbers*, WBC 5 (Dallas: Word, 1998), 186.
[27] Frankel, *Murmuring Stories*, 206.
[28] Glenda Stanley, and Judith Kearney, "The Experiences of Second Generation Samoans in Australia," *Journal of Social Inclusion* 8.2 (2017): 54–61; Anae, "Towards a NZ-Born Samoan Identity," 131.

5. Kingship

leader's ambition to return to the homeland, exhibit a similar scepticism towards out-of-touch leadership that we find in Qohelet.

ZERUBBABEL: THE KING AS REBUILDER

In the book of Ezra, complaint against leadership is not explicit in the case of Zerubbbael, but antagonistic attitudes towards Zerubbabel by the "people of the land" is clear. In fact, Ezra 4:1 refers to the "people of the land" as צרי "enemy" or "adversaries" (NRSV) of Judah and Benjamin. Immediately, this puts them in opposition to Zerubbabel and the heads of the families of Judah and Benjamin. Unsurprisingly, the label צר acts as a prelude to Zerubbabel's rejection of the request by the "people of the land" to help in the rebuilding of the Temple. Consequently, the "people of the land" take action through the bribing and intimidating of the *golah* (4:4), followed by a series of accusation letters to the kings of Persia (4:6–24), leading to the cessation of the rebuilding of Jerusalem till the second year of Darius' reign (4:24). The "people of the land" are evidently defiant against Zerubbabel and the returnees, as they are prevented from joining as allies (4:3).[29] This feeling of being marginalised, I would argue, is indicative of a diasporic attitude of scepticism—not literally, perhaps, but in a sociological sense.

To elaborate: The narrative takes place in Jerusalem, but there is an interesting interplay of diasporic attitudes between those who were exiled, or the *golah* community, and the "people of the land." The *golah* community in their exiled state are ostensibly the diasporic people, but their position of power in the land means that the surface of the language is not a reliable guide to the social dynamic. One could make a case for a diasporic identity even for "the people of the land." The relationship between the "people of the land" and the *golah* echoes a familiar position of diasporic people. The "people of the land" do not reside outside the land as diasporic people traditionally do, but they do in sociological terms.

Rocco Bernasconi points out that "beside the connection to the land, the observance of the law became a relevant criterion of definition of 'Israel' and eventually superseded it."[30] It is clear to Ezra that the *golah* by this definition are the true Israel and "the people of the land" are not. The distinction made here reflects a construction of identity based on religious observance and purity.[31] One could argue here that "the people of the land" take the position of diaspora, while the *golah* take the position of the true inhabitants of the land. In Ezra 9, the theme of mixed marriage enhances such a distinction as not only are "the people of the land" seen as foreign, they are also ceremonially unclean.[32] This seems to be a position that the redactor pushes, as Lester Grabbe argues: "any supposed

---

[29] Lester L. Grabbe, *Ezra-Nehemiah*, Old Testament Readings (London: Routledge, 1998), 16.
[30] Rocco Bernasconi, "Meanings, Function and Linguistic Usages of the Term 'Am Ha-Aretz in the Mishnah," *Revue des Études Juives* 170.3–4 (2011): 403.
[31] Smith-Christopher, *Biblical Theology of Exile*, 162.
[32] Smith-Christopher, *Biblical Theology of Exile*, 150.

'intermarriage' was not usually with non-Jews but with elements of the Jewish community not favoured by the author."[33]

The position is further developed through the description of the origins of the "people of the land." Ezra does state that the "people of the land" were brought to the land since the days of King Essar-haddon of Assyria (Ezra 4:2). This is the view of the redactor as H. G. M. Williamson points out, where the "people of the land" consisted of those "(or perhaps just some of those) who had been imported by the Assyrians into the territory of the old Northern Kingdom and who had adopted the local religion."[34] Lisbeth Fried has argued, we should note, that the term "people of the land" as used in Ezra 4:4 is consistent with the rest of the biblical corpus in that they are "the landed aristocracy of an area."[35] Fried implies then that the redactor makes the mistake of assuming that the "people of the land" descended from those people who were brought in by the Assyrian kings.[36] The redactor's view leads to a portrayal of the "people of the land" as outsiders. Their negative portrayal seems to arise from the hostile attitude of the *golah* community towards the "people of the land."

The redactor's view in Ezra 4:2 must therefore be questioned, particularly as Grabbe argues convincingly:

> The conclusion seems straightforward: the text simply refuses to admit that there were Jewish inhabitants of the land after the deportations under Nebuchadnezzar. Probably only a minority of the people were taken away, with the tens of thousands still left. These people continued to live in Judah, work the land, raise families, carry on their daily life. Presumably they would have quietly taken over any land abandoned because the owners had been killed in fighting or deported to Babylonia. There is no suggestion that any foreign peoples were brought in to replace those deported. Where are these people—Jews—in the books of Ezra and Nehemiah? They are absent. Instead we find references to the 'peoples of the land' who are identified as foreigners. One can only conclude that many, if not all, these 'peoples of the land' were the Jewish descendants of those who were

---

[33] Lester L. Grabbe, "The Reality of the Return: The Biblical Picture Versus Historical Reconstruction," in *Exile and Return: The Babylonian Context*, ed. Jonathan Stökl and Caroline Waerzeggers (Berlin: De Gruyter, 2015), 303.

[34] H. G. M. Williamson, *Ezra-Nehemiah*, WBC 16 (Dallas: Word, 1985), 49.

[35] Lisbeth S. Fried, "The 'am hā'āres in Ezra 4:4 and Persian Imperial Administration," in *Judah and the Judeans in the Persian Period*, ed. Oded Lipschits and Manfred Oeming (Winona Lake: Eisenbrauns, 2006), 125.

[36] Fried, "The 'am hā'āres," 125. Also see Antonius H. J. Gunneweg, "'Am Ha'aretz'—A Semantic Revolution," *ZAW* 95.3 (1983): 438. Gunneweg explains the development of the term throughout the corpus of the Hebrew Bible, from more positive nuances of being "full citizens of the state" and "full members of the cultic congregation of Israel" to the negative portrayal in Ezra that "denotes the hostile foreign people and pagans."

not deported. In the eyes of the author of Ezra, these peoples were no longer kin; the only 'people of Israel' were those who had gone into captivity.[37]

As one of my reviewers indicated, the so-called peoples of the land in Ezra themselves have a hybrid identity—they are ethnically Judaean, but from the point of view of the *golah* community they are not part of the true Israel. Perhaps identity was a very complex thing in postexilic Yehud, and Qohelet reflects a deep uncertainty about it all.

Accordingly, the misrepresentation of the history begins with the portrayal of the "people of the land" as "foreigners" (4:5; 6; 9–10)[38] who are at odds with the *golah* community and its leadership. The "people of the land" are therefore not diasporic in the physical sense given that they were not deported. I would argue that the "people of the land" in their defiance against Zerubbabel *paradoxically reflect a diasporic attitude of scepticism*. They are like the Israel who rebels in the wilderness.

In painting this picture of the "people of the land" the term עַם־הָאָרֶץ "people of the land" carries a negative sense different from the "more positive meaning of the expression 'people of the land' … in Hag 2:4 and Zech 7:5."[39] Specifically, the term "defile" used in Ezra to denote the defilement of the land by the "people of the land" carries connotations of "female menstrual impurity."[40] Southwood argues that the "people of the land" are viewed through this lens of impurity as "categorically and unconditionally untouchable."[41] As Grabbe notes of this terminology for defilement, "the term is not usually used of non-Jews."[42]

The context then for Ezra was conflicted, and as Antonius Gunneweg suggests, this was a conflict based on who was deemed as "God's true Israel-congregation."[43] By implication, the *golah* are colonial-type characters, as argued by John Kessler.[44] This provides an interesting milieu for the Persian edict to

---

[37] Grabbe, *Ezra-Nehemiah*, 135.
[38] Fried, "The 'am hā'āres," 134.
[39] Ralph W. Klein, "The Books of Ezra and Nehemiah," in *NIB* 3:695. Cf. Jacob L. Wright, *Rebuilding Identity: The Nehemiah-Memoir and Its Earliest Readers* (Berlin: de Gruyter, 2004), 62–66, 256. Wright emphasises that Neh 2 does not see the remainees as foreign. Also see Grabbe, *Ezra-Nehemiah*, 16.
[40] Katherine E. Southwood, *Ethnicity and the Mixed Marriage Crisis in Ezra 9–10: An Anthropological Approach* (Oxford: Oxford University Press, 2012), 137.
[41] Southwood, *Ethnicity*, 137.
[42] Grabbe, *Ezra-Nehemiah*, 16.
[43] Gunneweg, "'Am ha'aretz," 439. Cf. Peter R. Bedford, *Temple Restoration in Early Acharmenid Judah* (Leiden: Brill, 2001), 180.
[44] Kessler refers to the *golah* as a Charter Group who were returning to a land to which they held genealogical, religious and legal claim. At the same time, they also sought to exclude "foreigners" who did not have similar religious affiliation. See John Kessler, "Persia's Loyal Yahwists: Power Identity and Ethnicity in Achaemenid Yehud," in *Judah and the Judeans in the Persian Period*, ed.

rebuild the temple in Jerusalem. Zerubbabel had been tasked with the rebuilding of the temple under Persian king Cyrus's orders, but was met with hostility after having rejected the "people of the land" from working alongside them. Possible echoes of Eccl 4:16 are heard here, as "those who came later will not rejoice in him." The "people of the land" do not rejoice in Zerubbabel but in fact reject him as they send their letter of accusation "against the inhabitants of Judah and Jerusalem" (Ezra 4:6). In the case of Zerubbabel in Ezra, the diasporic space is ironically that of the "people of the land."

For the "people of the land," the building of the temple was seemingly irrelevant, as they had already been worshiping the same God as the *golah* community. Furthermore, Ralph Klein notes that "the leaders of the peoples of the land apparently saw the building of the Temple as a threat to their security."[45] Perhaps the "people of the land" found that the building of this new temple would repeat history. In any case, the temple would therefore be depicted as a point of vulnerability, endangering their own safety but also the Persian king through a "politically motivated revolt."[46]

It could be that the scepticism of the "people of the land" towards Zerubbabel deems the hype surrounding the returnees' mission to rebuild the temple as a "chasing of the wind." In short, the Samarians who evidently felt marginalised by Zerubbabel's arrival in Jerusalem express a kind of scepticism analogous to that which we find in Qohelet.

JEHOIACHIN: THE KING AS VASSAL

Jehoiachin is a rather ambiguous figure in the Hebrew Bible, who is treated differently in different texts. He is granted a favourable depiction in Kings, Chronicles, Jeremiah, and Ezekiel, particularly with the theological significance tied to his Davidic lineage.[47] On the other hand, Kings and Jeremiah are also critical of him, showing less favourable perspectives towards the exiled king. I pose a question as to whether such unfavourable perspectives towards Jehoiachin could stem from a diasporic context in Jeremiah and Kings.

Scepticism towards Jehoiachin in Jeremiah

In Jeremiah, the unfavourable perspectives appear in chapter 22, where firstly, Jehoiachin is called different names, Shallum (v. 11) and Coniah (vv. 24, 28) as

---

Oded Lipschits and Manfred Oeming (Winona Lake: Eisenbrauns, 2006), 101–2. Also cf. Mark G. Brett, *Locations of God: Political Theology in the Hebrew Bible* (New York: Oxford University Press, 2019), 75.

[45] Klein, "Ezra and Nehemiah," 695.

[46] Reinhard G. Kratz, "The Second Temple of Jeb and of Jerusalem," in *Judah and the Judeans in the Persian Period*, ed. Odel Lipschits and Manfred Oeming (Winona Lake: Eisenbrauns, 2006), 264.

[47] Matthew H. Patton, *Hope for a Tender Sprig: Jehoiachin in Biblical Theology*, BBRSup (Winona Lake: Eisenbrauns, 2017), 128.

opposed to his regnal name. Although Shallum and Coniah may be alternative names for Jehoiachin,[48] M. Goulder believes that the use of Jehoiachin's other names may be a refusal to acknowledge his kingship thus reflecting Jeremiah's contemptuous attitude towards Jehoiachin.[49]

Looking at verse 28, the scornful attitude of the prophet is clear towards Jehoicahin as he poses the question: "Is this man Coniah a despised broken pot, a vessel no one wants?" (NRSV).[50] The prophet's question reflects the intent of the passage as not only a pronouncement of judgment but to remove any hopes, in Babylon or Jerusalem, that Jehoiachin would eventually return to the throne.[51] The prophet's question also reflects the uncertainty and doubt that is characteristic of an exilic context, because the answer as to why Jehoiachin (Coniah) is "hurled into exile" is not forthcoming.[52]

In an attempt to provide possible answers, further study was carried out by C. L. Crouch in relation to ambiguous parts of the text. Crouch argues that verse 28 in particular, may have been copied incorrectly. For instance, Crouch understands the word העצב "pot" to be a scribal error, and should instead read העצם ("bone," "skeleton," "bodily frame").[53] She explains:

> If Jehoiachin's is the body in question, its description as *nibzœh* and *nāpûs* also begins to make sense: he is threatened with one of the most horrifying fates in the ancient world, the desecration of his corpse and denial of a proper burial.[54]

In addition, Crouch notes that the term כלי (vessel) (v. 28) might resonate better with the "weapon" expounded in Jer 48:38 and Hos 8:8. Crouch therefore suggests that a military meaning is more appropriate: כלי is "a weapon in which there is no delight."[55] This points to military failure, as Jehoiachin (or Coniah) is "the [weapon] no one wants."[56] It may be then that Jehoiachin was not a broken vessel, but as Crouch posits, a "humiliated vassal."[57]

---

[48] Patrick D. Miller, "The Book of Jeremiah," in *NIB* 6:743.
[49] M. Goulder, "Behold My Servant Jehoiachin," *VT* 52.2 (2002): 181.
[50] See Goulder, "Behold My Servant," 181. In Goulder's argument, he makes a case for the Suffering Servant in Isaiah 53 as Jehoiachin. He argues that the "words *nibzeh, hēpes, yislāh, yāmîm, zeraʾ*, in these two verses, all recur in Isa. liii 3,10. [Deutero-Isaiah] well knows what the people of Judah thought of Jehoiachin: they despised him and esteemed him not, but in the long run they were proved wrong—he did live on, and flourish, and 'see seed'."
[51] Miller, "Jeremiah," 743.
[52] Peter C. Craigie, *Jeremiah 1–25*, WBC 26 (Dallas: Word, 1991), 322.
[53] C. L. Crouch, "Jehoiachin: Not a Broken Vessel but a Humiliated Vassal (Jer 22:28–30)," *ZAW* 129.2 (2017): 234.
[54] Crouch, "Jehoiachin," 238.
[55] Crouch, "Jehoiachin," 240.
[56] Crouch, "Jehoiachin," 239.
[57] Crouch, "Jehoiachin," 234, 45.

Such an attitude towards Jehoiachin's reign is also evident in the LXX version of Jeremiah. John B. Job argues that in Jer 27:1–29:23 in the Septuagint, "there are remnants of a pessimistic view of Jehoiachin, portraying his exile as a disaster still to be completed."[58] The scepticism towards Jehoiachin threatened the pro-Jerusalem agenda of the temple and the fulfilment of the Davidic prophecy. As a captive, Jehoiachin was reduced to a fellow slave with the rest of the exiled Judahites, despite his fair treatment in Kings. The fall of Jehoiachin from monarchic figure to slave most likely promoted scepticism towards Jehoiachin.

The uncertainty towards Jehoiachin's reign in exile reflects an attitude of doubt towards the monarchic institution when outside its regnal realm. This finds resonance with a diaspora setting outside from where Jewish monarchic jurisdiction loses effect. In the diaspora, the exilic Jehoiachin's position as king is suspect as he yields to the foreign powers, while hope in a future return to Jerusalem becomes ambivalent.

Scepticism towards Jehoiachin in Kings

It seem that Kings prescribes hope in a future return. Gerhard von Rad and Jon Levenson among others think so, arguing that the ending of Kings (2 Kgs 25:27–30) exhibits a hopeful depiction which gives an ultimately positive view of Jehoiachin.[59] However, a closer reading points us towards a critical view of Jehoiachin. Jehoiachin, in his release, is not granted the throne by YHWH but instead, by a Babylonian king who serves the god Marduk.[60] The position he reclaims is not actually one of power and authority, but "merely a seat higher than other client kings."[61] Indeed, the amelioration of Jehoiachin's captive state may be perceived in a positive sense, but is actually limited in its application. Donald Murray writes:

> Crucially, this is a limit that in our text the Davidic monarchic line never promises to transcend, either in the person of Jehoiachin, who dies while still in this state, or in the person of a son and heir, who might have lived to see restoration.[62]

This points to the possibility of a suspicious view of Jehoiachin's stature. Jehoiachin has no real control over his own fate, so much that the higher seat that he receives is not claimed or earnt through a military exploit, but given to him.

The doubt towards Jehoiachin's future reign is accentuated by the lack of mention of a royal progeny for him in these last verses of Kings. I do not ask the

---

[58] John B. Job, *Jeremiah's Kings: A Study of the Monarchy in Jeremiah* (Aldershot, England: Ashgate, 2006), 96–97.

[59] Gerhard von Rad, *Deuteronomium-Studien*, FRLANT 40 (Göttingen: Vandenhoeck & Ruprecht, 1947), 52–64; Jon D. Levenson, "The Last Four Verses in Kings," *JBL* 103 (1984): 353–61.

[60] Donald F. Murray, "Of All the Years the Hopes—or Fears? Jehoiachin in Babylon (2 Kings 25:27–30)," *JBL* 120 (2001): 261.

[61] Murray, "Of all the Years," 261.

[62] Murray, "Of all the Years," 263.

question of whether Jehoiachin had an heir or not, and certainly 1 Chr 3:17–18 lists eight sons for him. I argue that a lack of progeny in Kings suggest a pessimistic view towards Jehoiachin and his future as king, for if the mention of an heir suggests royal succession, then the lack of mention of a son reflects a diminishing hope for the Davidic monarchy to be restored.[63]

Interestingly, Michael Chan and Ian Wilson suggest that the situation of exile would have generated memories of the exodus.[64] Chan focuses on a positive resonance between the exodus and Jehoiachin's exilic experience, arguing that "Both the family of Jacob at the end of Genesis and Jehoiachin find themselves in similar situations—enjoying the benevolence and bounty of a foreign ruler."[65] However, Wilson, in response to Chan, argues that the exodus is multivocal, and as such, the social memory of the Yehudites, would also have been multivocal. As seen through these opposite viewpoints, the exodus is indeed multivocal, as Wilson writes: "The exile/exodus, in Israel's story, symbolizes at once the people's oppression and its freedom, its failures and its successes, its struggles with apostasy and its devotion to Yahweh."[66]

The conversation between Chan and Wilson highlights that there is a tension in the mindset of the exilic Jews; a tension that has been influenced by mixed allusions and memories of Israel's exodus in the past. Despite the glimmer of hope that Kings portrays through the Jehoiachin story, remembering past exilic/exodus experiences of death and despair ensures that even if there were a sense of hope, it would be a "delayed and attenuated hope."[67]

DIASPORIC SUSPICION OF KINGSHIP IN CHRONICLES

The idea of remembering the past as hope for the future recalls the Chronicler's recounting of David's and Solomon's glorious reigns as hope for Yehud's future restoration. In fact, Johannes Hänel and von Rad, among others, understand that hope in the messianic Davidic monarchy is a central theme to the book.[68] This is conveyed through a heightened and glorified portrayal of David and Solomon.

Hence, the Chronicler offers a different portrayal of David and Solomon to that found in Samuel-Kings. The Chronicler's version is framed by a vision of where future restoration of Yehud is pinned on the rebuilding of the temple. The temple is significant for the Chronicler's purpose because it expresses divine

---

[63] Cf. Murray, "Of all the Years," 262–63.
[64] Michael J. Chan, "Joseph and Jehoiachin: On the Edge of Exodus," *ZAW* 125.4 (2013): 566–77.
[65] Chan, "Joseph and Jehoiachin," 574.
[66] Ian D. Wilson, "Joseph, Jehoiachin, and Cyrus: On Book Endings, Exoduses and Exiles, and Yehudite/Judean Social Remembering," *ZAW* 126.4 (2014): 527.
[67] Wilson, "Joseph, Jehoiachin, and Cyrus," 527.
[68] Johann Wilhelm Rothstein, and Johannes Hänel, *Kommentar Zum Ersten Buch Der Chronik*, Kat 18.2 (Leipzig: Scholl, 1927), xliii, xliv. See also pp. x–xi. Gerhard von Rad, *Das Geschichtsbild Des Chronistischen Werkes*, BWANT 54 (Stuggart: Kohlhammer, 1930), 119–32. Also see Sara Japhet, *I and II Chronicles: A Commentary* (Louisville: Westminster John Knox, 1993), 1077.

sovereignty.[69] Accordingly, a connection is made between temple and kingship, as "kingship plays a major role in the presentation of God's sovereignty in Chronicles."[70] This ensures that kingship in Chronicles serves a cultic or "religiously-tinted" purpose as opposed to a civic one.[71] David is therefore depicted as the cultic founder chosen by YHWH with a close affiliation with the temple (1 Chr 11:3b; 28:4), while Solomon is depicted as the temple builder.[72]

However, the portraits of kings in Chronicles are not all painted with the same brush as used for David and Solomon. In fact, in 2 Chr 36, we find a succession of kings who are shown in a more negative light. If kingship is crucial for the rebuilding and security of the temple, then what purpose does 2 Chr 36 serve? Why does Chronicles conclude with these heavily abridged kingship accounts? Samasoni Alama's argument is significant for our purpose here, as he writes:

> the Chronicler has rewoven the concept of the sovereignty of God via Israel's kingship, with the aim to ease the integration process among the various Israelite postexilic communities. It is through kingship, past and present, native and/or foreign, that the sovereignty of God is realized for postexilic Israel and its cultic institutions.[73]

In short, the restoration of Judean kings is not necessary. As mentioned above, the Chronicler links kingship with the temple as expressions of divine sovereignty. As such, the kings in 2 Chr 36 no longer represent God's sovereignty. What is articulated instead is a transition for Israel in exile, from the Davidic monarchy to the foreign kings who will continue God's promise in Israel's history.[74] Second Chronicles 36 depicts the transition from the Judean kings to the foreign kings. There is a list of examples in which foreign kings prevail.

Jehoahaz
2 Chr 36:3: Then the king of Egypt *deposed him* [ויסירהו]
2 Chr 36:4a: The king of Egypt *made* his brother Eliakim *king* [וימלך] over Judah and Jerusalem, and *changed* [ויסב] his name to Jehoiakim

Jehoiakim
2 Chr 36:6: Against him King Nebuchadnezzar of Babylon came up, and bound him with fetters to *take him* [להליכו] to Babylon

---

[69] Samasoni Moleli Alama, "Jabez in Context: A Multidimensional Approach to Identity and Landholdings in Chronicles" (PhD Thesis, University of Divinity, 2018), 145.
[70] Alama, "Jabez," 145.
[71] Jozef Tiňo, *King and Temple in Chronicles: A Contextual Approach to Their Relations* (Göttingen: Vandenhoeck & Ruprecht, 2010), 25.
[72] Alama, "Jabez," 172–73.
[73] Alama, "Jabez," 144.
[74] Alama, "Jabez," 162.

5. Kingship

Jehoiachin
2 Chr 36:10a: In the spring of the year King Nebuchadnezzar sent and *brought him* [ויבאהו] to Babylon
2 Chr 36:10c: and *made* his brother Zedekiah *king* [וימלך] over Judah and Jerusalem

Zedekiah
2 Chr 36:13a: He also rebelled against King Nebuchadnezzar, who had *made him swear* [השביעו] by God

For Jehoahaz, the root of the underlined verb in 2 Chr 36:3 above is סור "to turn aside" so the *hiphil* form would mean that the Egyptian king caused Jehoahaz to turn or to be deposed. In 2 Chr 36:4a, the root of וימלך is מלך "to rule" which in the *hiphil* form would mean that the Egyptian appointed Eliakim to rule over Judah and Jerusalem. In the case of Jehoiakim (2 Chr 36:6), it was King Nebuchadnezzar who took him to Babylon, or as the *hiphil* suggests, caused him to go להליכו. For Jehoiachin, Nebuchadnezzar brought him ויבאהו (2 Chr 36:10a) to Babylon and made Zedekiah king וימלך (2 Chr 36:10c) as his successor. Zedekiah was made by Nebuchadnezzar to swear a vow השביעו (2 Chr 36:13a) to him.

The language indicates two things. First, the foreign kings are now depicted as the new agents of God's sovereignty as the unrighteous Davidic kings lose their thrones. Second, the fact of the Judean kings' decline in power points to their diminished stature in the exile. The kings, in their imprisoned state, are also in no position to rebuild the temple, the temple being central to the Chronicler's agenda. As a result, Yehud have to accept the foreign kings as "their God-appointed leaders."[75] Chronicles appears to be ecumenical through the inclusion of these foreign kings who continue God's purpose for rebuilding the temple in Jerusalem. It envisions an inclusive Yehud, where foreigners and aliens are part of the "all-Israel" community. This is in line with the imperial openness of the Persians towards different cults,[76] only with Jerusalem as its centre.

Questions will arise regarding the Chronicler's ecumenical picture, particularly for the postexilic community. Indeed, the reality of exile would most likely provoke attitudes of scepticism towards the Davidic hope, as foreign kings determine the fate of Yehud in exile. Ironically, acceptance of the foreign kings would mean not accepting the Judean kings. This is an attitude most likely generated in the diaspora.

The Chronicler's text itself was not addressed to the diaspora but to the returnees. The Davidic hope was turned to affirm the rebirth of a Davidic temple, rather than a Davidic royal house. But this second temple was located precisely in Jerusalem, not in Gerizim and not in the diaspora. Gary Knoppers suggests that

---

[75] Louis C. Jonker, *Reflections of King Josiah in Chronicles: Late Stages of the Josiah Reception in II Chr. 34f* (Gutersloh: Gütersloher Verlagshaus, 2003), 87.
[76] Louis C. Jonker, *Defining All-Israel in Chronicles*, FAT 106 (Tübingen: Mohr Siebeck, 2016), 120.

there may have been opposition to a united leadership, stating that "Aside from the practical consideration that the Jews were under foreign domination and unlikely to regain their independence, there were those who saw no need, conditions permitting, to revitalize the Davidic monarchy.[77]

Diaspora peoples did not fit with the agenda of the Chronicler, particularly his "stress on the importance of the people, city, Temple, and land to those outside the land."[78] A sceptical response, I argue, would have come from people who did not want to return to Jerusalem. It may be that they were voices of Jews who preferred the diasporic lands where they were living and felt no need for a glorious return to Jerusalem or to a Davidic monarchy. And as already argued in relation to Ezra, one of those "diasporic" lands would be Samaria.

QOHELET'S ATTITUDE TO KINGSHIP

The attitudes towards Moses, Zerubbabel and Jehoiachin reveal an ability to show resistance and scepticism towards leaders deriving from different social settings, which would not be allowed in a traditional monarchic setting. This correlates with Qohelet's own sceptical attitude towards kingship, particularly in 4:13–16, where the fame and power of the king is a chasing of the wind.[79] The general reverence afforded to leaders and kings, traditionally understood to be divinely appointed, no longer constitutes a part of the cultural fabric of the societies that produced these texts. Even in the context that the Chronicler produced his portrayal of Jehoiachin and the Davidic kings, one cannot ignore the backdrop of conflicting views towards Davidic dynasty. While the Chronicler promoted a pro-Davidic and protemple agenda, Knoppers states that there is no reason to believe that all Jews felt the same. One could then imagine that the leaders were met with hostility and scepticism because social reality allows for such attitudes. This may be why Qohelet is sceptical towards kingship; he saw the inadequacy of traditional wisdom, as well as the impotence of Jewish kingship in the diaspora.[80]

There is a correlation among the three main figures discussed in this chapter, and it centres on the issue of Davidic lineage. Moses clearly does not associate with the Davidic line, however, Zerubbabel and Jehoiachin do, and there may be more to Moses's nonassociation with the Davidic line than meets the eye. Zerubbabel and Jehoiachin are both descendants of David, which might suggest that they were potential saviours for the community during and after the exile, in fulfilment of the Davidic prophecy. However, when they are met with criticism and

---

[77] Gary Knoppers, *I Chronicles 1–9: A New Translation with Introduction and Commentary*, AB 12 (New York: Doubleday, 2004), 113.
[78] Knoppers, *I Chronicles 1–9*, 114.
[79] Towner, "Ecclesiastes," 316.
[80] Cf. Mark R. Sneed, *The Politics of Pessimism in Ecclesiastes: A Social-Science Perspective*, AIL 12 (Atlanta: Society of Biblical Literature, 2012), 18.

resistance, their Davidic lineage is not mentioned. I would argue that in a diasporic context, Davidic lineage matters little. Similarly, a prophetic hope is immaterial as the reality of the diasporic situation presents itself, a reality where cultural and conventional practices from the homeland may not be appropriated.

As for Qohelet, there is no mention of the Davidic line when he speaks of kingship. In diaspora, we may imagine that Qohelet has become sceptical of the Judean kingship which has fallen under foreign powers. Such a pessimistic view questions the pertinence of a divinely instituted dynasty and a return to power of the Davidic throne. Importantly, however, there is no celebration of Persian power, as we find in Chronicles. As Smith-Christopher contends, perhaps this is wisdom best read from the worldview of those in the diaspora.[81]

CONCLUSION

The implications for Qohelet are significant, as the lack of mention of a Davidic ruler in Yehud besides the superscription in Eccl 1:1,[82] allows for reimagining Qohelet's social setting for, as Karin Schöplin points out, Qohelet reflects a certain disregard towards kingship. She writes: "The people just do not care about the quality of their ruler, whether he is qualified by wisdom or not."[83]

I therefore propose an alternative framework for interpretation in which Qohelet's discussion on kingship allows us to entertain the possibility of a diasporic location for the sage. This would go a long way towards explaining why he would have had issues with kingship. Accordingly, when Weeks finds that the absurdity (*hebel*) of kingship in 4:13–16 is hard to interpret,[84] the difficulty lies in failing to understand Qohelet's location. Positioning Qohelet in diaspora would help solve such an interpretive dilemma.

To be able to critique kingship implies a context that allows it. From my own reading perspective, I think for example of diasporic Samoan attitudes of scepticism shown towards leaders who try to uphold traditional modes of living in a foreign land. With this perspective, I could make a case for the location of suspicion towards kingship. For instance, I could recast Moses as representative of the homeland leaders and the Israelites as the first- and second-generation, who are in opposition within the wilderness context. In their diasporic existence they show scepticism and resistance towards their "king." Now that they are stranded in the wilderness, they may truly consider the experience *hebel*. Scepticism towards

---

[81] Smith-Christopher, *Biblical Theology of Exile*, 160.
[82] While the superscription may point to King Solomon, the language in the rest of the book suggests a date much later than Solomon. In reading 1:1, it is best to think of the author as adopting the persona of King Solomon, or the son of David. See Towner, "Ecclesiastes," 95; Seow, *Ecclesiastes*, 289.
[83] Karin Schöpflin, "Political Power and Ideology in Qohelet," *BN-NF* 161 (2014): 22.
[84] Weeks, *Ecclesiastes and Scepticism*, 115.

Moses potentially implies scepticism towards the torah of Moses, specifically, its ideas of reward and punishment.[85]

In the case of Zerubbabel, the marginalisation of the Samarians represents a common experience of diasporic identities being discriminated against in the host land despite being born in the host land. The Samarians or the "people of the land" are like the second-generation who, despite being born in the host land, are still deemed as outsiders. In their own "diasporic" experience, they are excluded, cast as outsiders and are being marginalised due to their "ethnicity"; although they are people of the land, they are rejected by Zerubbabel from building the temple. Zerubbabel then is a leader who seeks to marginalise members of society who do not "fit in." This type of colonial leadership cause suspicion for diasporic identities, whereby a diasporic setting allows them to voice their concerns against leadership.

The worldview of Chronicles presents itself as being ecumenical, and not overtly anti-Samaria as we find in Ezra-Nehemiah. This reflects a certain tension between diasporic people and those in the homeland. The voice of those in the diaspora speaks up in response to elements of oppression and marginalisation in the homeland.

AITAUMALELE

In Samoan circles, this diasporic voice is that of *aitaumalele*, a concept I will unpack in chapter 8, but in brief, it is the voice of those who provide service from afar, in urban centres, or in other countries. They are often downplayed by leaders in the homeland who consider them to be detrimental to the Samoan status quo. The leaders in the homeland are at times guilty of imparting a romanticised version of *faa-Samoa* (Samoan culture) which is often uncritically accepted by those in subordination.

The *aitaumalele* develop a different worldview after being exposed to a foreign context and are able to see the injustices that are ignored in the homeland. The traditional leaders rebuke such views as heretical, and their loyalty to the Samoan cause is questioned. Perhaps this is what is at play when Knoppers alludes to opposition to Jehoiachin and therefore against a united monarchy, which was concealed by the Chronicler.

I suggest that Qohelet was a sage who was dissatisfied with Jewish leadership, which in a diasporic context was simply *hebel*. Qohelet made the observation that regardless of who the Jewish king was, it did not matter, because later generations would no longer rejoice in him (4:16). This helps explain the lack of mention of the Davidic kings by Qohelet; an institution which Qohelet most likely considered as vanity.

---

[85] See chapter 7.

6. God's Presence

In this chapter, I will point to another indicator in Ecclesiastes that suggest a possible diasporic setting, namely the temple and the notion of God's presence. In my discussion of Qohelet's attitude towards the temple, I will highlight how his view of the temple points towards social settings which are critical of the cult not because of a prophetic concern for social justice, but for reasons that point to a different kind of social distance. I will discuss Qohelet's sceptical attitudes towards the temple before locating resonances throughout the Hebrew Bible. In reviewing some comparisons, I look to the aetiology of Bethel in the Jacob narratives in Genesis, the attitudes towards vows in Deuteronomy, and the notion of God's presence in relation to the temple in Ezekiel. There is an apparent diversity in these voices, but arguably, they all display a suspicion towards the idea of divine presence. I will draw implications from these comparisons for a diasporic understanding of Qohelet's own view of cultic practices.

The Temple in Qohelet

Qohelet offers a critique of the temple in 5:1–2 [Heb 4:17–5:1] where he says:

שמר רגלך כאשר תלך אל־בית האלהים וקרוב לשמע מתת הכסילים זבח כי־אינם יודעים לעשות רע

אל־תבהל על־פיך ולבך אל־ימהר להוציא דבר לפני האלהים בשמים ואתה על־הארץ על־כן יהיו דבריך מעטים

> Watch your steps when you go to the house of God; to draw near to listen is better than the offerings of fools; for they do not know of doing evil. ² Do not be hasty with your mouth, nor let your heart be quick to utter a word before God, for God is in heaven, and you on the earth; therefore let your words be few. (my trans.)

The instructions in this verse, which are part of the pericope in 5:1–7 (Heb 4:17–5:6), indicate a critique of the cult which is rare in biblical wisdom and in

Ecclesiastes specifically.[1] The very first word "watch" שמר signals an immediate caution to those who enter the "house of God." Given the significance and sanctity of the temple, Qohelet's instruction here might seem unusual and perhaps ironic as שמע "to listen" is a key word in the observance of law, covenant and sabbath (cf. Deut 6:4–5). Further irony is in the instruction to "draw near to listen," as opposed to actually stepping foot inside the temple. Ruth Fidler notes that "the addressee is better advised to be his own guard, against none other than the dangers and follies lurking in his temple visit!"[2] But what exactly does that imply? Could it be that Qohelet believes there is danger in going to the "house of God"?[3]

The phrase "house of God" (בית האלהים lit. "house of the gods") is intriguing. In the biblical corpus, בית האלהים appears overwhelmingly in late texts, whereas earlier traditions use בית אל as in Gen 28:19.[4] The Bethel sanctuary in Gen 28:19 is where Jacob renames Luz to mark the sacred place as revealed to him in a dream.

"House of God" appears in Judg 18, where it is juxtaposed with the Danite sanctuary in verse 31, to highlight the abominable state of the Danite sanctuary which attracts a different terminology.[5] With the "house of God" located in Shiloh, the Danite tribe had set up their own holy place for their idol. Strikingly, the callous manner with which the Danites acquired the land—by overpowering an unsuspecting community—implies that YHWH was not the true inspiration for their acquisition.[6] It also suggests that the divine presence was absent from the Danites, both in a geographical sense and also in their conquest. In short, the use of "house of God" in Judg 18:31 also alludes to a theological conclusion to the chapter, which claims God's presence at Shiloh and not at the Danite sanctuary.[7]

Elsewhere, בית האלהים is used of the Second Temple in Jerusalem as we find in the books of Ezra, Nehemiah, Chronicles and Daniel.[8] The Chronicler in 1 Chr 6:33 uses a variant phrase "tabernacle, house of God" which is important because by joining "house of God" with "tabernacle" "the Chronicler indicates a

---

[1] Fidler, "Qoheleth in 'The House of God,'" 8.
[2] Fidler, "Qoheleth in 'The House of God,'" 12.
[3] Seow, *Ecclesiastes*, 198.
[4] El and Elohim are both translated as "God" in English translations although a diachronic look at these terms in the Hebrew Bible points to an evolution of the name where El signifies memories of religions in the Southern Levant during the Bronze Age. See James S. Anderson, "El, Yahweh, and Elohim: The Evolution of God in Israel and Its Theological Implications," *ExpTim* 128.6 (2017): 261–62. Also see Aren M. Wilson-Wright, "Bethel and the Persistence of El: Evidence for the Survival of El as an Independent Deity in the Jacob Cycle and 1 Kings 12:25–30," *JBL* 138 (2019): 705–20.
[5] Barry G. Webb, *The Book of the Judges: An Integrated Reading*, JSOTSup 46 (Sheffield: Sheffield Academic, 1987), 187. Also see Dennis T. Olson, "The Book of Judges," in *NIB* 2:871.
[6] Roger Ryan, *Judges*, Readings: A New Biblical Commentary (Sheffield: Sheffield Phoenix, 2007), 140.
[7] Olson, "Judges," 871.
[8] Seow, *Ecclesiastes*, 194.

continuity of worship between the Mosaic legislation and the Chronicler's own day."[9] To further establish this continuity, the Chronicler synthesised the term "house of God" with other variants such as the "house of Yahweh" and "tent of meeting" which according to the Chronicler are all the same place to the extent that they fulfil essentially the same function.[10] To the Chronicler, it may not have mattered that the different terminologies that he uses interchangeably "originally referred to different things."[11]

When it comes to Qohelet, however, we do not find a range of different expressions for the cult, and the absence of "house of YHWH" seems more significant. If we are to assume that Qohelet is referring to the temple in Jerusalem, why is the temple then not referred to as "house of YHWH" בית יהוה? The name YHWH is lacking from the whole book of Ecclesiastes, generating a definite conundrum in understanding Qohelet's conception of God.[12] As Brittany Melton writes:

> The giving of the name YHWH (Exod 3) entailed assurance of God's presence; "I will be with you" (Exod 3:12). The absence of the personal name of God in Ecclesiastes ... leads one to further question God's presence.[13]

To clarify: YHWH is the personal name of God for the Israelites while the name Elohim is not.[14] If this is the case, then one might think that in Jerusalem, with the postexilic Jewish community reestablishing the cult, the temple would honour YHWH as a mark of their personal relationship. Complicating matters would be the contention over whether YHWH's temple was in Jerusalem, or in Gerizim where the Samarians would claim YHWH's jurisdiction.[15] Perhaps Qohelet's lack of reference to YHWH might imply a critique of the temple in Jerusalem, and specifically, the idea which "Deuteronomic texts emphasize that the temple houses the divine name of YHWH."[16] Could there also be scepticism towards the Samarian temple? Or could the author have been critical of the tension between

---

[9] James T. Sparks, *The Chronicler's Genealogies: Towards an Understanding of 1 Chronicles 1–9* (Atlanta: Society of Biblical Literature, 2008), 42–43.
[10] Sparks, *Chronicler's Genealogies*, 44.
[11] Sparks, *Chronicler's Genealogies*, 45.
[12] Sneed, *Politics of Pessimism*, 1.
[13] Brittany N. Melton, *Where Is God in the Megilloth? A Dialogue on the Ambiguity of Divine Presence and Absence*, OtSt (Leiden: Brill, 2018), 8.
[14] Karel van der Toorn, "Yahweh," in *Dictionary of Deities and Demons in the Bible*, ed. Karel van der Toorn, Bob Becking, and Pieter W. van der Horst (Leiden: Brill, 1999), 910.
[15] Gary N. Knoppers, *Jews and Samaritans: The Origins and History of Their Early Relations* (New York: Oxford University Press, 2013), 171; Reinhard Pummer, *The Samaritans: A Profile* (Grand Rapids: Eerdmans, 2016), 35.
[16] Melody D. Knowles, *Centrality Practiced: Jerusalem in the Religious Practice of Yehud and the Diaspora in the Persian Period*, ABS 16 (Atlanta: Society of Biblical Literature, 2006), 1.

Yehud and Samaria? Could his reference to the בית האלהים have been an unbiased reference to either Gerizim or Jerusalem?

Qohelet claims that God is in heaven (v. 2) using language common in late texts, but what does this reference to heaven imply? Scholars often argue that Qohelet's statement is not a contradiction of the theology of God's omnipresence, but an expression of the distinction between God and humans. In the Hebrew Bible, the conception that God is in heaven is understood differently across various texts. One understanding is linked to the absence of the temple, but highlights God's sovereignty when understood as "a divine rule exercised at a distance from the local details of political tragedy."[17] Brett explains:

> The basic problem is articulated in Ps 115:2, which assumes the loss of the temple. "Why do the nations say, 'Where now is their Elohim?' Our God is in heaven." The existence of Yhwh's temple is no longer necessary, and divine sovereignty is reasserted in the symbolism of a heavenly throne (e.g., 1 Kgs 8 and Pss 2:4; 33:13-14; 103:19, and 123:1). From this lofty position, God can see all and intervene in the world at will.[18]

Another perspective on the name "God of heaven" is evident in late texts. The term occurs in Ezra, Nehemiah, Chronicles, Daniel and Jonah not just to emphasise transcendence, but for an additional reason.[19] Douglas Stuart notes in the book of Jonah:

> The epithet "God of Heaven" (אלהי השמים) was a convenient way for the Israelites to describe Yahweh's identity to syncretistic, polytheistic foreigners. The sounds in the name Yahweh meant little to non-Israelites.... The "God of Heaven" was logically the supreme deity. We find the term thus commonly used after the exile (2 Chr 36:23; Ezra 1:2; Neh 1:4, 5; 2:4) by Jews and Persians (in their dealings with Jews) alike.[20]

Particularly in the Aramaic letters from Elephantine, the phrase "God of heaven" was a title that implicitly conflated YHWH with Ahuramazda.[21]

---

[17] Brett, *Locations*, 129.

[18] Brett, *Locations*, 129.

[19] Thomas Bolin, "The Temple of יהו at Elephantine and Persian Religious Policy," in *The Triumph of Elohim: From Yahwisms to Judaisms*, ed. Diana Edelman (Kampen: Kok Pharos, 1996), 127–42. In addition to the texts mentioned by Bolin which appear in Hebrew, there are Neh 2: 20 and Jonah 1:9, while in Aramaic form, "God of heaven" appears in Ezra 5:11–12; 6:9–10; 7:12, 21, 23; and Dan 2:18–19, 37, 44.

[20] Douglas Stuart, *Hosea-Jonah*, WBC 31 (Dallas: Word, 1987), 461.

[21] Bolin, "Temple of יהו at Elphantine," 139–40. Also see Brett, *Locations*, 117; H. G. M. Williamson, "Ezra and Nehemiah," in *New Bible Commentary: Twenty-First Century Edition*, ed. D. A. Carson et al. (Downers Grove: Inter-Varsity, 1994), 426.

6. God's Presence

For Qohelet, it is not just that God lives in a transcendent realm. There is a question about whether that heavenly rule can be comprehended by humans. Murphy argues that the statement is made to highlight the difference between God and humans, that is, to emphasise God's supremacy.[22] But this does not quite capture Qohelet's questions about the doctrine of retribution. The rule of God may not cohere with human conceptions of justice and order.

Qohelet drives a wedge between humanity and God; God cannot be manipulated by words and does whatever God pleases (cf. Ps 115:3).[23] For Qohelet then, as Seow explains, "God and mortals do not belong in the same realms, and so one ought not rush to bring forth every inane matter, as if the deity is an earthly agent available to respond to every human whim and fancy."[24] This engenders a fascinating paradigm for considering the presence of God in the temple. Where does God's jurisdiction lie? More specifically, is Qohelet suggesting that God's authority is away from the temple, and hence outside Jerusalem?[25] And outside Gerizim?

The use of "Elohim" in Qohelet—which is the name of God used throughout the book—might help us to form a response to these questions. Sneed observes that it is in affirmation of the "gulf between mortals and the Immortal."[26] The use of Elohim is particularly striking in Qohelet's comment on vows in 5:4–5. In those verses, Qohelet quotes, almost verbatim, Deut 23:21 [22], but instead of Deuteronomy's YHWH, he uses Elohim.[27] (I discuss the matter of vows below).

Secondly, the importance of the name YHWH in worship is further highlighted through its association with Jerusalem.[28] Accordingly, Deuteronomic texts (Joshua–2 Kings) emphasise that the temple—in Jerusalem—"houses the divine name of YHWH."[29] Qohelet's use of the name Elohim therefore in reference to the temple, generates questions about YHWH's mobility and jurisdiction. I am suggesting, of course, that "house of Elohim" may reflect the words of one who no longer worships in the Jerusalem temple, but lives in diasporic lands. It might be that the absence of the Tetragrammaton resonates with lands who do not use YHWH to designate God, that is, those lands outside Jerusalem.

In the ensuing paragraphs, I pursue these questions by highlighting resonances in the rest of the Hebrew Bible with Qohelet's critique of the temple. By doing so, I aim to show how such resonances underline the temple critique in chapter 5 as an indicator of a diasporic setting for Qohelet.

---

[22] Murphy, *Ecclesiastes*, 50.
[23] Towner, "Ecclesiastes," 316.
[24] Seow, *Ecclesiastes*, 199.
[25] Cf. Eep Talstra, "The Name in Kings and Chronicles," in *The Revelation of the Name Yhwh to Moses: Perspectives from Judaism, the Pagan Graeco-Roman World, and Early Christianity*, ed. George H. van Kooten (Leiden: Brill, 2006), 55.
[26] Sneed, *Politics of Pessimism*, 149.
[27] Bartholomew, *Ecclesiastes*, 206.
[28] Knowles, *Centrality*, 1.
[29] Knowles, *Centrality*, 1.

Temple and Presence of God in the Hebrew Bible

The temple plays a significant role in the Hebrew Bible. It designates the place where God is situated, and where humans could offer up sacrifices and pronounce vows in exchange for God's protection and blessings.[30] Nevertheless, even Deuteronomy signals a note of caution in relation to vows, as we shall see.

Our discussion begins with the story of a vow in Jacob's narrative in Genesis. I also look to the story of Ezekiel and how the glory of God departing from Israel is congruent with the destruction of the temple. Then I will consider the negative attitudes of the "people of the land" towards rebuilding the temple in Ezra.

"House of God": Bet-El in Genesis

The first mention of the "house of God" in the Hebrew Bible comes in Gen 28:10–22. I will first discuss Gen 28, before analysing its parallel account in Gen 35. Obviously, the context in Gen 28:10–22 does not speak to a cultic centre or a temple. The conversation then must focus on מקום "place" which is significant in part because Jacob is a refugee in Gen 28:10–22 and refugees at the worst of times, do not have a place. In this passage, the word מקום is mentioned six times. The regularity of מקום is no coincidence according to J.P. Fokkelman. He argues that for מקום to be a key word integrated into the narrative, it would have to anticipate the main theme of the story, which it does, or at least acts as a "precursor to it."[31] Understanding Jacob as a refugee highlights the theme of "place" in a more precarious sense. What might this mean then for understanding the "house of God"?

As a theme, the word מקום undergoes a shift from being an anonymous place to a specific place: the "house of God." In that dream, YHWH promises Jacob multitudinous offspring extending out "west, east, north and south" (28:14); directions which "leaves the scope of the promised land unspecified, but which envisages Bethel as the centre of Jacob's 'place.'"[32]

Jacob's place is named Bethel בית־אל in recognition of God's presence, which prior to his dream he had not known. The fascinating aspect to the narrative is the transformation of the מקום "place" as Jacob awakes from his dream; an ordinary place has become sacred.[33] (Re)naming the place "Bethel" ("House of God")—which was originally Luz—coincides with the identification of שער השמים "the gate of Heaven." Jacob's delineation of the place as "the gate of

---

[30] Michael B. Hundley, *Gods in Dwellings: Temples and Divine Presence in the Ancient near East*, WAWSup 3 (Atlanta: Society of Biblical Literature, 2013), 3.
[31] J. P. Fokkelman, *Narrative Art in Genesis: Specimens of Stylistic and Structural Analysis*, 2nd ed. (Oregon: Wipf & Stock, 2004), 49, 63.
[32] Mark G. Brett, *Genesis: Procreation and the Politics of Identity* (London: Routledge, 2000), 93.
[33] Terence E. Fretheim, "The Book of Genesis," in *NIB* 1:542. Also see Fokkelman, *Genesis*, 64; Yitzhak (Itzik) Peleg, *Going up and Going Down: A Key to Interpreting Jacob's Dream (Genesis 28:10–22)*, trans. Betty Rozen (London: Bloomsbury T&T Clark, 2015), 55.

Heaven" stems from his dream, in which he sees a ramp connecting earth to heaven with angels ascending and descending that ramp. The connotations with temple theology is obvious here, particularly if we are to imagine a temple as a place where worshippers connect to the deity.[34] Further, Jacob displays religious piety as he feels awe at the presence of God, demonstrated by his dedication of a stone to mark the "house of God" and swearing a vow of tithing to God in return for his protection in his journey.[35] With Jacob's religious acts here, the connection with the temple and its cultic function is evident (even if Bethel is not Jerusalem).

In light of these cultic associations, it is ironic that the setting of the story, before and after the consecration of the place as "Bethel" since that name seems contrary to the experiences of a traveler, who is displaced and seeking refuge.[36] Jacob is a migrant, a displaced one at that, who is seeking his own מקום but instead locates the place where YHWH is (28:16). The movement of bodies is evident in this narrative as the angels also move up and down the ramp which stresses the "travelling" theme even more.[37] It is from his migrant experience that Jacob encounters God and undergoes a transformation. The experience also brings Jacob to an understanding of God's presence, which leads to his consecration and renaming of the place to commemorate God's presence.

The correlation between Jacob's refugee state and the experience of diasporic people is apparent, and one could draw implications of such an experience with understanding the "house of God." I call attention to how Jacob's leaving his home[38] leads to incidents of transformation,[39] culminating in finding the "place" where God is. Amit argues that "even in a long exile, one can preserve his identity. Jacob's case teaches that exile does not force one to adopt new identity. That is a

---

[34] See Fidler, "Qoheleth in 'The House of God, 10. Fidler outlines this comparison through an intertextual reading of Ecclesiastes 5 with the Bethel story.
[35] Gordon J. Wenham, *Genesis 16–50*, WBC 2 (Dallas: Word, 1994), 223. Also see Fidler, "Qoheleth in 'The House of God,'" 10.
[36] Wenham frames Jacob among other "biblical stories of travelers." in Wenham, *Gen 16–50*, 221. Brett notes that the narrative conveys that "Jacob really belongs elsewhere" in Brett, *Genesis*, 93. Also see C. A. Strine, "Your Name Shall No Longer Be Jacob, but Refugee: Involuntary Migration and the Development of the Jacob Narrative," in *Scripture as Social Discourse: Social-Scientific Perspectives on Early Jewish and Christian Writings*, ed. Jessica M. Keady, Todd E. Klutz, and C. A. Strine (London: T&T Clark, 2018), 51. Victor Hamilton notes the original name of the place as Luz which he argues may originally have been "Lauz, Loz" and vocalised as "Luz." The meaning of which is "place of refuge" which is consistent with the function of Bethel, see Victor P. Hamilton, *The Book of Genesis: Chapters 18–50*, NICOT (Grand Rapids: Eerdmans Publishing Co, 1995), 246..
[37] Hamilton, *Genesis 18–50*, 240.
[38] Cf. Fretheim, "Genesis," 541. Also see Yairah Amit, "The Place of Exile in the Ancestors' Narratives and in Their Framework," in *The Politics of the Ancestors: Exegetical and Historical Perspectives on Genesis 12–36*, ed. Mark G. Brett and Jakob Wöhrle, FAT 124 (Tübingen: Mohr Siebeck, 2018), 137.
[39] Hamilton, *Genesis 18–50*, 247.

matter of choice."⁴⁰ Yet, one may be able to preserve identity and undergo change at the same time. Leaving home and migrating to a different place, leading to change and transformation, reflects a typical diasporic experience.

There is no overt scepticism in Gen 28, but in highlighting Jacob's migrant state, which would have had a bearing on his perception of God's presence, the attitudes and impression of the "holy place" emerge as Jacob crosses from one place to another. The determination of the place as holy arises out of a migrant experience, and perhaps a diasporic experience (or at least northern, non-Judean experience), that distinguishes the new place from an earlier one. Consequently, the actions and speeches (vows) which ensue evince a diasporic character. The narrative is certainly contrived as such as Gordon Wenham argues that

> the narrative in Gen 28 and the whole Jacob cycle presuppose a situation in which a vow is fully appropriate. Jacob is in a distressed state, running away from home, which is equivalent to being under threat of death.⁴¹

Jacob's genuine vow in 28:20–22 is provoked by his state of desperation and his consequent transformation.

Bearing in mind Qohelet's attitude towards "house of God," Fidler has argued, that Qohelet's discussion of the temple offers, by implication, a subversive reading of Gen 28:10–22.⁴² But in what sense is it a subversive reading? Erhard Blum points out an alternative perspective that throws fresh light on the suggestion by Fidler. As noted before, Gen 28:10–22 is repeated in Gen 35:9–15 with small variations. Blum notes that no attempt has been made to harmonise the two accounts and hence asks the question of how the juxtaposition of the two stories is supposed to be understood.⁴³ In answering his question, Blum argues:

> As *hieros logos*, Gen 28 deals mainly with the place whose holiness Jacob discovers, and with the stone that he dedicates as a *Massebah*. Genesis 35 employs exactly these two elements, in part in identical language. At the same time, however, the message is inverted: Bethel is no longer the place at which YHWH dwells—the "house of God" or the "gate of heaven" (as in Gen 28)—but is now described three times, redundantly, as "the place at which he (God) spoke with him" (vv. 13, 14, 15) and from which God "ascended" (v. 13). Accordingly, the cult stele in Gen 28 now functions as a memorial to the divine speech (v. 14a) and the anointing of the *massebah* appears transformed into an ad-hoc libation (v. 14b). This means that Gen 35 employs the narrative framework of the *hieros logos* in order to negate its etiological point! In other words,

---

⁴⁰ Amit, "Place of Exile," 142.
⁴¹ Wenham, *Gen 16–50*, 224.
⁴² Fidler, "Qoheleth in 'The House of God,'" 11.
⁴³ Erhard Blum, "The Jacob Tradition," in *The Book of Genesis: Composition, Reception, and Interpretation*, ed. Craig A. Evans, Joel N. Lohr, and David L. Petersen (Leiden: Brill, 2012), 191.

the Priestly tradent of Gen 35 has revised the old Bethel story by juxtaposing his "contra-version" to it.[44]

In short, the kind of subversion suggested by Fidler is already undertaken in Gen 35, according to Blum.[45] There is no reason to found a temple in Bethel; it is simply a place where Jacob spoke with YHWH.

Given the Priestly character of Gen 35, Blum's argument suggests suspicion towards the northern temple which in turn legitimises the temple in Jerusalem. But Qohelet has gone a step further, raising a question about both temples. There is every likelihood that such attitudes had filtered to diasporic communities, which may have even intensified given their location away from these temple centres.

Further, it is interesting to note that Jacob's renaming of Bethel has implications for another kind of scepticism. The name Bethel is paired with the description of שער השמים "gate of heaven" which according to Wenham is the only time such a description appears in the Hebrew Bible and is also reminiscent of the name of Babylon whose etymology is the "gate of the god."[46] Such an observation may be suggestive of a countering of Babylon's "gate of the god."

The juxtaposition of the two accounts of Bethel, the etiological significance of Bethel in Gen 28:10–22 and its deconstruction in Gen 35:9–15 implies a collocation of two different attitudes. One seeks to acknowledge and define the significance of God's presence in a מקום while the other signals an attitude of scepticism towards Bethel as the מקום of God's presence. The latter seems to reflect a similar attitude to what we see in Qohelet's own scepticism towards God's presence in the temple. Qohelet might well have seen and understood the subversive reading that takes place in Genesis 35 but pursues the questions and attitudes of the Priestly editor further as he reflects in his own מקום in the diaspora.

VOWS IN DEUTERONOMY

In light of Jacob's vow, the more general significance of vows invites discussion. In the Hebrew Bible, the institution of a vow has a specific function which connects the person or people to the deity, and also as Micha Roi highlights, often to a specific place.[47] While vows tend to be performed in the Hebrew Bible mainly by individuals, there are also "group vows."[48]

In 5:4, Qohelet does not focus solely on either individuals or groups in his address, as vows made both by an individual (תדר נדר) "When you [second person

---

[44] Blum, "Jacob Tradition," 191–92.
[45] Blum, "Jacob Tradition," 191–92.
[46] Wenham, *Gen 16–50*, 223.
[47] Micha Roi, "Conditional Vows—Where They Are Made and Paid," *BN* 167 (2015): 3–24.
[48] Jacques Berlinerblau, *The Vow and the 'Popular Religious Groups' of Ancient Israel: A Philological and Sociological Inquiry*, JSOTSup 210 (Sheffield: Sheffield Academic, 1996), 48; Tony W. Cartledge, *Vows in the Hebrew Bible and the Ancient Near East*, JSOTSup 147 (Sheffield: JSOT Press, 1992), 13, 28–29.

singular] make a vow") and by a group (כסילים "fools") are indicated. Qohelet's scepticism towards vows is formulated through a restatement of the law of vows in Deut 23:22–24 [MT].[49] It is important then to examine the law of vows in Deuteronomy in order to ascertain the context that generated such law. In turn, the discussion might lead us to locate the source of Qohelet's suspicion towards vows.

The law of vows in Deut 23:22–24 in the MT states:

כי תדר נדר ליהוה אלהיך אל תאחר לשלמו כי־דרש ידרשנו יהוה אלהיך מעמך והיה בך חטא
וכי תחדל לנדר לא־יהיה בך חטא
מוצא שפתיך תשמר ועשית כאשר נדרת ליהוה אלהיך נדבה אשר דברת בפיך

> If you make a vow to the Lord your God, do not postpone fulfilling it; for the LORD your God will surely require it of you, and you would incur guilt. But if you refrain from vowing, you will not incur guilt. Whatever your lips utter you must diligently perform, just as you have freely vowed to the LORD your God with your own mouth. (Deut 23:21–23 NRSV)[50]

The gist of the law concerning the fulfilment of vows in Deuteronomy's context is economic.[51] Ronald Clements explains:

> Vows to present goods and produce to the sanctuary at the end of the harvest or of some commercial enterprise could readily prove to be inconvenient, or even hopelessly optimistic, in their calculation. Behind all such actions often lay the unexpressed belief that such vows might serve as a form of inducement to God so that the enterprise would be blessed. Any delay in paying what had been vowed is here prohibited out of the theological conviction that words spoken to God, even in secret, were binding promises in which the integrity and good faith of the giver were at stake.[52]

The theological conviction of a promise made to God is what made a vow binding and emphasised the responsibility one or group has when such a vow was made.[53]

The "law" of vows in Deuteronomy does not sound like typical Deuteronomic laws, but as scholars have noted, it is "more like a wisdom saying."[54] Moshe

---

[49] Murphy, *Ecclesiastes*, 50.
[50] Deut 23:22–24 in the MT corresponds to Deut 23:21–23 in the NRSV and other English translations.
[51] Ronald E. Clements, "The Book of Deuteronomy," in *NIB* 2:467.
[52] Clements, "Deuteronomy," 467.
[53] Cartledge, *Vows*, 13.
[54] Richard D. Nelson, *Deuteronomy: A Commentary*, OTL (Louisville: Westminster John Knox, 2002), 282; Gerhard von Rad, *Deuteronomy: A Commentary*, trans. Dorothea Barton, OTL (Philadelphia: The Westminster, 1966), 148; Jeffrey H. Tigay, *Deuteronomy: The Traditional Hebrew Text with the New JPS Translation*, ed. Nahum M. Sarna, The JPS Torah Commentary

Weinfeld and C. Brekelmans among others, have extended the discussion regarding the extent of wisdom influence on the book of Deuteronomy.[55] Yet both fall short of claiming Deuteronomy's origins in wisdom tradition, opting instead for readers to "rethink the entire problematic" and not ignore the sapiential tendencies of the book of Deuteronomy.[56]

Deuteronomy 23:22–24 [Heb] might be perceived as "words of advice" against a vow-maker who fails to fulfil their deed promptly.[57] Though, "words of advice" might not have the authoritative tone associated with Deuteronomy's legal character, especially if Deut 23:22–24 [Heb] is identified as "law of vows." Pursuing Weinfeld's and Brekelmans' line of questioning in regards to wisdom origins may highlight a wisdom tangent in understanding the law of vows in Deuteronomy.

A closer look at the "law of vows" reveals a problem in interpretation to which Levinson calls attention. The problem arises in the structure of verses 22–24 [MT] whose sequence he finds "curious to the point of being problematic." Levinson summarises the sequence as such:

v. 22: A   If you vow, pay promptly; otherwise, it is sin.
v. 23: B   If you do not vow, no sin.
v. 24: C   Be sure to pay promptly what you vow.[58]

Levinson argues that the sequence reaches an awkward point at C where the law "urges the addressee to be careful to fulfill what the lips utter."[59] Levinson claims that the admonition "to fulfil what the lips utter" in the sequence is "a non sequitur" meaning that "it is difficult to see how it follows B logically (v. 23), since it presupposes the uttering of a vow (A, v. 22)."[60] Not many scholars have accounted for this curious sequence, preferring to read verse 23 as a formal subcondition which elaborates the immediately preceding law.[61] Levinson concludes that verse

---

(Philadelphia: The Jewish Publication Society, 1996), 218; Duane L. Christensen, *Deuteronomy 21:10–34:12*, WBC 6B (Dallas: Word, 2002), 555; Jack R. Lundbom, *Deuteronomy: A Commentary* (Grand Rapids: Eerdmans, 2013), 666.

[55] See Moshe Weinfeld, *Deuteronomy and the Deuteronomic School* (Winona Lake: Eisenbrauns, 1972). Also cf. C. Brekelmans, "Wisdom Influence in Deuteronomy," in *La Sagesse De L'ancien Testament*, ed. M. Gilbert, BETL 51 (Louvain: Louvain University, 1978), 28–38.

[56] Brekelmans, "Wisdom," 38.

[57] von Rad, *Deuteronomy*, 148; Lundbom, *Deuteronomy*, 666.

[58] Bernard M. Levinson, *A More Perfect Torah: At the Intersection of Philology and Hermeneutics in Deuteronomy and the Temple Scroll* (Winona Lake: Eisenbrauns, 2013), 47.

[59] Levinson, *More Perfect Torah*, 47–48. In making this judgment, Levinson argues that verse B "represents the antithesis" of verse A.

[60] Levinson, *More Perfect Torah*, 48.

[61] Levinson, *More Perfect Torah*, 67. Cf. Gottfried Seitz, *Redaktionsgeschichtliche Studien Zum Deuteronomium*, BWANT 93 (Stuttgart: Kohlhammer, 1971), 177–78. Ironically, at the centre of

23 breaks the continuity between verses 22 and 24 and must therefore be an insertion.[62] The significance of Levinson's conclusion generates questions about the attitudes towards vows in Deut 23:21–23. It might be, as Levinson claims, that verse 23 had been added by a redactor, who urged that refraining from vows is the ideal course of action.[63] Levinson argues further that the insertion "can be explained in terms of wider Second Temple reservations about the wisdom of vowing."[64]

The scepticism towards the wisdom of vowing is further highlighted in the reworking of the "law of vows" in Eccl 5:4–6. Levinson aptly explains Qohelet's reworking and revising of the law of vows which transforms it from Torah legislation to instruction "against the dictates of wisdom and good sense."[65] Levinson outlines Qohelet's revising of Deuteronomy's law of vows as follows:[66]

Deut 23:22	כי תדר נדר ליהוה אלהיך לא תאחר לשלמו
Qoh 5:3	כאשר תדר נדר לאלהים אל תאחר לשלמו
Deut 23:22	כי דרש ידרשנו יהוה אלהיך מעמך והיה בך חטא
Qoh 5:3	כי אין חפץ בכסילים את אשר תדר שלם
Deut 23:22	If you make a vow to Yahweh your God, do not delay in fulfilling it
Qoh 5:3	When you make a vow to God, do not delay in fulfilling it
Deut 23:22	for Yahweh your God will surely require it of you, and it will count against you as a sin
Qoh 5:3	for there is no delight in fools: What you vow, fulfill

Levinson points out that with the exception of the "near-verbatim correspondence between the opening verses in Deuteronomy and Qoheleth" as indicated by the

---

Seitz's chiastic structure of the law of vows is verse 23, which he had already described as a subcondition! Also see Gerhard Liedke, *Gestalt Und Bezeichnung Alttestamentlicher Rechtssätze: Eine Formgeschichtlich-Terminologische Studie*, WMANT 39 (Neukirchen-Vluyn: Neukirchener Verlag, 1971), 21–22.

[62] Levinson, *More Perfect Torah*, 32.
[63] Levinson, *More Perfect Torah*, 32.
[64] Levinson, *More Perfect Torah*, 50.
[65] Levinson, *More Perfect Torah*, 58. Also see Thomas Krüger, "Die Rezeption Der Tora Im Buch Kohelet," in *Das Buch Kohelet: Studien Zur Struktur*, ed. Ludger Schwienhorst-Schönberger, Geschichte, Rezeption Und Theologie (Berlin: de Gruyter, 1997), 306–07.
[66] Figure 2.2 in Levinson, *More Perfect Torah*, 57. Note: Levinson follows the numbering of verses in the MT.

underlining above, Qohelet is not citing Deuteronomy "as a divine command or as Torah legislation but as an instruction by Qoheleth himself."[67]

The parallel to Deut 23:22 [Eng. 23:23] is in Eccl 5:3 [Eng. 5:4] but with a different tone. While the motivation behind Deut 23:22 [Eng. 23:23] is to avoid sin and guilt, the impulse behind Eccl 5:3 [Eng. 5:4] is to avoid an unfulfilled vow. One might ask why the issue of guilt is not prevalent for Qohelet in 5:3 [Eng. 5:4], and why he is concerned mainly with circumventing a broken vow. Levinson does not provide a rationale other than to point out that the author of the Targum version of Qohelet "reinserts the deity's name into the motive clause, once again making the desire not to sin against the deity the primary rationale for honoring one's vows."[68] This is striking and warrants further *talanoa*. Positioning Qohelet in a diasporic setting provides an alternative reasoning behind Qohelet's concern. I contend that Qohelet's sceptical attitude towards unfulfilled vows points to the problem of location and related complications faced by those in migration.

Going back to the earlier question of whether the law of vows might seem out of place in Deuteronomy, there may be a case for such reasoning. The ritual of vows seemed to be doing more harm than good; due to the voluntary and often private nature of vows, there may be nobody—besides YHWH—to guard one's honesty in keeping a vow. As Jeffrey Tigay explains, the law of vows "warns against procrastination in fulfilling the vow once the desired goal has been achieved."[69] The wisdom, or lack thereof, lies in the delay and the procrastination. As a result, despite the voluntarily nature of vows, they were also non-retractable and non-negotiable.[70] This might also be in line with Rogerson's argument, where the interpolation of verse 22 [MT v. 23] may have been part of the "expansions to the legal sections of Deut 19–25 to meet new situations that had arisen after the return."[71] And what of those who did not return?

What might have been the nature of such "new situations"? Stopping the practices of vow-making altogether was difficult as Tony Cartledge argues:

> Vow-making was such a popular means of religious expression that Israel's 'organized religion' took steps to control the practice through the imposition of strict regulations. Such structures placed limits on who could make vows, what could be promised, and where payment could be made. However, religious authorities could neither require nor forbid the practice (Deut. 23.21–23 [MT 22-24]).... In the extant sources, however, Israel preserves more specific regulations

---

[67] Levinson, *More Perfect Torah*, 57–58.
[68] Levinson, *More Perfect Torah*, 59. Also see Lohfink, *Qoheleth*, 77.
[69] Tigay, *Deuteronomy*, 218.
[70] Roi, "Conditional," 11.
[71] John W. Rogerson, *Deuteronomy*, Eerdmans Commentary on the Bible (Grand Rapids: Eerdmans, 2003), 27.

concerning the practice, perhaps indicating that vows were more prevalent (or problematic) among the Hebrews.[72]

The sceptical attitudes towards vows, as indicated by the insertion of verse 22 [MT v. 23] in Deut 23 might have been in response to a general complacency in vow-making by diasporic Jews as "some of the widespread debates about the wisdom of religious vows was read back into the Pentateuch."[73]

For diasporic people, the wisdom about vow-making at the temple would have provoked a particular problem. If as Levinson claims, the insertion of Deut 23:22 [MT 22.23] was during the Second Temple period, I would argue that vow-making might have been particularly useless for diasporic Jews given the time and effort to travel to Jerusalem in order to fulfil such vows. This is well illustrated in later rabbinic literature, for example, where we could envisage such a scenario as Nahum the Mede:

> It was this mistake that Nahum the Mede made when those under a nazirite vow made a pilgrimage from the Diaspora and found the temple destroyed. Nahum the Mede said to them, "If you had known that the temple was destroyed, would you have made a nazirite vow?" They replied, "No." So Nahum the Mede released them. But when the matter came before the Sages they said, "Whoever vowed before the temple was destroyed, his vow is valid, but those who vowed after the temple was destroyed, his vow is void." (m. Nazir 5.4)[74]

Vow-making in this instance could be construed as a foolish act, if one had depended on the temple for a vow to be valid, while oblivious to the fact that the temple was already destroyed! This points to a similar reasoning behind Qohelet's own scepticism, linking unfulfilled vows to fools (Eccl 5:4).

The scepticism towards vow-making makes good sense in a diasporic location. Particular problems discussed above would have been generated from living at a great distance from the temple(s), consequent delays in having vows fulfilled, and the resultant economic stress that unfulfilled vows may have caused. It is likely the interpolation of Deut 23:22 [Heb] is in response to such problems. Perhaps then, Qohelet in his own response to the issue, proposes that it is better and legally safer to stay in the diaspora and not make a vow at all.

---

[72] Cartledge, *Vows*, 28.
[73] Levinson, ""Better That You Should Not Vow,"" 36. Levinson argues that the interpolation could be dated around the fifth to fourth centuries BCE.
[74] See Jonathan R. Trotter, *The Jerusalem Temple in Diaspora Jewish Practice and Thought During the Second Temple Period* (Leiden: Brill, 2019), 105.

Departing Glory of God: Ezekiel 10

Questions concerning the presence of God in Jerusalem arise in Ezek 8–11, which "describe the Glory vacating the Temple."[75] In chapter 10, the prophet sees a vision of God's glory depicted through a sapphire-like throne, cherubim, and wheelwork (10:1–2), while the mention of fire and coal anticipate the impending destruction of Jerusalem (10:2).[76] The destruction of Jerusalem is particularly threatening as the "man clothed in linen" who appears in 9:2 changes role from scribe to incendiary.[77] The wheelwork and cherubim function as a conveyance that serves to transport the Glory outside the temple realms. The vision thus builds up effectively towards chapter 11 as the mobility of the conveyance takes Ezekiel also, with the purpose of casting judgment on the "officials of the people" (11:1).

Yet while the vision that Ezekiel sees takes place in the domain of the Jerusalem temple, it is witnessed in the context of exile, outside of Jerusalem. Elizabeth Keck points out how the Glory in Ezekiel is reminiscent of the Glory in the pre-Tabernacle community in the wilderness (Exod 16:10), but also stresses the similarity of contexts, connecting "the exilic community (or Ezekiel's perception of it) with the Priestly presentation of the dislocated Israelite community that wandered outside the land of Canaan."[78] God's glory in Ezekiel thus invites a reimagining of the presence of God from an exilic point of view—or as Keck suggests, Ezekiel's perception of it.

From a position of exile, Keck is correct to point out that it provides the only context for which the glory appears outside its sanctuary.[79] The implication here is that the mobile glory is a response to a temporary loss of the temple during the exile. This is also indicative of Priestly theological reflections of the glory of God in the desert, as Brett suggests:

> Instead of locating the divine name in one particular place that could be destroyed by Babylonian armies, the Priestly compositions discover the glory of God even in desert wandering and exile.[80]

One of the major differences between the Priestly traditions and Ezekiel is that the glory leads and provides for Israel in the wilderness but in Ezekiel, the vision is of the glory leaving the temple, along with the mobile cherubim, constituting "divine abandonment."[81] This provides an insight to God's presence from

---

[75] Elizabeth Keck, "The Glory of Yahweh in Ezekiel and the Pre-Tabernacle Wilderness," *JSOT* 37.2 (2012): 205.
[76] Leslie C. Allen, *Ezekiel 1–19*, WBC 28 (Dalls: Word, 1994), 151.
[77] Allen, *Ezekiel 1–19*, 151. Also see Katheryn Pfisterer Darr, "The Book of Ezekiel," in *NIB* 6:1182.
[78] Keck, "Glory of Yahweh," 202.
[79] Keck, "Glory of Yahweh," 204–5.
[80] Brett, *Locations*, 60.
[81] The theme of "divine abandonment" defines chapters 8–11. See: Allen, *Ezekiel 1–19*, 155.

an exilic or migrant position, where God's presence escapes the human sphere, in contrast with God's providence and immanence. The notion of the glory leaving the temple bespeaks a condition of dislocation and being separated from the homeland (the social conditions of diaspora). Curiously, in light of the changed social setting, Ezekiel turns more to the practice of ethics in exile, rather than envisaging a transformation of cultic practice—although he does remain concerned about idolatrous practices.

In reinterpreting God's presence in exile, there is a "shift of moral focus away from the grand, institutional sins that have brought about the fall of Jerusalem towards a smaller, more circumscribed moral world of exile."[82] The clearest evidence of this comes in chapter 18, where Ezekiel brings to the exilic community's attention "their complicity in the events of the current national crisis."[83] As such, Ezekiel composes a list of standards to which the exilic community must adhere in accordance with the Torah.[84]

Ezekiel commends attention to three areas: idolatry, sexual ethics, and economics.[85] One could infer that exilic ethics have no need for a temple. The first injunction is against idolatry, which in chapter 18 is depicted through the phrase "eat upon the mountains" as if to refer to worship on high places, a sin which Ezekiel condemns in chapter 6.[86] Andrew Mein argues that the language used is "more part of Ezekiel's general condemnation of idolatry,"[87] while Gordon Matties contends that "The language belongs to an inner Ezekielian concern and is expressed in terms independent of Israel's legal traditions" bearing close "resemblance to the judgment oracles in Ezek 1–24 which castigate prevailing idolatrous practice."[88] It is likely that Ezekiel's use of "mountain" and "idols" was adopted to form part of his general admonishment of idolatry.[89]

Moving on from religious ethics, Ezekiel speaks of sexual ethics, specifically adultery (18:6, 10, 15). Defilement and taboo of intercourse during menstruation are clear in legal codes that guard against such behaviour in Num 5:14, 20, 27–29; Lev 18:20.[90] Yet in terms of the ethical standards expected to consolidate the

---

[82] Mein, *Ezekiel*, 198.
[83] Mein, *Ezekiel*, 190.
[84] Moshe Greenberg, *Ezekiel 1–20*, AB 22 (New York: Doubleday, 1995), 342.
[85] Mein, *Ezekiel*, 191.
[86] Mein, *Ezekiel*, 191–92. Also see: H. G. May, "The Book of Ezekiel," in *The Interpreter's Bible 6*, ed. G. A. Buttricke et al. (New York: Abingdon, 1956), 158–59; John William Wevers, *Ezekiel*, NCB (Greenwood: Attic, 1969), 109; Walther Zimmerli, *Ezekiel: A Commentary on the Book of the Prophet Ezekiel*, trans. R. E. Clements, Hermeneia 26 (Philadelphia: Fortress, 1979), 380; Joel S. Kaminsky, *Corporate Responsibility in the Hebrew Bible* (Sheffield: Sheffield Academic, 1995), 161.
[87] Mein, *Ezekiel*, 193.
[88] Gordon H. Matties, *Ezekiel 18 and the Rhetoric of Moral Discourse*, SBLDS 126 (Atlanta: Scholars Press, 1990), 164. Also see Greenberg, *Ezekiel 1–20*, 329; Zimmerli, *Ezekiel*, 453.
[89] Mein, *Ezekiel*, 194.
[90] Allen, *Ezekiel 1–19*, 274.

community while in exile, such sexual acts threaten "the disintegration of the community by striking at the family bonds which are its basic building-blocks."[91]

The third area of ethics in Ezekiel's list is social behaviour, specifically, family and business ethics. Even in exile, Babylonia was a "land of opportunity."[92] Ezekiel therefore calls for a moral obligation between individuals as they perform trade, to preserve social justice within the exilic community.[93]

Mein's premise that Ezekiel's list of ethics in chapter 18 was tailored to fit an exilic context, seems apt.[94] As Walther Eichrodt states: "What is enumerated by Ezekiel here is independent of any tie with soil of Palestine or the temple of Jerusalem."[95] Indeed, the understandings of God's presence outside of Jerusalem may reflect the attitudes of a people who were not only away from the temple and Jerusalem, but a people who had shifted from sanctuary practice to ethics. (Similarly, observance of circumcision and sabbath did not require a temple.)

Ezekiel still envisaged a glorious return to Jerusalem and a transfigured homeland but for Qohelet, the Ezekelian pattern of judgment and exile with its resultant ethics does not have to foresee a return to Jerusalem and the temple. In other words, Qohelet may have perceived Ezekiel's ethics as a clear indication that there is no need for a temple. In diaspora, the sacred may be realised in other ways.

SUMMARY

The question of divine presence in the temple and its associated rituals—namely, vows—is probed in the three instances discussed, which all suggest an ability to pursue those questions at locations which do not require a temple. Instead, the inquiry into the divine presence, at times, reflects the mindset of a community that exists outside the traditional religious sphere, which might be a diasporic context. As a result, attitudes of scepticism towards the temple seem to be fuelled by a disparity between contexts, whereby rituals such as vows seem convenient for those near the temple, but inconvenient for those who live afar. These attitudes are analogous with Qohelet's own attitude towards the temple and divine presence.

The Bethel story, as highlighted earlier, represents a migrant narrative. The experiences of Jacob are that of a refugee; an "asylum seeker who subsequently

---

[91] Mein, *Ezekiel*, 194.
[92] Hans M. Barstad, *The Myth of the Empty Land: A Study of the History and Archaeology of Judah During the 'Exilic' Period*, Symbolae Osloenses Sup 28 (Oslo: Scandinavian University Press, 1996), 75.
[93] Mein, *Ezekiel*, 198. Also see Moshe Weinfeld, "Instructions for Temple Visitors in the Bible and in Ancient Egypt," *ScrHier* 28 (1982): 235–36.
[94] Mein, *Ezekiel*, 191.
[95] Walter Eichrodt, *Ezekiel: A Commentary*, OTL (Philadelphia: The Westminster, 2003), 238–39.

repatriates by choice."⁹⁶ It is this experience, as mentioned earlier, that leads to Jacob's transformation, but more importantly for this chapter, the experience of migration is crucial in locating the "place" of God's presence, which Jacob names Bethel. It is the naming of this place Bethel that has parallels with Qohelet, who also names the place of the institutionally framed divine presence as the "house of God." Fidler's intertextual reading of Bethel between the Jacob narrative and Qohelet pointed towards literary parallels. I go a step further and emphasise that these literary parallels implicitly reveal a migrant or diasporic setting for Qohelet. For Qohelet, the place of the divine takes the name "house of God" as it did for the migrant Jacob, and significantly, this is not the house of YHWH in Jerusalem.

The distance from Jerusalem affects religious piety and ritual performance, highlighted by the pessimistic attitude towards vow-making in Deuteronomy. Being away from Jerusalem meant that it was difficult for vows to be fulfilled, considering that they had to be effectuated at the sanctuary. Qohelet's scepticism towards vow-making might be suggestive of this, but more importantly, this certainly would give further clarity to Qohelet's words: "It is better that you should not vow than that you should vow and not fulfill it" (Eccl 5:5 NRSV). Qohelet's revising of the law of vow reflects a move away from Torah legislation into the sphere of sapiential teaching, and it also reflects a community who has moved away from the temple in Jerusalem into a whole new diasporic religious setting.

This new move could be further explained by Ezekiel's expounding of the divine presence leaving Jerusalem, and taking its place among the exiles in Babylon. Mein aligns the escape of God's presence from Jerusalem with the loss of privilege of the Jews in exile. Such is the reality of diasporic communities who experience loss of land; lands which represent honour and prestige. Qohelet speaks from the diaspora, and as a result, he understands the loss of privilege associated with the loss of land.

Questioning the wisdom behind vow-making and other temple-related practices is more meaningful from a diasporic vantage point. "House of God" from such a vantage point allows us to consider the possibility of other temples outside Jerusalem, such as Elephantine and Samaria. But these were Yahwist temples, so he does not embrace them either. For Qohelet, God is in heaven.

SAMOAN HERMENEUTICS

The foregoing are grounds for probing into the possibility of a diasporic location for Qohelet. The lack of use of the name YHWH as well as his critique of the temple and its practices point to issues in Qohelet's community. Those allow us

---

[96] See Strine, "Your Name," 51. Strine's definition here of Jacob as an asylum seeker is set within the framework of the United Nations High Commissioner for Refugees (UNHCR). Also see Frankel, *Land of Canaan*, 221–23.

to reimagine and reinterpret Qohelet's social setting. A diasporic location could provide an apt way of explaining the nature of Qohelet's religious stance.

Fidler's intertextual reading of Eccl 5:1–7 [Heb Qoh 4:17–5:6] through the Bethel story in Gen 28:10–22 reveals "the author's 'other voice': his subtle irony, his capacity for counter-textuality, and his critical view of accepted religion."[97] A diasporic location stresses the ironic and critical voices of Qohelet even more, because diaspora is a context that allows for such voices. It is clear throughout Ecclesiastes that Qohelet is speaking against a system "that is fixed and constantly recycled."[98] One of those systems is the religious institution with which Qohelet has reservations. Qohelet accepts the demise of institutional religion but he also questions the substitution of ethics for religious practice which Ezekiel proposed. In reference to the rest of the Hebrew Bible and the attitudes found towards the temple and place of the divine, one can make the case for Qohelet's concerns to resonate with the diasporic and migrant experience.

In Samoa, the church building(s) marks the visual centrepiece of any Samoan village, somewhat reflecting the central role the church plays in the Samoan lifestyle.[99] Samoans are used to the church being the physical centre, and as the Samoan term for church implies, the *falesā* is a house (*fale*) which is holy (*sā*) but also acts as a deterrent (*sā*) for inappropriate behaviour. Yet when Samoans migrate, they endure a real struggle of finding that place in foreign lands, similar to the way Jacob struggled to find his מקום (*maqom*). One might therefore see Jacob, not just as an asylum seeker, but also a seeker of God's house. Jacob used a rock to designate the "house of God" which was a temporary mark of God's presence.

Some Samoan churches in Australia gather in their own places of worship, which may be church buildings or renovated factories. But the majority of Samoan churches however worship in temporary locations, such as churches that belong to *palagi* and other denominations, school and community halls, local community facilities and in some cases, in the garage of the minister's residence. They would rather worship in a *maqom* that belongs to them, but like Jacob, sometimes the migrant cannot choose nor own. They can however reimagine God's presence in a temporary location, which may be what Qohelet intimates in the "house of God" (5:1 Heb 4:17)—a temporary place to envisage God's presence for those in the diaspora. As such, God's presence shifts from the homeland to a new land.

There are remaining problems in being shifted to a different context, as the discussion of vow-making above purports. In migration, there are elements that cannot be carried from one place to another. Most Samoan churches in Australia have their headquarters in Samoa, and thus its authorities are also located there.

---

[97] Fidler, "Qoheleth in 'The House of God,'" 21.
[98] Katharine J. Dell, *Interpreting Ecclesiastes: Readers Old and New*, Critical Studies in the Hebrew Bible 3 (Winona Lake: Eisenbrauns, 2013), 83.
[99] Cf. Va'a, *Saili Matagi*, 106.

General meetings, conferences and certain religious ceremonies can only be carried out in Samoa.

On a cultural level, Samoans in foreign lands can only perform certain rituals, such as the bestowal of *matai* titles, on Samoan land. Similarly, while God's presence can be reinterpreted in new lands, religious piety in the form of vows can only be fulfilled in the temple at Jerusalem.[100] A diasporic reading would call attention to this issue, and certainly for Qohelet, which would highlight the wisdom (or lack thereof) of making religious commitments, such as vows, where jurisdiction and distance from the temple might prove to be problematic.

The question of jurisdiction is a major contention in diaspora, particularly for Ezekiel's struggle with the notion of God's glory. For Ezekiel, God's presence has left Jerusalem and has shifted to Babylonia. This would undoubtedly give rise to scepticism as those in diaspora might come to doubt that their homeland no longer holds jurisdiction in religious and cultural matters. This is certainly reflective of the tension between first- and second-generation Samoans living in Australia. The former holds an idealised and celebrated version of the culture and the church, while the latter cast suspicion towards such notions. Qohelet might be like these second-generation Samoans, who find that restricting God to Jerusalem would be inconvenient for diasporic Jews, so that a better understanding of God's presence that would entail all Jewish existence ("and you upon earth" 5:2), is to locate God in heaven (5:2).

It seems from the foregoing discussions that critique of the temple and the divine presence could be situated within a diasporic context. The resonance that these texts have with attitudes of scepticism towards the temple and the divine place provide a reimagining of Qohelet's own scepticism towards the temple from outside Jerusalem. It might be that Qohelet was frustrated with romanticizing notions of God's presence in Jerusalem which sought to marginalise the religious experience and status of those outside Jerusalem.

We could imagine Qohelet as a friend of Ezekiel who never returned; a sage who was a friend of Deuteronomy's editor but disagreed with centralization. Ezekiel might have imagined a return to Jerusalem, but for Qohelet, there is no return! Qohelet draws on certain tangents of these reading contexts, and applies them to the purposes of those in the diaspora, not envisaging a return home. Qohelet, like Jacob, only sees Jerusalem as a place where Jews had a conversation with God, but not YHWH's final place of residence. Qohelet follows the tracks set out by Ezekiel and the editor of Deuteronomy, but for him, it leads him out of Jerusalem and into diaspora.

---

[100] See Jacob Milgrom, *Numbers*, The JPS Torah Commentary (Philadelphia: The Jewish Publication Society, 1989), 488. Milgrom argues that all biblical vows are fulfilled at the sanctuary, which could only be understood as being the temple in Jerusalem. Cartledge also notes other requirements to pay vows at the temple in the ancient Near East, cf. Cartledge, *Vows*, 87.

One could also argue that Qohelet was suspicious towards acts of religious observance and piety which proved inauthentic and pretentious. As Qohelet instructs in 5:5, Jews would be better off to not say a vow at all. The problem of not fulfilling a vow might be better understood as a call to consider the social distance in fulfilling a vow at the temple (Jerusalem or Gerizim) for Jews in diasporic lands. For Qohelet, to travel all that way just to honour a vow is vanity.

7. Moral Order

As observed in the previous chapter, ethics plays an important role for the exilic community. The significance of ethics was a concern for Qohelet, especially if we are to imagine a situation where a return to Jerusalem and the temple is not to be anticipated, as Jews establish their homes in the diaspora. Continuing this line of thought I focus in this chapter on Qohelet's critique of moral order and its wisdom. I argue that Qohelet's critique is also an important indicator of a diasporic setting.

The discussion will review Qohelet's critique of moral order in relation to what he observed, looking at selected texts from the book. This will be followed by a survey of instances in the Hebrew Bible which resonate with Qohelet's sceptical attitude. Specifically, I will inquire into Joseph's strained relationship with his brothers in Genesis, the Psalmist's observations of moral chaos in Ps 14, and the prosperity of the wicked Ninevites in Jonah. These texts speak against the expectations of moral order. It is from these contexts of reading that I draw further implications for a diasporic understanding of Qohelet's own critique.

MORAL ORDER IN QOHELET

Qohelet questions moral order throughout the book, observing wicked people not receiving their just deserts, while righteous people were not benefiting from their virtuous behaviour as expected. This point is emphasised in 8:14:

יש־הבל אשר נעשה על־הארץ אשר יש צדיקים אשר מניע אלהם כמעשה הרשעים
ויש רשעים שמגיע אלהם כמעשה הצדיקים אמרתי שגם־זה הבל

> There is an incomprehensible situation which happens on (the) earth, there are righteous people to whom it happens according to the wicked and there are wicked people to whom it happens according to the righteous. I say, this is also incomprehensible. (my trans.)

What Qohelet outlines here is a reversal of the deeds-consequence formula and with that he is frustrated.[1] Understanding Qohelet's dejection might be highlighted by how we interpret the word הבל in this verse. There is debate about the term הבל which I have translated as "incomprehensible" as opposed to the common translation as "vanity." Where most translators would translate הבל as "vanity," others have found that the context in 8:14 might render a different meaning. Those who translate הבל as "vanity" and other related words such as "futility," "emptiness" or "meaningless" seek to maintain continuity with other appearances of הבל in the book. For those authors, it indicates how disturbed Qohelet is with such a "deplorable situation."[2] However, others have argued that such a translation may be "too strong" and that defining the situation as "futile" or "vanity" ignores that "Qoheleth here describes a real situation, so *hevel* cannot mean 'emptiness' or 'meaningless' as is found in many translations."[3] Graham Ogden and Lynell Zogbo, among others, translate הבל as "incomprehensible."[4]

I follow Ogden and Zogbo's translation to highlight the fact that the situation is more incomprehensible than it is meaningless.[5] For this chapter, the intrigue in social conditions that generated attitudes of scepticism would make it appropriate to treat Qohelet's dilemma as a real-life situation. Conversations with other realities observed in the Hebrew Bible and with diasporic realities would not be meaningless; they would be evidence that informs the statement of the problems at issue.

Indeed, the situation is הבל in the sense that Seow explains as the "impossibility of control" whereby humans are not able to "change the ephemeral nature of human life."[6] But Ogden and Zogbo's translation of הבל as "incomprehensible" is better because "Qoheleth does not necessarily reject these explanations, although he certainly points out that they are inadequate. He is about to show that the explanations quoted are not always true in real life."[7] The incomprehensible reality which Qohelet observes is one of injustice—a "topsy-turvy world."[8] Qohelet affirms the conventional theology of blessings and curses (8:12–13), but in 8:14 he does not show the same faith because he also witnesses the opposite.

What may have caused this turn for Qohelet? On this, I turn to 8:11:

---

[1] Murphy, *Ecclesiastes*, 85.
[2] Krüger, *Qoheleth*, 161. Also see Seow, *Ecclesiastes*, 288.
[3] Graham S. Ogden and Lynell Zogbo, *A Handbook on Ecclesiastes*, UBS Handbook Series (New York: United Bible Societies, 1998), 303. Also see Fox, *Ecclesiastes*, 59.
[4] Ogden and Zogbo, *Handbook on Ecclesiastes*, 305.
[5] The term "meaningless" disassociates Qohelet from any potential emotion he may have felt. Where the fundamentals of conventional wisdom have been betrayed, it is hard to imagine Qohelet being neutral.
[6] Seow, *Ecclesiastes*, 295.
[7] Ogden and Zogbo, *Handbook on Ecclesiastes*, 304.
[8] Towner, "Ecclesiastes," 337.

7. Moral Order 143

אשר אין־נעשה פתגם מעשה הרעה מהרה על־כן מלא לב בני־האדם בהם לעשות רע

> Because sentence for the evil deed is not executed quickly, therefore the hearts of the sons of men among them are fully set to do evil.

Qohelet raises the issue of sentencing against evil deed, which is not executed מהרה "quickly" enough. The word מהרה resonates with Deut 11:17 where on that occasion, the anger of YHWH will be kindled against the apostasy of the wicked who will perish "quickly" (cf. Deut 7:10)—suggesting that there is no delay in punishment. Levinson argues that Deut 7:10 transforms the Decalogue doctrine in Deut 5:9–10 by deleting "references to the transgenerational consequences of sin and instead asserts that God now punishes the sinner 'to his face.'"[9] This then is the turn for Qohelet: he contradicts the Deuteronomy notion of a quick punishment because in his world, the punishment against the wicked is not מהרה, but it is delayed.

Qohelet questions the delay in divine justice and the text suggests that it might have to do with his location. The question of moral order presses specifically against moral order within his social conditions. The evidence in 8:14 (translated above) provides locational clues. This "topsy-turvy world" in 8:14 is denoted as "the earth" (על־הארץ) as opposed to the usual place of chaos—"under the sun" (תחת השמש).[10] This becomes an interesting distinction and one which has not been sufficiently appreciated. Crenshaw, among others, contends that "the earth" is the equivalent of "under the sun."[11] Yet Thomas Krüger believes that there is more to it than just an alternating between terms, arguing:

> [That the use of על־הארץ] perhaps indicates that for the deplorable situation lamented in v. 14 (as well as in v. 10) it is not God but human beings who are responsible. For in 8:16a the expression הענין אשר נעשה על־הארץ *hāʿinyān ʾăšer naʿăśâ ʿal-hāʾāreṣ* is clearly related to human activity, which is juxtaposed to the "work of the Deity" in v. 17.[12]

The divine work "under the sun" cannot be found, 8:17 suggests. The distinction between "the earth" and "under the sun" becomes a point of differentiation of responsibility, that is, between humans ("on the earth") and the divine ("under the sun"). Understanding the earth as the realm of humans is clear, while J. Gerald Janzen notes that the sun, in ancient Israel, had connotations with the divine: "During the former days, life under the delegated rule of the sun was—so far as

---

[9] Bernard M. Levinson, *Legal Revision and Religious Renewal in Ancient Israel* (New York: Cambridge University Press, 2008), 74.
[10] See Krüger, *Qoheleth*, 161.
[11] Crenshaw, *Ecclesiastes*, 156; Ogden, and Zogbo, *Handbook on Ecclesiastes*, 304.
[12] Krüger, *Qoheleth*, 161–62.

Israel's epic and cultic calendars were concerned—expressive of the ultimate rule of God."[13]

Krüger's argument goes against the understanding that the contradictions Qohelet witnesses fall within the purview of divine responsibility. Advocating the "divine responsibility" interpretation, Murphy remarks that Qohelet "does not separate the world from divine causality; he well knows that the 'contradictions' in it are the divine responsibility."[14] Krüger's distinction on the other hand suggests that Qohelet is frustrated more with humanity in 8:14; the juxtaposition with the "work of the Deity" in 8:17 affirms this. It also provides an opportunity to inquire from an alternative perspective—one which focuses on the vicissitudes of human activity. In this "human" position, על־הארץ "the earth" as opposed to the generic "under the sun" focuses our attention, as Marie Turner puts it, on the "Earth as the stage we live our lives."[15]

In Turner's Earth Bible commentary on Ecclesiastes, she prioritises "Earth" in her exegetical explorations. While the environmental significance is evident, prioritising the earth in reading also has sociological implications because it brings our discussion away from "heavens" to focus on the earth in front of us, more specifically, what is in front of Qohelet's eyes.[16] I argue that this allows for an inquiry into Qohelet's jaundice with the moral order, that centres more on the social and human conditions ("on the earth"), rather than trying to speculate about the divine ("under the sun").

This generates a number of questions: How might we conclude that Qohelet's frustration was aimed at the role of humanity in upsetting the moral order? What sort of social conditions may have allowed for such injustice? How may these social conditions have caused delay in punishment against the wicked? I suggest that the topsy-turvy world that Qohelet witnesses applies especially in diasporic conditions. What Qohelet knows, is that God is just and so it makes no sense to Qohelet that God would act unfairly.[17] As mentioned above, it is the delay in justice that is frustrating for Qohelet. Therefore, Krüger's argument that the injustice may be due to human activity is a possibility.

In the next section, we shall look into the rest of the Hebrew Bible at some of the human conditions which contradict the conventional moral order, and how they might resonate with a diasporic setting.

---

[13] J. Gerald Janzen, "Qohelet on Life 'under the Sun,'" *CBQ* 70 (2008): 481.

[14] Cf. Murphy, *Ecclesiastes*, 86.

[15] Marie Turner, *Ecclesiastes: Qoheleth's Eternal Earth*, Earth Bible Commentary (London: Bloomsbury, 2017), 103.

[16] Turner, *Ecclesiastes*, 1. Turner's environmental reading of Ecclesiastes places emphasis on the Earth—highlighted by the capitalisation of the letter "e"—as a way of recognising Earth's priority in Ecclesiastes.

[17] Cf. Murphy, *Ecclesiastes*, 86.

7. Moral Order

MORAL ORDER IN THE HEBREW BIBLE

I turn to parts of the Hebrew Bible where the question of moral order fails to uphold the position of orthodoxy as prescribed by Deuteronomy and Priestly theology. First, our discussion will entail a close examination of Joseph (a diaspora novella) and the question of moral justice of his brothers' actions. Second, the discussion will call further attention to the delay in divine justice through an analysis of an implied delay in Ps 14. Finally, I will discuss Jonah's encounter with the wicked Ninevites, and the questions generated around wickedness and punishment. All three of these contexts of reading give us further implications for considering a diasporic setting for Qohelet.

JOSEPH AND HIS BROTHERS

The story of Joseph and his brothers portrays a version of ethics that is similar to what Qohelet witnesses. We see the "righteous" Joseph being sold by his brothers as a slave to Midianite traders, and later thrown into prison for a crime he did not commit, while his "wicked" brothers, as Barton writes, "who, far from 'reaping what they have sown', end up settling in a favourable part of Egypt and eventually returning to Israel as rich men."[18] Indeed, this assumes that in the narrative, Joseph represents the righteous (צדיקים) while the brothers embody the wicked (הרשעים).[19] Barton presents an important observation here, because it represents a similar ethical dilemma as highlighted by their father Jacob's early life:

> In this they are like their father Jacob, who tricks Esau yet in the end is unharmed by him, and suffers no ill consequences from his deception of Laban (who of course is equally deceitful himself).[20]

From this, one might ask: What is the point to acting righteously then, if as seen in this sequence of moral contradictions, there would be no consequence following acts of deception and cruelty?

This question is raised subtly in Gen 45:4–5:

---

[18] John Barton, *Ethics in Ancient Israel* (Oxford: Oxford University Press, 2014), 221.
[19] See J. Gordon McConville, "Forgiveness as Private and Public Act: A Reading of the Biblical Joseph Narrative," *CBQ* 75 (2013): 637. Contrary to McConville, some scholars argue that Joseph's status as righteous may be difficult to argue and that Joseph could even be viewed as sinister. Nahum M. Sarna for instance, sees that Joseph may have had intentions of revenge only for those intentions to be tempered by his concern for his father and younger brother. See Nahum M. Sarna, *Genesis*, The JPS Torah Commentary (Philadelphia: JPS, 1989), 293.
[20] Barton, *Ethics*, 221. Also see Holger Delkurt, *Ethische Einsichten in Der Alttestamentlichen Spruchweisheit*, Biblischtheologische Studien 21 (Neukirchener: Neukirchen-Vluyn, 1993), 152–53.

ויאמר יוסף אל־אחיו גשו־נא אלי ויגשו ויאמר אני יוסף אחיכם אשר־מכרתם אתי מצרימה
ועתה אל־תעצבו ואל־יחר בעיניכם כי־מכרתם אתי הנה כי למחיה שלחני אלהים לפניכם

> Then Joseph said to his brothers, "Please come near to me." And they came closer. And he said, "I am Joseph your brother, whom you sold into Egypt. And now do not be distressed and do not be angry with yourselves because you sold me here, for God sent me before you to preserve life." (my trans.)

In these words, Joseph offers reassurance to his brothers but also rebukes them by reminding them that he was the brother "whom you sold" (45:5), which seems to be an ironic dig, as if to say: "I shall behave as a brother should even though you were unbrotherly."[21] But then there is a double irony, because Joseph delayed his self-revelation and left the brothers in their confusion.

Drawing out the subtle ironies here further amplifies the brothers' guilt. It also focuses our attention on the human element of the injustice that Joseph experienced. This element is often overshadowed by the role that God plays, who in spite of the brothers' wicked act, is the one in control. Nevertheless, the question of moral order in relation to human activity returns in 50:20. As Terence Fretheim posits of the brothers' behaviour: "Human actions could have resulted in different ends."[22] Their actions do not end in punishment, but why not?

While the narrative answers this question through God's role as an orchestrator, it is interesting to note the virtuous behaviour of Joseph. Indeed, Joseph is not just virtuous, but a virtuous foreigner, and as Hyun Chul Paul Kim points out, "this motif of the virtuous foreigner is not uncommon throughout many of the patriarchal narratives in Genesis."[23] Other examples which Kim lists include

> the virtuous pharaoh whose trust and benevolence contrast with Abraham's distrust and trickery. King Abimelech of Gerar, and of the Philistines, likewise provides hospitality to the deceptive aliens Abraham and then Isaac. Readers also encounter Hagar (literally, "the alien") and her son, Ishmael, who are equally, if not more notably, blessed by God. In addition, Esau, the forefather of the Edomites, is portrayed as more forgiving than Jacob, the "heel-catcher."[24]

Virtue and honour are not specific to foreigners, but the patriarchs have all been on the receiving end of compassion amidst hostility from a foreigner. Joseph, who is a migrant and a foreigner (to Egyptians and to his brothers), continues on the path of righteous conduct by the foreigners listed.[25] In these narratives, why is it common for foreigners to show mercy and compassion, particularly in

---

[21] Sarna, *Genesis*, 308.
[22] Fretheim, "Genesis," 644.
[23] Hyun Chul Paul Kim, "Reading the Joseph Story (Genesis 37–50) as a Diaspora Narrative," *CBQ* 75.2 (2013): 223.
[24] Kim, "Reading the Joseph Story," 223.
[25] Kim, "Reading the Joseph Story," 223.

response to unethical behaviour by the patriarchs? Joseph, like Jacob and Abraham, are migrants, and it is in these migrant spaces that they encounter benevolence at the mercy of foreigners. In turn, this might also suggest that the context of honour and ethical behaviour in the patriarchal narratives, including the story of Joseph, resonate with diasporic and migrant settings.

Reading the Joseph story as a "diaspora narrative" offers a way of considering the ethical questions further.[26] Consequently, our reading shifts from the familial space between Joseph and his brothers to an inter-national space between Joseph the Egyptian administrator and Israelites seeking foreign aid. As such, we see Joseph not as a patriarch, but as a foreigner who reflects a similar ethical ethos to that of the foreign rulers in Genesis. In this light, the ethical balance is reversed much in the same way that Joseph's foreign predecessors have shown, where the unjust are treated as though they were just, and the foreigners turn out to be just, against expectations. Reconsidering Joseph's story this way alludes to a migrant-based subverted ethics in the Genesis narrative, where the patriarchal figures do not get their just deserts after clearly doing unethical things. Moreover, the reversed ethics in Joseph's story occurs in a diasporic space, between two nations and on foreign land—ultimately a land that Jacob and his family would later migrate to and occupy. But what causes this imbalance to occur?

In these foreign lands the questions regarding this moral dilemma linger on, which is highlighted in chapter 50 when Jacob dies. The brothers in particular ask: "What if Joseph still bears a grudge against us and pays us back in full for all the wrong that we did to him?" (50:15 NRSV). The brothers seem to be aware of the natural order of moral justice, that their horrible act warrants punishment. A culture of revenge seem appropriate, but what the brothers might not have expected was the act of forgiveness by Joseph. It is this act of forgiveness that provides a paradox in biblical ethics.

The expectation of revenge against a wrongful act and the ensuing punishment is critical in the ethical equation. It is necessary for "restoring equilibrium between offender and victim."[27] The brothers knew this and were anxious that Joseph might follow this talion form of ethics. However, Joseph upsets the balance by showing pity as he says in 50:20, "Even though you intended to do harm to me, God intended it for good, in order to preserve a numerous people, as he is doing today" (NRSV). Harm is meant to be offset by punishment and revenge in order to end disparity between two parties caused by the offence.[28] However the disparity remains as Joseph does not punish but forgives.

---

[26] Kim, "Reading the Joseph Story," 219–38.
[27] Barton, *Ethics*, 106, Eckart Otto, ""Um Gerechtigkeit Im Land Sichtbar Werden Zu Lassen ... ": Zur Vermittlung Von Recht Und Gerechtigkeit Im Alten Orient, in Der Hebräischen Bibel Und in Der Moderne," in *Recht—Macht—Gerechtigkeit*, ed. Joachim Mehlhausen (Gütersloh: Christian Kaiser, 1998), 118–19.
[28] Otto, "Um Gerechtigkeit Im Land," 109.

This "unusual" trait of pity in the context of talion ethics is drawn out by Josephus in his construction of Joseph.[29] Sarah Pearce explains:

> In his epitaph for Joseph, Josephus praises the patriarch for his extraordinary virtue; he is to be remembered as a man who controlled everything by the use of "reason," using his authority sparingly (*Ant. 2.198*).... This is a God-given opportunity for Joseph to show himself the best kind of ruler; by exercising his authority as a "humane" (φιλάνθρωπος) leader, Joseph's superiority is distinguished by extending his humaneness even to those who deserve the severest punishment (*Ant. 2.145–46*).[30]

In supporting this "pity" motif, Josephus highlights Judah's appeal to Joseph to save Benjamin and offer himself up as substitution, where Judah asks Joseph to have concern for his father. Judah's appeal, for Josephus, emphasises the importance of pity as a way "to match God in kindness (χάρις) by saving the guilty (indeed, as many as possible of them), not by destroying them (2.153)."[31]

In the view of Josephus, Joseph is the paradigm of the virtuous foreigner. As Kim suggests, much of his ethical character is a result of the different location of viewpoints due to his hybridity.[32] Joseph is both Israelite and Egyptian, and his moral compass is shaped by these two contexts. Moreover, other traits such as his wisdom, justice, courage, temperance and piety are drawn out by Josephus as virtues which the Greeks of his time found impressive.[33] The implications of this for diasporic Jews is significant, as "it would not be difficult for the Diaspora Jews to empathize with this Hebrew-Egyptian, who presents a model of justice, mercy, and humility in his walk with God (cf. Mic 6:8)."[34]

On the other hand, Joseph may not always exhibit the ideal model of morality when considering how he reduces the entire land of Egypt to slavery (Gen 47:21). This provides further implications because when read as a diaspora novella, Joseph can also be a symbol of hindrance for conventional ethics. In the face of wickedness, such a righteous character, in the eyes of those whom the wicked behaviour seeks to harm, can be disruptive. While the Greeks may have admired Joseph's ethical stance, Qohelet might find his pity as repulsive, because the wicked are "let off the hook."

Qohelet might well have seen the virtue of "pity" which Josephus draws out, as characteristic of Joseph's exemplary reign. But while diaspora Jews have

---

[29] Sarah Judith Pearce, "Pity and Emotion in Josephus's Reading of Joseph," *JBL* 133 (2014): 859.
[30] Pearce, "Pity and Emotion," 859.
[31] Pearce, "Pity and Emotion," 860.
[32] Kim, "Reading the Joseph Story," 222. Cf. Bhabha, *Location of Culture*, 313: "Hybrid hyphenations emphasize the incommensurable elements—the stubborn chunks—as the basis of cultural identifications."
[33] Fred Guyette, "Joseph's Emotional Development," *JBQ* 32.3 (2004): 185.
[34] Guyette, "Joseph's Emotional," 224.

empathised with the Hebrew-Egyptian, Qohelet also signals other problematic dimensions of diasporic ethics. As I have discussed, the notion of forgiveness and pity towards extremely wicked behaviour is seen, by implication, as vanity (cf. Eccl 8:14). But the vanity of pity in the Joseph story is made even more alarming through the "topsy-turvy" world in Genesis, similar to Qohelet's. That world looks as such: Joseph's brothers represent the wicked who are treated as righteous, and the Egyptians reduced to slavery may also be innocent (Gen 47:21).

Read this way, the Joseph story reads as a subversive response to the Exodus, as the roles of oppressor and oppressed are reversed.[35] Joseph may have saved his family, after a pronounced delay, but the economic reality of Egypt in the end is not redemptive—according to the land-based sensibilities of Israel's prophets, and according to the Jubilee norm of land restoration.[36] Is this the point of the irony in Gen 16, where the mistreatment of Hagar matches the exodus story?[37]

If Hagar stands for the Egyptians more generally, or especially for the lower classes of Egypt, Genesis 16 seems to be affirming the possibility that Israelites (represented by Abraham and Sarah) are also capable of being oppressive. Such an irony fits well within Qohelet's observations of the world.

JUDGMENT DELAY IN PSALM 14

Lament arising from delayed justice is often voiced, with considerable passion, in the Psalms. Although Ps 14 is commonly classed as a lament psalm and may thus stand as an example of a wider pattern of lament, there are other features within this psalm that may enrich our discussion.[38] In addition to the wisdom motifs which resonate with Qohelet, there is also the important question regarding the divine presence (cf. Ps 14:1) which evokes similar sentiments to the seemingly smaller and isolated experience of those in the diaspora. Consequently, the moral focus shifts from the grand populace of Jerusalem to the smaller and more circumscribed community in exile.[39] In exile, it may not be unusual to question the divine presence, especially in experiences of trauma and uncertainty which exilic conditions may generate.[40] This allows us to envisage how such interrogation of the divine presence may revise one's moral perspective.

---

[35] Thomas Römer notes a number of ironical allusions of the Joseph story to Exodus motifs, in Thomas Römer, "The Exodus in the Book of Genesis," *SEA* 75 (2010): 10–11.
[36] Cf. Barton, *Ethics*, 109, Jeffrey A. Fager, *Land Tenure and the Biblical Jubilee: Uncovering Hebrew Ethics through the Sociology of Knowledge*, JSOTSup 155 (Sheffield: Sheffield Academic, 1993), 51.
[37] Römer, "Exodus," 15.
[38] Cf. Mitchell Dahood, *Psalms I:1–50: Introduction, Translation, and Notes*, AB 16 (New Haven: Yale University Press, 2008), 80.
[39] Mein, *Ezekiel*, 198.
[40] Joel S. Burnett, *Where Is God? Divine Absence in the Hebrew Bible* (Minneapolis: Fortress, 2010), 154; Melton, *Where Is God*, 32.

Psalm 14 adopts vocabulary that is characteristic of the wisdom tradition, for example, in Proverbs. The psalmist here—and in the repeated (near verbatim) Ps 53[41]—labels some people as נבל "fool." Psalm 14:1 reads:

למנצח לדוד אמר נבל בלבו אין אלהים השחיתו התעיבו עלילה אין עשה־טוב

> To the leader. For David. A fool says in their heart: "There is no God." They are corrupt. They do abominable deeds. There is no one who does good. (my trans.)

As some scholars have argued, to establish a precise meaning of נבל in this psalm might not be straightforward.[42] In Ps 14, it is evident that this group of people referred to as נבל stand in opposition to the righteous (14:5) but they also stand in opposition to YHWH for they do not call upon YHWH's name (14:4). Their opposition to YHWH is highlighted by the term התעיבו (14:1) which "implies deeds which are an abomination in the eyes of God."[43] So while the condemnation of נבל may indicate wisdom motifs,[44] the text implies that the term נבל might be more of a moral (or immoral) articulation than a wisdom polemic.

Analogous to other parts of the Hebrew Bible, we are also reminded of the "aggressive perversity, epitomized in the Nabal of 1 Sam 25:25."[45] Even the wisdom traditions link the נבל to immoral behaviour as Fox explains that in Proverbs "a *nabal* is a species of fool, base and worthless and an object of scorn. He is never merely stupid, but, like the *'ĕwil*, morally deficient."[46] For Pss 14 and 53, the moral deficiency of the נבל lies in "practical atheism" as J. Clinton McCann explains:

> What the fools say to themselves in v. 1*a* should not be understood as a statement of philosophical atheism. Rather, the issue is a much more subtle and widespread practical atheism—that is, acting as if there is no God to whom one is accountable in any way. Thus foolishness turns out to be synonymous with wickedness— that is, autonomy, being a "law unto oneself."[47]

---

[41] It is well attested that Pss 14 and 53 constitute a doublet, with some substantial differences in the latter verses of the two psalms. There's also a key difference in the name of the divine where Ps 14 denotes the divine as YHWH while Ps 53 uses the more generic name of Elohim. See Karl Budde, "Psalm 14 Und 53," *JBL* 47 (1928): 160–83; Robert A. Bennett, "Wisdom Motifs in Psalm 14 = 53 — *Nābāl* and *'Ēsāh*," *BASOR* 220 (1975): 15–21; PJ Botha, "Ironie as Sleutel Tot Die Verstaan Van Psalm 14," *Verbum et Ecclesia* 16 (1995): 16–27; Carolin Neuber, "'Es Gibt Keinen Gott': Die Möglichkeit Der Gottesleugnung Und Das Gottesbild in Psalm 9/10; 14; 53," *PzB* 29 (2020): 26–46.
[42] Tremper Longman, *Psalms: An Introduction and Commentary*, TOTC 15–16 (Nottingham: InterVartsity, 2014), 98.
[43] Peter C. Craigie, *Psalms 1–50*, WBC 19 (Dallas: Word, 1983), 147.
[44] Bennett, "Wisdom Motifs," 15–21.
[45] Derek Kidner, *Psalms 1–72*, TOTC 15 (Downers Grove: InterVarsity, 1973), 95.
[46] Michael V. Fox, *Proverbs 10–31: A New Translation with Introduction and Commentary*, AB 18B (London: Yale University Press, 2009), 627.
[47] J. Clinton McCann, "The Book of Psalms," in *NIB* 4:729.

The נבל acts as though there is no God; they are a person "who disregards God, who convinces himself or herself that God does not matter."[48] So what context might we envisage that could have conjured up such a figure?

Carolin Neuber argues that Ps 14 portrays a society where the wicked can go about their business regardless of their impurity, while the pious find themselves in distress.[49] It suggests a world where the נבל acts freely, eats up God's people and does not call on YHWH (14:4); the נבל also devises plans against the "wretched poor" (14:6).[50] Where does this take place? It is not difficult to assume an Israelite context, however, P. J. Botha notes that the term בני־אדם "people/humanity" (14:2) stands in contrast with "my people" (14:5), and could therefore point us to the possibility that the antagonists belonged to nations outside and in opposition to Israel. Certainly, as Botha argues, when 14:7 is considered, it might be that the protagonists and antagonists represent conflicting hostile nations, whereby the terms "Zion," "Israel," "his people," "Jacob" and again "Israel" are descriptions that demarcate Israel as a homogenous whole from other nations.[51]

This setting allows for us to reconsider the theodicy problem in Ps 14, because ultimately, the pressing issue is that in spite of the Psalmist's ideas about moral order, there still lacks an act of divine justice.[52] This might be the attitude of the psalmist, and the context might be speaking to the attitudes of scepticism towards God's jurisdiction and/or existence. As Botha has suggested, the conditions for such doubt might be better understood in a political dynamic involving two nations. Indeed, it is not unlikely that the Psalmist speaks from a diasporic context, as Peter Craigie writes:

> With respect to date, it is commonly argued that the psalm must be a postexilic composition, first on the basis of the mixed form, and second on the basis of v 7b, which could be translated: "when the Lord brings back the captivity of his people" (cf. AV), which in turn could be interpreted as a reference either to the Diaspora or the Exile.[53]

I argue that the social dynamics of the "fools" in light of verse 7, seem more understandable from a diasporic context. Such a society could not have been Jerusalem and McCann affirms this by suggesting "v. 7 to be a post-exilic addition to the psalm in order to make it especially applicable to a situation in which Israel was dominated by other nations."[54] The discourse of אין אלהים thus point to a

---

[48] Robert G. Bratcher, and William David Reyburn, *A Translator's Handbook on the Book of Psalms*, UBS Handbook Series (New York: United Bible Societies, 1991), 127.
[49] Neuber, "'Es Gibt Keinen Gott,'" 41.
[50] Botha, "Ironie as sleutel," 22.
[51] Botha, "Ironie as sleutel," 22.
[52] Neuber, "'Es Gibt Keinen Gott,'" 42.
[53] Craigie, *Psalms 1–50*, 147.
[54] McCann, "Psalms," 730.

society where Israel is captive to or in conflict with foreign nations who do not accept God's jurisdiction.[55] Moreover, אין אלהים might reflect a context where God's presence is called into question because God's judgment upon the wicked has been delayed. After all, verse 7 envisages hopes of redemption, but if this verse was a later addition, by implication, we could argue that the psalmist is still waiting for such redemption.

Verse 7 therefore serves a significant purpose in the conclusion of the psalm as a final prayer that brings hope for the protagonists ("company of the righteous") (14:5) against the antagonist ("fool"). Yet there is still uncertainty, because it remains an unfulfilled hope. As Botha raises: "The certainty with which the narrator makes statements in verses 1–6, is thus considerably tempered in verse 7."[56] The psalmist hopes for YHWH to change their fate, and to give them joy, but the reality is that the people of YHWH still lie "in the dark shadows of the statements of laments of v. 1."[57] If this is the case, then verse 7 implies delay in the divine judgment. Consequently, this generates significant implications for understanding the statement by the נבל that "there is no God."

So what might an alternative meaning of "there is no God" look like? I contend that the delay in divine judgment is better understood in the context of the diaspora because diasporic conditions, particularly notions of exile, reinforce distance from Jerusalem and the temple which accentuates the conception of delay.[58] From a diasporic perspective then, one may view the irony in אין אלהים "There is no God" whereby the Israelite God-followers are not speaking of divine presence but of divine abandonment. The statement "there is no God" therefore could be asking the question "Where is God?" or more specifically "Where is God when we need God?" It may be that in response to God looking down from heaven searching if there are any that are wise and seek God (14:2), the righteous are looking back up to heaven or to Zion (14:7) and wondering if God will ever deliver them. It is a theological dilemma that remains unsolved for the people of YHWH in Ps 14 because for them, "the 'righteousness' of Yahweh can ... be seen when the harm that has been set in motion by the hostile powers falls back upon its instigators."[59] This is perhaps what Qohelet had in mind, although rather than supplying a prayer of hope, Qohelet comes to the realisation that justice does not come and so he gives no hope at all: "I said that this also is incomprehensible." For Qohelet, the absence of God might be a metaphor for divine delay.

---

[55] Cf. Bratcher and Reyburn, *Handbook on Psalms*, 128.

[56] Botha, "Ironie as sleutel," 22. My translation: "Die sekerheid waarmee die verteller in vers 1–6 uitsprake maak, word dus in vers 7 aansienlik getemper."

[57] Hans-Joachim Kraus, *Psalms 1–59*, A Continental Commentary (Minneapolis: Fortress, 1993), 223.

[58] Cf. Adele Berlin, "On Writing a Commentary on Lamentations," in *Lamentations in Ancient and Contemporary Cultural Contexts*, ed. Nancy Lee and Carleen Mandolfo, SBLSymS 43 (Atlanta: Society of Biblical Literature, 2008), 9.

[59] Hans-Joachim Kraus, *Theology of the Psalms: A Continental Commentary*, trans. Keith Crim (Minneapolis: Fortress, 1992), 155.

THE WICKED NINEVITES

Let us consider further implications of divine delay, by examining another example of justice towards antagonistic character(s), and here I bring our discussion to the Ninevites in the book of Jonah. It is clear that the Ninevites are the antagonists from the onset. In Jonah 1:2, it reads:

קום לך אל־נינוה העיר הגדולה וקרא עליה כי־עלתה רעתם לפני

"Arise and go to Nineveh the great city and call upon it, for their wickedness has come before me." (my trans.)

Highlighting the antagonistic character of Nineveh, the narrator immediately identified them by their wickedness (root: רעה "wicked") while Jonah is ordered to call against it. To the ancient readers of Jonah, this comes as no surprise given the history of Israel with the Assyrians, as Nineveh "stands as a synecdoche for the brutally oppressive Assyrian empire itself."[60] This presents conflict for ancient hearers of the Jonah story, who expect divine justice to rain down upon the Ninevites. Yet, as it turns out, the Ninevites are shown mercy which could hardly have been applauded by the implied readers.[61]

In antiquity, it was self-evident that the gods would exact punishment for any immoral deeds against them.[62] In the book of Jonah, a similar expectation is held by the Israelites of their God, through the viewpoint of the narrator. Such a position is reflected by Étan Levine's argument that God "as the dispenser of good and evil he *must* punish as well as reward; otherwise he would come to resemble the remote, inactive gods (*dei otiosi*), withdrawn in the sky and departed from human life."[63] Furthermore, God as *deus otiosus* "would lose religious currency as a party to the covenant" should God fail to act.[64] However, while God is expected to exact punishment—in line with this ancient thought—Jonah was familiar with and complicated by the other side to God's nature. This other side is noted elsewhere in the Hebrew Bible, particularly in Exod 34:9 which Jonah quotes almost verbatim in Jonah 4:2: "for I knew that you are a gracious God and merciful, slow to anger, and abounding in steadfast love, and ready to relent from punishing" (NRSV). These words are the foundation of Jonah's conflict. Jonah

---

[60] Stuart, *Hosea-Jonah*, 449; See also Jack M. Sasson, *Jonah: A New Translation with Introduction, Commentary, and Interpretation*, AB 24B (New Haven: Yale University Press, 2008), 70. Despite the association with the Assyrian reign, there is strong evidence that the book was written or composed in its final form during the Persian era. See the argument by Étan Levine, "Justice in Judaism: The Case of Jonah," *The Review of Rabbinic Judaism* 5.2 (2002): 171–72.
[61] Cf. Philip Davies, "Rough Justice?," in *Bible and Justice: Ancient Texts, Modern Challenges*, ed. Matthew J. M. Coomber (London: Routledge, 2014), 51.
[62] See discussion in Levine, "Justice in Judaism," 184–86.
[63] Levine, "Justice in Judaism," 185.
[64] Levine, "Justice in Judaism," 185.

did not want God to act according to his merciful nature and complains against God's goodness.⁶⁵ The irony of prophecy comes to the fore here, for while he was called in 1:2 to cry against the city of Nineveh, he in fact cries against God. Phyllis Trible notes that by doing so, "Jonah produces an oxymoron. He subverts divine love into accusation, condemns compassion, and demands vindication from the 'merciful' God who coerced obedience from him."⁶⁶

Significantly, it may sound that Jonah's despair is selfish, yet in his cry (קרא) he stands with his countrymen in opposition to God. On the other hand, God, by implication, is on the side of Israel's wicked enemies.⁶⁷ In some sense, as Havea argues, one could "hear justice in Jonah's anger" for a "colonial power (read: Nineveh) should not be let off the hook but called to account for its past and ongoing violent actions."⁶⁸ We may interpret Jonah's call to God then, as a call for justice. On that account, we may perceive Jonah's stance against God as engendering a deep concern for moral order to be restored, by which his recalcitrant actions and demeanour reflect his desperation for God to punish the oppressors.

The prophet is crafty in his rebellion, manipulating the terms of God's order the second time he is told to call against the Ninevites (3:3–5). First, he truncates his walk, taking just one day to conduct his call in a city that takes three days' walk to cover, raising some doubts as to whether he reached everyone in the city. By doing so, he delays the completion of his mission so as to raise the likelihood of the Ninevites not being able to save themselves.⁶⁹ Second, the "call" which God instructs Jonah to perform involves not only a declaration of imminent doom but also a plea for repentance, giving Nineveh the chance to redeem themselves and be saved.⁷⁰ But Jonah does not encourage repentance from the protagonists, as he instead obscures the message. In proclaiming that Nineveh will be "overthrown" נהפכת in forty days (3:4), the narrator shrewdly conceals the message of hope in an alternative meaning of that verb, "offering only a faint indication that the 'upending' of the city could take the form of a transformation of its conduct."⁷¹ The actions of the prophet are deliberate and zealous, and perhaps Gershom Scholem is right, that in the end it is not prophetism that the prophet carries out here, but "what he does is essentially politics."⁷² The politics is highlighted by the irony in his actions, as the problem of delay in the destruction of Nineveh—which will

---

⁶⁵ Stuart, *Hosea-Jonah*, 502.
⁶⁶ Phyllis Trible, "The Book of Jonah," in *NIB* 7:518.
⁶⁷ Hans Walter Wolff, *Obadiah and Jonah: A Continental Commentary* (Minneapolis: Augsburg, 1986), 168.
⁶⁸ Jione Havea, "Adjusting Jonah," *International Review of Mission* 102.1 (2013): 48–49.
⁶⁹ Sasson, *Jonah*, 231, Yitzhak Berger, *Jonah in the Shadows of Eden* (Bloomington: Indiana University Press, 2016), 28.
⁷⁰ Berger, *Jonah in the Shadows*, 29.
⁷¹ Berger, *Jonah in the Shadows*, 29–30.
⁷² Gershom Scholem, "On Jonah and the Concept of Justice," *Critical Inquiry* 25.2 (1999): 356.

come to pass much later[73]—is countered by Jonah attempting to make haste of Nineveh's fate by minimising the opportunity for the Ninevites to repent in time. Jonah's actions may be reflecting a great deal of frustration and pain of the prophet but also the readers of this text, particularly if we recognise the implied audience to be Jews in exile. They are a nation who had suffered greatly at the hands of an oppressive colonial power, who like the prophet, were conflicted by the notion of a God who administers divine justice, yet who at the same time, is frustratingly merciful and slow to anger.

Arguably, the conflicts around the notions of justice and moral order in the book, are rooted in a conflict between nations. At the same time, we are reminded of other nuances of exile, such as being distanced and cast as an outsider. Henceforth, in the book of Jonah, we are also invited into the world of Jonah the "outsider." The notion of Jonah being an outsider certainly raises the possibility of diasporic conditions, and such social conditions may have formulated some of the questions and arguments in the book of Jonah.[74] Smith-Christopher argues that it would seem clear that "Jonah derives much of its power and meaning by being read 'in diaspora.'"[75] The exasperations of Jonah, through a diasporic perspective, reveal much more than an uncooperative prophet, but also an outsider who struggles to "fit in."[76] Whether it be on the boat, in the belly of the great fish, or in Nineveh, the story of Jonah can be reimagined as Jonah's struggle to "fit in" the places which he moves to and from. His conflict mirrors that of the postexilic community, where "the displacement and dislocation that Jonah experiences within the narrative evokes Israel's banishment from the land."[77]

In the question of ethics and justice, further diasporic proclivities emerge as Jonah also feels displaced and conflicted between the ideas of justice, mercy, and a sovereign God.[78] Indeed, Jonah's anger with divine justice resonates with Qohelet's own struggle to comprehend the moral chaos of the world around him. But while Jonah learns a valuable lesson about the extent of divine compassion that is beyond his own "narrow and rigid concept of justice,"[79] Qohelet discovers

---

[73] Stuart, *Hosea-Jonah*, 508.

[74] Most scholars would date Jonah from postexilic to as late as the third century BCE, with influences of Persian thought prominent throughout the book. See Levine, "Justice in Judaism," 171–72. Also see the discussion by Sasson in Sasson, *Jonah*, 27.

[75] Daniel L. Smith-Christopher, *Jonah, Jesus, and Other Good Coyotes: Speaking Peace to Power in the Bible* (Nashville: Abingdon, 2007), 64.

[76] See Lois Baer Barr, "The Jonah Experience: The Jews of Brazil According to Scliar," in *The Jewish Diaspora in Latin America: New Studies on History and Literature*, ed. David Sheinin and Lois Baer Barr (New York: Garland, 1996), 33.

[77] David J. Downs, "The Specter of Exile in the Story of Jonah," *Horizons in Biblical Theology* 31 (2009): 43.

[78] Davies, "Rough Justice?," 51.

[79] Thomas M. Bolin, *Freedom Beyond Forgiveness: The Book of Jonah Re-examined*, JSOTSup 236 (Sheffield: Sheffield Academic, 1997), 159–60.

that the breadth of divine compassion is "not concerned with justice as a principle: rain falls on everyone and death comes to good and bad alike."[80]

MORAL CHAOS IN DIASPORA

The three readings above provide interesting intersections that allow us to reconsider the notion of morality from a diasporic perspective. Certainly, all three stories could speak from diasporic locations, and when read alongside one another, we could imagine a debate by the authors of these texts over the conditions of ethics in the diaspora. Hence, it is worth discussing the diversity of views offered in dialogue, and the implications the discussion has for (re)viewing Qohelet's pessimistic attitude towards moral order. These readings help us to understand (and maybe appreciate) the complexity of Qohelet's ethical stance.

The conception of the virtuous foreigner may have been viewed in a positive light with regards to the Joseph story, and in the rest of the patriarchal narratives in Genesis, but as discussed above, it could also prove to be a hindrance to moral order. In particular, foreign rulers who show mercy point to a diasporic reality where justice does not always occur as expected. Thus while Qohelet is not explicit, the way morality is distorted could, by implication, be the result of a merciful foreign leader(s). This may offer one possible explanation for Qohelet's incomprehensible (הבל) "topsy-turvy" world. What is incomprehensible is the rationale behind what Qohelet sees, as to the actual event itself. To understand this, we must observe alternative dynamics.

The mercy Joseph shows to his brothers seems illogical from a familial point of view, as he does not penalise their act of cruelty. On the other hand, the political dynamic to the story sees Joseph, the powerful and tyrannical Egyptian administrator, showing pity to migrant Israelites. If an Egyptian ruler could make slaves of his fellow Egyptians (Gen 47:21), then the idea of foreigners receiving freedom seems absurd. This may have been a similar sentiment to what Qohelet was feeling when he exclaims: שגם־זה הבל "this is incomprehensible." Qohelet may have bemoaned a similar act of mercy by a foreign ruler towards an undeserving group, all while those who deserve compassion are being made slaves by the foreign tyranny. Indeed, it may well be that the "incomprehensible situation" for Qohelet is actually the "incomprehensible ruler." Carolyn Sharp argues that Joseph becomes like God to the people "but his divinity has not been performed in a reliable way."[81] Similarly, we might infer that Qohelet's frustration in 8:14 is over a ruler who tries to play "God" but performs in an unreliable way.

In Ps 14, it is not a foreign ruler but God who seems to perform in an unreliable way. The Psalmist ascribes those who make the claim אין אלהים "there is no

---

[80] Davies, "Rough Justice?," 52.
[81] Carolyn J. Sharp, *Irony and Meaning in the Hebrew Bible* (Bloomington: Indiana University Press, 2009), 58.

God" as foolish נבל. But are they foolish? There may be room to draw another conclusion from this statement: that in lands where God's presence and jurisdiction are in question, the hope for justice may be lost while the demand for justice moves towards desperation. To clarify, those who claim there is no God reflect the position of reality: that the justice the Psalmist cries for does not actually eventuate, because God is not around to grant it. It is a cry for hope, yet the language Ps 14:5–6 suggests that the fate of the נבל will take place in the future, so justice is still impending. For that moment then, the statement "there is no God" is analogous to divine abandonment, and may speak to an attitude of uncertainty by diasporic people as to how God is acting in the diaspora.[82] The uncertainty and doubt over God's presence seem to reflect an uncertainty of diasporic people with religion.[83] For Qohelet however, it is not so much the divine presence that is the focus, but that there is no divine justice.

However, while the נבל of Ps 14 may push God away, Jonah and oddly the Ninevites bring God back into the realm of moral justice, but not without controversy. As discussed earlier, the story of Jonah suggests that the frustration with God's justice lies in the breadth of God's compassion. Understanding God's compassion in a universal sense may exhibit the nature of God as preached throughout the Hebrew Bible, but when considering the context of a people who are oppressed by a colonial power, such divine compassion could only be viewed with frustration. The reality is that judgment does not always fall upon the wicked, and as 8:11 suggests, it does not happen quickly enough. Frustratingly, it is the repentance of the Ninevites that actually leads to the delay in judgment and consequent mercy.[84] Human agency is again at play, as human repentance (Ninevites) leads to divine mercy, which then leads to no justice for Jonah and the Israelites.

Ironically for the Israelites, their own human actions are pointless as it seems that nothing they do could incur immediate divine justice.[85] So while the Israelites cannot relieve themselves of the iniquities of their fathers' sins, they, and specifically Qohelet, may not understand why the same transgenerational consequence of sin cannot be said for their enemies and oppressors.

This may have been the incomprehensible topsy-turvy world that Qohelet witnessed. A world where people's fates could result from the unpredictability of human behaviour: humans interfering, humans manipulating, and humans repenting. In diaspora, the human element is more diverse, consisting of different ethnic

---

[82] Melton, *Where Is God*, 68.

[83] Melton, *Where Is God*, 68. Also see the discussion by Sidnie Ann White about the uncertainty of diaspora in relation to the ambiguous purpose of the book of Esther, in Sidnie Ann White, "Esther: A Feminine Model for Jewish Diaspora," in *Gender and Difference in Ancient Israel*, ed. Peggy L. Day (Minneapolis: Fortress, 1989), 161–77.

[84] Stuart, *Hosea-Jonah*, 495.

[85] See Levinson, *Legal Revision*, 59, who argues that the injustice of the doctrine of the transgenerational consequence of sins "inevitably creates an overwhelming sense of the futility of historical action altogther, inasmuch as the progeny cannot free themselves from the consequences of the past."

groups. Naturally, the ideas about morality are disparate and conflicting, and what ensues is the creation of further moral chaos. From the vantage point of diaspora, we could envisage Qohelet's frustration in 8:11, where his indignation is a result of the delay in divine justice, and in that delay, the complexities of conflicting peoples and cultures seek to interfere, manipulate, change and shift the world out of place. Once again, in this chapter, we see that it is possible to understand Qohelet's position as the result of a theological conversation with other texts and genres, rather than an isolated wisdom sceptic.[86]

Samoan Diaspora Hermeneutics

The complexity of Qohelet's concerns regarding moral order provides further evidence of a diasporic location for the sceptical sage. A diasporic setting illuminates the intricacy of the moral debate when considering the variety of voices discussed earlier, side-by-side. The three readings in this chapter depict typical diasporic experiences and attitudes, which provide significant implications for understanding Qohelet's critique of moral order from a diasporic perspective. To provide further hermeneutical reflection, I discuss my own diasporic experience.

As Samoan diasporic communities establish themselves in the host land, there is transition from an ethnic group to a distinct community where culture and religion are intertwined but not with traditional lands, so as to maintain some semblance of their traditional identity. In maintaining their traditional identity, traditional notions of morality and ethics are upheld. It might be easier to imagine justice in a monocultural community as is typical of a Samoan village, but in a multicultural and multiethnic society such as Australia, notions of justice are more complicated. As migrants will often find, the immediacy of justice may not be forthcoming in the new context, because the old processes which determined justice in the homeland do not apply in the host land. Indeed, not all elements of one's *maota* can be carried into new lands.

To add to the complexity, the existence of a dominant culture may also affect how justice is contemplated. In a utopian view of society, one could imagine an ecumenical approach to justice, but in reality, justice does not always arrive and is often delayed. For many diasporic people, when they are wronged, justice becomes a lengthy wait. Some of the injustices that migrant Samoans experience include racism and discrimination. In Australia, the experience of racism (particularly against Indigenous Australians and people of colour), discrimination, gender inequality, the detaining of asylum seekers, and the damaging Lombok Treaty that has led to oppression and murder against native West Papuans, are proof that justice is often elusive and delayed. What hope is there for moral order, if this is what is witnessed? Much like the Egyptians who are enslaved by Joseph,

---

[86] Kynes, *Obituary*, 217.

7. Moral Order

the desperate Psalmist in Ps 14:7, the exasperating Jonah, and the frustrated Qohelet, justice becomes a "waiting game."

Like Samoans in the diaspora, we can readily envisage Qohelet as a conflicted diasporic hybrid identity. Arguably, the experience of migrant Samoans in Australia exhibits similar difficulties to that of ancient diasporic Jews who in transitioning from an ethnic group to a religious community, are tussling with this distinction in ethics:

> between the ethics of pre-exilic Yahwism might be expected to be paraenetic, reflecting the life of a people not trying to distinguish themselves from the surrounding world; that of the post-exilic Jewish communities protreptic, since it required a commitment to live differently from the surrounding population.[87]

This distinction might have fuelled Qohelet's perturbation, who was probably vacillating between preexilic Yahwism and a diasporic understanding of Jewish ethics. I argue that for Qohelet the issue was this: neither understanding of ethics gives him a satisfactory explanation of the injustice that he witnesses.

Moreover, I contend that Qohelet knew the deficiency of Deuteronomistic and Priestly notions of justice when considered from the point of view of diaspora; Deut 28 and Lev 26 presume a moral universe with promised land at the centre of things. The national Deuteronomic theology evidently assumes a uniformity of religion whereas the Priestly tradition conveys an intercultural vision of morality and justice.[88] However, for Qohelet neither of these notions seem to account for the diasporic experience.

In sum, we see in the three contexts of reading (Joseph novella, Ps 14, and Jonah) that justice is curtailed by this same assumption and as a result we are made to question divine justice and the moral order. Similarly, Qohelet expresses his frustration but in more profound terms. We could imagine Qohelet having a response to the psalmist's question Ps 14:7: *When will the salvation from Zion come for Israel?* The sceptical sage might well have read this question and responded to the psalmist that salvation is delayed, and if you are in the diaspora, salvation might not come at all!

---

[87] Barton, *Ethics*, 151, draws on the distinction between 'protreptic' and 'paraenetic' ethics as discussed by Michael Wolter in relation to New Testament ethics. As Barton explains: "The first can be seen where early Christian converts from paganism are challenged to change their ethical commitments to fit in with the ethical style of the religion to which they were now migrating; the second is to be found in exhortations to live a good life within the community on an ongoing basis. The former is likely to show more signs of distinctiveness than the second." For more on this distinction, see Michael Wolter, *Theologie Und Ethos Im Frühen Christentum*, WUNT 236 (Tübingen: Mohr Siebeck, 2009), 122–69.

[88] Mark G. Brett, "Whakawhiti Kōrero: Theology and Social Vocation," in *Holding Forth the Word of Life: Essays in Honor of Tim Meadowcroft*, ed. John de Jong and Csilla Saysell (Eugene: Wipf & Stock, 2020), 219–20.

8. Qohelet's *Maota Tau Ave*

There are significant implications from diaspora contexts for reading, as articulated in the previous chapters. Reading as an Australian-Samoan, I first configure *Maota Tau Ave* as a hermeneutical lens for reading Ecclesiastes. In utilising this hermeneutic, I pursue two possibilities. First, I use the notion of *Maota* metaphorically to represent Qohelet's "house" of thematic concerns, themes that he deconstructs from a diasporic location. Second, the question of Qohelet's scepticism as a by-product of his *tautua* (service) will be discussed. Ultimately, the discussion will reframe the scepticism in the book of Ecclesiastes.

Maota Tau Ave as Hermeneutical Lens

Maota Tau Ave (the house to carry) represents movement of people from one land to another. *Maota Tau Ave* embodies the journey of diasporic people, in this case, diasporic Samoans. The statement *Maota Tau Ave* is literally imperative, but for Samoans in diasporic locations, *Maota Tau Ave* seems more to be indicative, so rather than the house that *is carried*, I contend that it is the house *to carry*.

The movement of bodies which had been bordered by cultural and religious constraints in the homeland, generate new perspectives due to the change in social conditions. As such, *Maota Tau Ave* signifies a new worldview for Samoans migrating to new lands, an outlook shaped by change, but also by the awkwardness of trying to fit into the new context. As an Australian Samoan, I am a descendant of first-generation Samoan migrants who carried (*tau ave*) their Samoan *maota* to Australia. In their *maota*, they brought their cultural traditions and customs, their *lotu* and their language. Attempting to situate their *maota* on the new land, which through the dominant Anglo culture had its own customs and traditions, its own spiritual identity and its own language, was obviously complicated.

The transition from homeland to the new land required negotiation and compromise; to set aside some of the traditions and customs, while learning new skills and a foreign language. In the process, our people also learnt to conduct their *lotu* away from their extravagant and grandiose church buildings in Samoa, to the inside of garages and shacks, and renting out old town halls. This "institutional replication" was the reality of first-generation Samoan migrants in the 1980s and was perhaps envisaged by "parent" communities in Samoa.[1]

However, the emergence of the second-generation added a different dimension to the migrant experience. Significantly, their existence would pose a threat to the parent communities by way of challenging institutional replication. In other words, the second-generation is the voice of dissonance against *Maota Tau Ave*. Their worldview is cluttered with uncertainty and disillusionment as they were born in the host land whilst having little to no knowledge of the homeland. As a result, second-generation Samoans, in their own unique experience might ask: Why is there be a need for institutional replication? What relevance is there for cultural traditions and customs in a foreign land? Why must we worship the Samoan way when we struggle to speak our mother tongue? Anae poses questions regarding culture which articulate the sceptical attitude of the second-generation:

> Is culture primordial—'in the blood'—as many people will insist, or is it shaped by external influences? Are cultural traditions invented, as some scholars claim, and used to validate a traditional past? Is culture a whole way of struggle, or does the anthropological notion of culture as a 'whole way of life' reign supreme?[2]

Following this line of questioning, carrying the *maota* generates a number of serious questions. These questions reflect a desire by the second-generation to renegotiate terms.

The standpoint of the second-generation represents a space for interrogating inherited norms, such as culture and tradition, but also the biblical text. It is an in-between space which Bhabha refers to as the "third space"—a space

> which constitutes the discursive conditions of enunciation that ensure that the meaning and symbols of culture have no primordial unity or fixity; that even the same signs can be appropriated, translated, rehistoricized and read anew.[3]

In this third space, the second-generation still *tau ave* the *maota*, but with attitudes of scepticism and pessimism, in order to find the relevance of their *maota* among other *maota* in the host land. It is from this third space that I construct a hermeneutic: a *Maota Tau Ave* hermeneutic.

The structure of this hermeneutic has two parts. As indicated in the introduction, the first part is the word *maota*. A traditional Samoan *maota* has a round-shaped foundation, with a thatched-roof supported by wooden poles. Visitors would normally sit at the front poles of the house while the hosts occupy the back poles. When visitors meet the hosts, they sit face-to-face from their respective

---

[1] Cluny Macpherson, "From Moral Community to Moral Communities: The Foundations of Migrant Social Solidarity among Samoans in Urban Aotearoa/New Zealand," *Pacific Studies* 25.1–2 (2002): 72, 75.
[2] Anae, "Towards a NZ-Born Samoan Identity," 131.
[3] Bhabha, *Location of Culture*, 37.

positions in the *maota*. As such there is an unoccupied space in the middle which is known as *va*. Nobody sits in the middle for it is deemed *tapuia* (sacred) and the space is therefore known as *va tapuia*. The reason this *va* is *tapuia* is because it is a space for *talanoa* (conversation/ dialogues) and negotiation; to decide and resolve matters; for peace and reconciliation. The *va* therefore, as Sa'iliemanu Lilomaiava-Doktor notes, is "not empty space, not space that separates, but space that relates."[4] By implication, serious *talanoa* or conversations are sacred. The conversation itself can be uneasy and awkward, it can also be controversial and petulant, however the sacredness of the *va* ensures that respect is maintained.

In fact, the Samoan word for respect is *fa'aaloalo* which is aptly represented by this sitting in a *maota*, because the root word for *fa'aaloalo* is *alo*, which means "to face" and this implies that respect is shown face-to-face like those sitting in the Samoan *maota*. *Maota* constitutes the standpoint from which I read. Specifically, as a second-generation Australian Samoan, *maota* represents the third space: a space for *talanoa* and renegotiation.

The second part to the hermeneutical framework rests in the word *tau ave* and I emphasise the prefix *tau* in this deliberation. The word *tau* has the sense of an ongoing process, or even an unfinished process. While *ave* means "carry," the prefix *tau* implies that the carrying is ongoing. By this analogy, there is a constant deliberation (*tau ave*) of the terms of culture (*faa-Samoa*), worship (*lotu*) and familial links (*aiga*) by second-generation Samoans in Australia who are conflicted by disparities between the two contexts, but also between themselves and first-generation. In carrying the *maota*, the second-generation are constantly negotiating their position, to ensure their *maota* can be placed among other *maota* in the new context.

However, the second-generation are different from the first-generation in that the first-generation do not challenge the customs and traditions of the homeland but seek to make compromises so that these customs and traditions can be upheld. Significantly, there is a Samoan tradition that states: *E sui faiga ae tumau faavae* ("the processes/practices change but foundations remain" [my trans.]). In this saying, compromise is allowed, for it "depicts the philosophical view that the transformation of modern thinking to our cultural norms when traditional practices are implemented does not change the principles that underpin the essence of practice."[5]

The second-generation however are not so accommodating and may even seek to challenge the foundations as well as the processes. This is because they are conflicted by the expectations of *maota* in the homeland, and their own reality.

---

[4] Sa'iliemanu Lilomaiava-Doktor, "Beyond "Migration": Samoan Population Movement (Malaga) and the Geography of Social Space (Vā)," *The Contemporary Pacific* 21.1 (2009): 12.

[5] Aliitasi Su'a-Tavila, "Contemporary Pacific Values and Beliefs," in *Pacific Social Work: Navigating Practice, Policy and Research*, ed. Jioji Ravulo, Tracie Mafile'o, and Donald Bruce Yeates (New York: Routledge, 2019), 29.

A typical example is the difference between *fa'alavelave* (Samoan ritual exchanges), and the capitalist exchanges in the Western economies of the lands to which Samoans migrate.[6] In this example, the two forms of exchanges highlight tension between first-generation and second-generation Samoans. Ilana Gershon notes that

> when migrants made requests from a Samoan perspective, they did not take into account how limited other people's resources were. For those being asked, it feels as though their elders' initial assumption is that other people are potentially boundless resources and this potential wealth can be tapped into through carefully established strategies. Those asking for resources were consistently overlooking other people's position in a capitalist system, and, in doing so, refusing to manage the intricacies of capitalism and *fa'alavelave* at the same time.[7]

While Gershon speaks of the relationship between migrants and Samoans back in the homeland, there is a different tension that exists between first- and second-generation Samoan migrants in Australia. The first-generation will often promote the necessity of contributing to Samoan ritual exchanges as well as to the church. They see the value of a capitalist system but often give preference to their cultural and religious responsibilities. The second-generation on the other hand question the validity of donating excessive amounts to church and *fa'alavelave*. Attitudes of scepticism are therefore prevalent and can also be seen towards other forms of Samoan customs.

Additionally, another voice of dissonance can be heard due to the different type of *tautua* that emerges from diasporic settings. One such *tautua* is the *tautua aitaumalele* which refers to those who provide service from outside the village. This includes those living in urban centres, as well as Samoans living overseas and in Samoan diasporic communities. As an Australian Samoan, I am situated away from my home villages and in the diaspora (at the time of writing), and it is from this space that I *tautua*.

This is in contrast to those who perform *tautua* in the village who are known as *tautua tuāvae*. The word *tuāvae* can mean "behind the legs or feet" or "dependant on the legs or feet." There are two meanings of *tuāvae*. The first meaning refers to the close proximity of the *tautua* to their home, that is, right behind one's legs or feet. This meaning refers to the *tautua* who lives on the land.[8]

---

[6] See Ilana Gershon, *No Family Is an Island: Cultural Expertise among Samoans in Diaspora* (Ithaca: Cornell University Press, 2012), 25.

[7] Gershon, *No Family*, 27.

[8] One who grew up and lives on the land is known as *taumalae*, hence the term *aitaumelele* stands on the opposite spectrum to *taumalae* and *tuāvae*, see Mema Motusaga, "Women in Decision Making in Samoa" (PhD diss., Victoria University, 2016), 99. See also Pratt's discussion of *taumalae* as the same as *anomalae*, which defines "those living nearest the *malae*" with the *malae* being the family land, in Pratt, *A Grammar and Dictionary of the Samoan Language*, s.v. "Anomalae."

The second meaning of *tuāvae* resonates with the Samoan idiom *vae ma lima* (feet and hands). *Vae ma lima* is a common Samoan phrase that explains service with *vae* (feet), emphasising the haste of one's *tautua*, whereas *lima* (hands) describes the strength and dexterity of the *tautua*.[9] It "describes figuratively the alertness and readiness to act immediately whenever one is called for."[10] Thus, *tautua tuāvae* emphasises how the *tautua*'s family depend upon him/her to provide haste and strong service to the *aiga*.

The force of *aitaumalele* lies in the root *lele*. *Lele* refers to the action of flying and thus alludes to migration, just like a bird that flies or migrates away from its nest or home.[11] The notion of a bird flying or migrating away from its nest is congruous with the Samoan proverb: *E lele le toloa ae maau i le vai* which translates as "A wild duck may fly away, but will always return to its habitat."[12] This Samoan proverb means that irrespective of where Samoans traverse to, they know where home is. If we imagine the *tautua* as the *toloa*, then *aitaumalele* embodies the spirit of the proverb. Accordingly, I want to expound further nuances of *aitaumalele* by envisioning *aitaumalele* as the *toloa*. Similar to my explanation of *faatauvaa*, I acknowledge *aitaumalele* as a construct of the words *'ai, tau, ma,* and *lele*. The word *'ai* means "eat"; for the word *tau*, I take the meaning "to snatch,"[13] *ma* is the conjunction "and" while *lele* as explained above means "to fly." *Ai-tau-ma-lele* therefore is "to snatch one's food and fly" which resonates with the dabbling and eating for which the *toloa* is known.[14]

The *toloa* is a "great wanderer" and is "found across a huge geographic area, extending from Indonesia to French Polynesia, and south to New Zealand and Australia."[15] This feature of the *toloa* has diasporic connotations for the *tautua aitaumalele*. As *aitaumalele*, the *tautua* no longer lives on the land as he/she

---

[9] Cf. Pa'u Tafaogalupe Mulitalo-Lauta, "Pacific Peoples' Identities and Social Services in New Zealand: Creating New Options," in *Tangata O Te Moana Nui: Evolving Identities of Pacific Peoples in Aotearoa/New Zealand*, ed. Cluny Macpherson, Paul Spoonley, and Melani Anae (Palmerston North, NZ: Dunmore, 2001), 255.

[10] Gataivai L. Nepo Auva'a, "A Theological Study of 'Tautua' (Service) in the Light of the Christian Faith, with Special Reference to the Ministry of the Congregational Christian Church in Samoa" (Pacfic Theological College, 1990), 12.

[11] Tamari Mulitalo-Cheung, *"E lele le toloa 'ae ma'au i le vai": Toe taliu mai i fanua le 'au Sa'ili Matagi* (National University of Samoa, 2008), 2.

[12] Seulupe Falaniko Tominiko et al., "The Transnational Matai and the Foreign Homeland: Does the Toloa Still Return to the Water" (paper presented at the 7th Measina Sāmoa Conference, NUS Fale Samoa, 2016), 2.

[13] I have explained the various meanings of *tau* in chapter 1 and in this chapter.

[14] The *toloa* is known as the 'dabbling duck' due to its action of not diving under the water, but dipping in its head and snatching its food before flying away. See: International Business Publications, *Samoa (American): Doing Businsess, Investing in Samoa (American) Guide—Strategic Information, Regulations, Contacts* (Washington DC: International Business Publications, 2007), 187.

[15] International Business Publications, *Samoa (American): Doing Business*, 187.

crosses borders, and carries their *maota* into new and foreign lands.[16] Efi further explains that in spite of their distance, the *tautua aitaumalele* still *tautua* (serve) for the village.[17] In other words, with regards to their *aitaumalele* status, they still have *monotaga* (village membership).[18] Efi's statement about *monotaga* is important because it explicates that one's connection to the *fanua* (land), *aiga* (family), and *nuu* (village) is not just physical but spiritual and hence permanent. *Monotaga* guarantees that even if the *aitaumalele* lives outside the village, the *aitaumalele* still has a say in village and family matters.[19] The *aitaumalele* therefore has the ability to critique cultural practices and customs, despite being physically absent from the *fanua*, *aiga*, and *nuu*.

TEXT IS GUEST

This is how the *maota* is transplanted by Samoans in diaspora, especially by the second-generation people and the *aitaumalele*: rather than idealise and romanticise the culture and *lotu*, they question them and point out the realities of the new context. This shift is what occurs in the space (*va*) in the middle of the *maota*. In some respects, it is a new *maota* and prompts a new *talanoa*.

In configuring *Maota Tau Ave* as a hermeneutical lens, I want to clarify that as *Maota Tau Ave* represents diasporic departure, analogously, this signifies the reader's departure from traditional readings and entering into a new space (*va*). This *va* becomes the platform for a *talanoa* from where new meaning and other possibilities in reading emerge. Yet, while Samoans depart to foreign lands, there is always a longing to return to the homeland. Similarly, the reader "returns" to his/her position of reading equipped, challenged, informed and emancipated by the new meanings and readings, which would allow for further dialogue and critique. Such a return resonates with the return of the *aitaumalele*.

In this chapter, I adapt *maota* as a framework for reflecting on Ecclesiastes in light of the previous chapters. The *maota* becomes the meeting place between the reader and text, where the text is the visitor who sits at the front poles while I, the reader, sit at the back poles as host.[20] The text is not merely an object that can be read, but a guest who is invited to engage with the reader. Ultimately, I am engaging in *talanoa* with the text.

Tau ave (to carry) frames the questions I ask in *talanoa* with the text. I call this form of query *talanoa tau ave*. *Tau ave* is dialogical, underlined by the face-to-face framework of *maota*. The *maota* becomes the space where questions are asked of the text by the second-generation. It is with this mindset that I pose

---

[16] Cf. Motusaga, "Women in Decision Making," 99.
[17] Tui Atua Tupua Tamasese Ta'isi Efi, "O Samoa o le Atunuu Tofi, e lē se Atunuu Taliola" (paper presented at the NUS Measina Conference, Samoa, 2012), 5.
[18] Efi, "Samoa o le Atunuu Tofi," 5.
[19] Efi, "Samoa o le Atunuu Tofi," 5.
[20] Cf. Martin Buber, *I and Thou*, trans. Ronald Gregor Smith (Edinburgh: T&T Clark, 1937).

questions of the text, for the purpose of gauging an alternative understanding of scepticism in Ecclesiastes. As such, I employ a hermeneutic of *Maota Tau Ave* in this reading, where I *talanoa* (dialogue) *tau ave* with the text in the *maota* as third space.

Qohelet's Diasporic *Maota*

Using the hermeneutical framework, I revisit the concept of "house" בית as a space for conversation. Indeed, Qohelet's *maota* is characterised by sceptical and pessimistic attitudes towards various themes. Essentially, Qohelet's viewpoint places him in a critical teaching role in "wisdom" tradition.[21] Qohelet's doubt, in particular, serves as an antithetical response to a host of themes, including toil, wealth and wisdom itself. Indeed, scepticism in Job and Ecclesiastes, could be taken to be a crucial part of wisdom literature, providing critical reflection of wisdom traditions in conversation with the more conventional forms found in Proverbs.[22] Moreover, scepticism may render another nuance of biblical wisdom, particularly if the term חכמה "indicates the ability more generally to assess complex situations, determine the issues involved, and then make the best possible decisions."[23] In other words, assessing complex situations requires one to be critical, and hence, sceptical. As a result, we can be convinced that this affirms the canonical place of Ecclesiastes in wisdom tradition.[24] However, as we have seen in previous chapters, similar attitudes of scepticism appear elsewhere in the Hebrew Bible.

From what we have seen in previous chapters, Qohelet seems to be targeting certain elements of the lived reality of Jewish people in antiquity, most likely in the Persian period. In his critique, I have made a claim that it is likely Qohelet is doing so from afar, possibly in a diasporic setting. To push this claim further, I reimagine Qohelet's interrogative space as *Maota Tau Ave*: as a *maota* that Qohelet carries to diasporic lands.

---

[21] Dell, *Interpreting Ecclesiastes*, 17.
[22] See Gerald H. Wilson, "The Words of the Wise: The Intent and Significance of Qoheleth 12:9–14," *JBL* 103 (1984): 175.
[23] Douglas B. Miller, "Wisdom in the Canon: Discerning the Early Institution," in Sneed, *Was There a Wisdom Tradition?*, 89.
[24] Crenshaw, *Old Testament Wisdom*, 246, argues that "the mere attribution of Proverbs and Ecclesiastes to Solomon hardly assured these works a place in the canon. Instead, Job, Proverbs, and Ecclesiastes gave authentic voice to the sages' fundamental understanding of reality, and in so doing, functioned to orient generation after generation with regard to the world into which they had been thrust." Also see Roland E. Murphy, "Ecclesiastes (Qoheleth)," in *Jerome Bible Commentary*, ed. Raymond Brown, Joseph A. Fitzmyer, and Roland E. Murphy, vol. 1 (London: Prentice Hall, 1968), 540.

RESITUATING QOHELET

In this conceptual framework, Qohelet takes the position of the diasporic Samoan, carrying his *maota* into a distant land. In Qohelet's *maota*, it contains the cultural and religious traditions of ancient Israel, and the ideas of wealth, toil and wisdom which are dictated by traditional understandings, namely, the deeds-consequence formula. Yet, there is tension as Qohelet's *maota* is transplanted to a different context where expectations and results are not as one carrying the *maota* might hope. The tension is highlighted throughout the book, but I have highlighted three sayings in particular, which reflect Qohelet's frustration with the results and expectations that do not come to fruition. Those discourses are:

1. רעות רוח /רעיון רוח "chasing after wind"
2. תחת השמש "under the sun"
3. הבל "*hebel*"[25]

These describe the futility of events, but they may also point to the tension experienced in the diaspora. How might we envisage this? Previously, I analysed Qohelet's scepticism via an intertextual *talanoa* with other texts in the Hebrew Bible. In the following paragraphs, I utilise *Maota Tau Ave* as a way of *talanoa* with Qohelet to envisage the diasporic locale from which these sayings or discursive judgments were uttered. In this framework, I use my position as an Australian-Samoan as a lens for rereading.

Before I discuss the sayings listed above, I set markers to outline how the discussion will unfold. In *Maota Tau Ave*, I am the host while the text is the visitor. The *va* is the space within the *maota*, between me and the text; namely, the space in which I engage with Qohelet. As an Australian Samoan, the *maota* is transplanted, uprooted from the land (*fanua*) of the homeland, and situated on "these lands now called Australia."[26] The terms are different and therefore the *va* will generate different questions. Undoubtedly, conflict may eventuate as a result of this exchange which in itself, could provide further implications for understanding scepticism from a diasporic point of view.

---

[25] The translation of הבל has undergone extensive scrutiny by scholars, as discussed in chapter 7. Aside from the common translation of "vanity," Fox renders the translation of "absurdity" in "The Meaning of *Hebel* for Qohelet," *JBL* 105 (1986): 427, while others such as Daniel C. Fredericks prefer "breath" to suggest transience, in *Coping with Transience: Ecclesiastes on Brevity in Life*, The Biblical Seminar 18 (Sheffield: JSOT Press, 1993), 11–12. Like Fredericks, Miller translates הבל as "vapor" with a similar emphasis on transience, see Douglas B. Miller, "Qohelet's Symbolic Use of הבל," *JBL* 117 (1998): 437–54. For other meanings, see discussion by Choon-Leong Seow, "Beyond Mortal Grasp: The Usage of *Hebel* in Ecclesiastes," *Australian Biblical Review* 48 (2000): 1–16.

[26] Brooke Prentis, "What Can the Birds of the Land Tell Us?," in *Grounded in the Body, in Time and Place, in Scripture: Papers by Australian Women Scholars in the Evangelical Tradition*, ed. Jill Firth and Denise Cooper-Clarke (Eugene: Wipf & Stock, 2021), 31.

Further, the *talanoa* observed in previous chapters consisted of conversations with other texts in the Hebrew Bible corpus. However, the intertextual *talanoa* in this book also involves engaging with cultural texts. Significantly, the analysis that follows would take the form of Barton's hard intertextuality. The conversations that proceed from this point on, engage with the cultural texts of my own diasporic background; as a way of highlighting, from a logical point of view as opposed to linguistic, how Ecclesiastes might be a "permutation of texts, an intertextuality: in the space of a given text, several utterances, taken from other texts, intersect and neutralize one another."[27] In essence, the purpose of this exercise is to *talanoa* by way of reading these intertexts (or *talanoa* partners) and how their juxtapositions can produce new meanings.

"CHASING AFTER WIND" AND "SAILI MATAGI"

The saying "chasing after wind" in its forms רעיון רוח and רעות רוח appears 10 times in Ecclesiastes.[28] The saying communicates the idea of striving or pursuing for wind.[29] Seow argues that the term רוח "wind"

> is frequently a metaphor for things that have no abiding value or are insubstantial. Thus, the sages spoke of inheriting wind (Prov 11:29), restraining wind (Prov 27:16), gathering wind (Prov 30:4), windy knowledge (Job 15:2), and windy words (Job 16:3; cf. 6:26; 8:2). In every case "wind" indicates futility or meaninglessness (see Isa 41:29).[30]

In essence, the saying signifies the striving for something meaningless and futile, or something transitory.[31]

However, such an expression is not without ambiguity, mostly due to the translation of the word רוח. Michael Eaton acknowledges this ambivalence: "The Hebrew *rûaḥ* may mean "spirit" or "wind." The context equally suits two notions: frustration by the insoluble (*vexation of spirit*), or ambition for the unattainable (*striving after wind*)."[32] Here, I invite the text into my *maota*, to *talanoa* with the purpose of coming to an alternative understanding. How might the ambiguity of רוח render a different understanding in this *talanoa*? How could we understand "chasing after wind" from an Australian-Samoan perspective?

---

[27] Kristeva, *Desire in Language*, 36.
[28] Seow notes that the two forms are synonymous in meaning, see: Seow, *Ecclesiastes*, 121.
[29] Others such as Crenshaw translate רעיון and רעות as "shepherding" in addition to "pursuit" or "feeding." See Crenshaw, *Old Testament Wisdom*, 128–29, 42; Peter J. Leithart, "Solomon's Sexual Wisdom: Qohelet and the Song of Songs in the Postmodern Condition," in *The Words of the Wise Are Like Goads: Engaging Qohelet in the Twenty-First Century*, ed. Mark J. Boda, Tremper Longman, and Cristian G. Rata (Winona Lake: Eisenbrauns, 2013), 450.
[30] Seow, *Ecclesiastes*, 122.
[31] Towner, "Ecclesiastes," 295.
[32] Michael Eaton, *Ecclesiastes: An Introduction and Commentary*, TOTC 18 (Downers Grove: InterVarsity, 1983), 74–75 (italics are original).

A common Samoan word for "wind" is *matagi*. As an Australian-Samoan, I am constantly variegated by the wisdom of my Samoan ancestors while living away from the homeland. When I hear the word *matagi*, I am reminded of its many nuances. One of those is depicted in the Samoan proverb: *E le falala fua le niu* which translates as "The coconut tree (*niu*) does not sway without cause." The implication in this proverb is that the coconut tree sways because of the wind (*matagi*). The proverb therefore speaks to the idea that everything has a reason.[33]

Another nuance of *matagi* is captured in the Samoan concept of *saili matagi* (searching for the wind) which means "looking for good fortune."[34] The idea that *matagi* means purpose therefore resonates with "good fortune" as this indeed provides the impetus for Samoans to migrate overseas. This idea of *matagi* as fortune echoes the ideals of *Maota Tau Ave* as mandated by the elders who remain in the homeland. As one *saili* (searches) for *matagi* (fortune) in other lands, the expectation is that there are riches and opportunities awaiting. According to *Maota Tau Ave*, success will come for the Samoan who carries their *maota* to new lands.

As they migrate to new lands, they struggle to compromise the old with the new. For instance, as Gershon explains:

> To hold a Samoan wedding, funeral, or to bestow a *matai* (chiefly) title, many people have to move resources (cash and commodities) from capitalist exchanges into Samoan ritual exchanges (*fa'alavelave*). Capitalist exchanges don't operate by the same principles as Samoan ritual exchanges, so that Samoans are constantly moving among two distinct and, on the surface, incompatible exchange systems.[35]

While Gershon highlights this dilemma for diasporic Samoans, constant moving between "incompatible exchange systems" reflects the hybrid experience in diaspora. Gershon explains in an interview with Samoan migrants that for Samoans,

> being a cultural person means participating in some form in Samoan ritual exchanges. By contrast, capitalist exchange is widely understood to be acultural. People are constantly involved in both forms of exchange relationships, they were frequently moving between exchanges they considered cultural and exchanges they considered acultural.[36]

In other words, Samoans have a hybrid understanding of money. This is particularly true in a diasporic context where the capitalist system of exchange seems

---

[33] Pemerika L. Tauiliili, *Anoafale O Le Gagana Ma Le Aganuu*, 2nd ed. (Keynes: AuthorHouse, 2010), 73.
[34] Va'a, *Saili Matagi*, 14.
[35] Gershon, *No Family*, 25.
[36] Gershon, *No Family*, 26.

economically viable, yet in the traditional Samoan exchange or *fa'alavelave*, the money given at times overwhelmingly outweighs what is received.[37]

Perhaps "chasing after wind" is more than just a pursuit of what is worthless. As an expression, it may also reflect Qohelet's frustration with how culture obstructs one's search for fortune. A diasporic context would be likely to generate this attitude. In other words, it is not that רוח (what is being pursued) itself is worthless, but that the *act* of pursuing רוח is being hindered. Eaton mentions another possible translation of the phrase as "ambition for the unattainable."[38] Why might it be unattainable? It may be that in a diasporic context, Qohelet observes that seeking רוח is impeded by cultural tension; between what is cultural and what is intercultural. Qohelet, like the Samoan migrant, may seem more inclined towards a hybrid position.

"UNDER THE SUN" AND "TOLOLA"

I here revisit Qohelet's saying תחת השמש "under the sun" as discussed in chapter 7. As mentioned there, the saying and its cognate expression found elsewhere in Ecclesiastes (1:3; 2:3; 3:1) refers to the "universality of human experience."[39] I note Seow's argument that "in the ancient Near East, the light of the sun is equated with life and its blessings, while the deprivation of its rays means death."[40] It has also been argued that the sun points to the divine realm or divine responsibility.[41]

But as Qohelet and I face each other inside the *maota*, I ask: why under the sun? Why not under the moon, the stars, or under the skies? Is there a preference for the daytime? I ask these questions because for Samoans, traditional folklore also points to the sun representing the divine; in other words, the sun represents the heavenly realm that constituted the creation of the world.

I thus recall one of our stories of creation: the tale of the sun and the woman.[42] In the story, the sun is attracted to a beautiful woman and begins a quest to court her and to win her affection. However, the woman is coy and repeatedly avoids the sun. Efi notes that the Samoan female name *Aloalolela* comes from this story, as "Samoans use the word aloalo to mean 'resisting

---

[37] See John R. Bond, and Faapisa M. Soli, "The Samoans," in *People and Cultures of Hawai'i: The Evolution of Culture and Ethnicity*, ed. John F. McDermott and Naleen Naupaka Andrade (Honolulu: University of Hawai'i Press, 2011), 244. Here, Bond and Soli write of the experiences of Samoans living in Hawai'i which are analogous to the experiences of Samoans in Australia. Cf. Va'a, *Saili Matagi*, 170.

[38] Eaton, *Ecclesiastes*, 75.

[39] Seow, *Ecclesiastes*, 104.

[40] Seow, *Ecclesiastes*, 105.

[41] See the discussion in chapter 7.

[42] See Tui Atua Tupua Tamasese Ta'isi Efi, "Whispers and Vanities in Samoan Indigenous Religious Culture," in *Whispers and Vanities: Samoan Indigenous Knowledge and Religion*, ed. Tamasailau M. Suaalii-Sauni et al. (Wellington, New Zealand: Huia, 2014), 45–46.

overtures'; in this case the overtures of the sun."[43] The woman, after a while, becomes attracted to the sun and agrees to be with him, which leads to an expedition to try and catch the sun. As she waits for the sun to set, the sun gets to a certain point where she is able to net him. After netting him, the woman gives herself to the sun and they engage in sexual intercourse, which delays the setting of the sun. The chiefly title *Tolola* from the village of Safune in Savaii, Samoa commemorates this delay, as *tolo* means delay while *la* refers to the sun. Consequently, "a child was born to the woman from her union with the sun. He was called Tagaloaui. According to the fagogo of the custodian, this child became one of the original forefathers of Samoa."[44]

The intriguing features of this story which may provide useful intertexts for Qohelet's idiom, are the important names that emerge from the tale. The first name, *Aloalolela* means resisting overtures of the sun. The name suggests that the sun is oppressive, intrusive and harsh. The name *Aloalolela* is therefore a name of resistance and perhaps resilience. When Qohelet's saying "under the sun" is read against *Aloalolela*, we are reminded of the harsh nature of the sun, especially for those who are toiling and being enslaved under the sun. That means that those who are "under the sun" are not enjoying it.

On the other hand, the name *Tolola* is not concerned with the harsh nature of the sun, but the picturesque nature of the sunset. Delaying the sunset, as the sun mates with the woman, is an attempt to savour the moment, but also suggests that one does not want the moment to end. Those who are "under the sun" in this instance are enjoying it and might even be experiencing romance.

What we gain from this tale are two sides of the sun, the cruel side which people try to avoid or *aloalo*, and the graceful side which people try to savour. These two sides point to the reality of the sun, but also to the reality of human nature: that there are times in which we feel like *aloalo* from what is harsh and oppressive, but also times we want to *tolo* what is good and peaceful.

For Qohelet then, "under the sun" might also be pointing to these human desires—that there are times we seek to *aloalo* from the sun, and there are also times we desire to *tolo* the sunset. In a metaphorical sense, there are times we want to escape curse and death, and there are also times we want to prolong blessings. Ironically, these desires might reflect attitudes of disgruntlement against the lived reality, where curses are being prolonged while blessings are minimal, especially if Qohelet "saw under the sun that in the place of justice, wickedness was there, and in the place of righteousness, wickedness was there as well" (Eccl 3:16). This might well constitute the "universality of the human experience."

---

[43] Efi, "Whispers and Vanities," 45.
[44] Efi, "Whispers and Vanities," 45. *Fagogo* refers to traditional Samoan folk stories.

"Hebel" and "Faatauvaa"

The final idiom commonly used by Qohelet is the term הבל. As discussed earlier, scholars are divided on the translation of the term. The ambiguity of its meaning could be viewed intertextually. As I sit across from Qohelet in the *maota*, I wonder if we have obsessed over trying to find the real meaning of הבל when perhaps understanding the term involves a web of different meanings in conversation. An intertextuality! I am reminded of the way conversation is practiced throughout Pasifika, which is through *talanoa*.

To provide a further nuance from a Samoan point of view, I emphasise the flexibility of the *talanoa* process. To recap, *talanoa* can be viewed etymologically as the construct of two words: *tala* and *noa*. The word *tala* means "story" or "conversation" and can also mean "to open up" whereby telling a story involves one "opening up." The word *noa* means "nothing" or "nakedness" but can also mean a place that is not specified. This latter meaning of *noa* which when combined with *tala*, implies a conversation that leads to no specified destination, because the motivation behind *talanoa* is that the conversation is ongoing but also as Havea implies, "fluid."[45]

I engage הבל, as used in Ecclesiastes, in *talanoa* with other meanings in order to maintain the fluidity of conversation. Fox states that "the *hebel* leitmotiv disintegrates if the word is assigned several different meanings."[46] But meaning does not disintegrate through *talanoa*, because *talanoa* allows for different voices to be heard. As the word implies, the conversation continues: into the *noa*.

I consider the Samoan translation of הבל: *faatauvaa*. The word *faatauvaa* is often taken to mean "insignificant, of no real worth or use, unimportant, trivial, inferior."[47] This is the common meaning, however, I am interested at how this meaning came about, because Samoan words are usually formed by constructs. Penehuro Fatu Lefale also notes that Samoan words often undergo a pattern of etymology, through observation.[48] For example, he points to the Samoan name for the constellation of stars known commonly as Belt of Orion. In that instance, Samoans observe the stellar pattern to resemble a person carrying coconuts, and thus give it the name *amoga* meaning "load" which refers to the load of coconuts carried. I follow this frame of thinking to deconstruct the word *faatauvaa* so as to ascertain its layers of meaning. This resonates with the flexibility and fluidity of *talanoa*.

---

[45] Jione Havea, "Diaspora Contexted: Talanoa, Reading, and Theologizing, as Migrants," *Black Theology* 11.2 (2013): 186.
[46] Fox, *Qohelet and His Contradictions*, 36.
[47] *Tusiupu Samoa: The Samoan Dictionary of Papaali'i Dr Semisi Ma'ia'i*, s.v. "Faatauva'a."
[48] Lefale, "*Ua 'Afa Le Aso*," 323–25.

The word *faatauvaa* is made up of two words, *faa* and *tauvaa*. The word *faa* is a "causative prefix that means 'to be'."[49] It can also mean "like" or "as." *Tauvaa* is a term used in Samoan fishing and refers to one who "remains in the boat." To provide context for *tauvaa*, there is a Samoan proverb: *e au i le tauola e au foi i le fagota* which translates as "one must become *tauola* before becoming a *fagota*." The phrase points to the usual father-son dynamic in Samoan fishing, specifically, the father who is *fagota* (fisher) and his son who has not matured yet to fish, but remains in the boat to hold the *ola* (fish basket) for the *fagota* to put the fish. The child here is called the *tauola* (holder of the fish basket). The lesson from this fishing proverb is the importance of patience in succession, that for one to become a *fagota*, one must first be a *tauola*. *Tauola* then is a position of observance and learning, before they eventually rise to the important and lifegiving role of *fagota*.

The word *tauvaa* is analogous to the *tauola*, while the term *fagota* represents the *tautai*. *Faatauvaa* therefore means "to be like a *tauvaa*," which implies that one has little or no knowledge or skill like the *tauvaa*. However, it also means that to be like a *tauvaa* does not mean that there is no hope, but that they are in a space of learning with anticipation that they too, after years of absorbing new knowledge and skills, will rise to be a fisher. Significantly, the *tauvaa* also acknowledges its humility before the *tautai*.[50] How *faatauvaa* has come to mean "inferior" or "unimportant" then, requires further probing.

Let me clarify. In the Samoan context, the most significant aspect of the *fa'a-Samoa* (the Samoan way) is *fa'aaloalo* (respect). One of the profound manifestations of *fa'aaloalo* is humility. Samoans are reluctant to receive praise and would much rather give credit to their colleague or even their opponent. This reflects the essence of humility in *fa'aaloalo*, that one lowers oneself before the other. In recognition of this fact, *faatauvaa* could imply that despite the significance of *tauvaa*'s role in attending to the boat and holding the *ola*, it acknowledges that the *tautai* holds greater importance. While the *tauvaa* enters an important learning stage, the term *faatauvaa* directs praise to the *tautai* who has come through the rigorous learning process of the *tauvaa*. *Faatauvaa* therefore is not so much defining insignificance, but a designation of *fa'aaloalo* towards others by lowering oneself.

In this *talanoa*, and from a Samoan perspective, הבל as *faatauvaa* could mean that Qohelet does not discard the importance of toiling (for instance), but that in the manner of *fa'aaloalo*, there are other aspects of one's life that deserve more attention. The idea of הבל as vanity could therefore seem ineffectual. Moreover,

---

[49] Latu Latai, "Changing Covenants in Samoa? From Brothers and Sisters to Husbands and Wives?," *Oceania* 85.1 (2015): 96.

[50] I must acknowledge with gratitude Lauvao Paulo Anetelea for his *talanoa* on the origins of *faatauvaa*.

the idea that הבל represents something "'worthless' is hard to reconcile with the theme of a worthwhile, immanent חלק [portion]."⁵¹ As Phillip Lasater contends,

> When the writer laments situations where somebody is not enabled by God to enjoy their חלק (see 5:17–6:6), the negative issue is not the worldly חלק itself, but rather being unable to *enjoy* it. Its own worthwhileness is not questioned.⁵²

Rather than worrying about one's toil and wealth, Qohelet prefers that the person "Go, eat your bread with enjoyment, and drink your wine with a merry heart; for God has long ago approved what you do" (Eccl 9:7).

TAUTUA AITAUMALELE AS QOHELET'S THIRD SPACE

Having considered Qohelet's *Maota* intertextually, through a hard Samoan intertextuality, it seems that Qohelet's arguments about life and his renegotiation of the terms of Jewish teachings and wisdom took place in a third space. Qohelet might well have carried his *maota* into a diasporic location, and from this space his voice of scepticism has emerged. Before proposing a way of rereading scepticism in Ecclesiastes, I draw further implications for understanding Qohelet's works, by implicating him as a *Tautua Aitaumalele*.

The voice of the *aitaumalele* has gained significant traction over the last three decades, as more Samoans migrate beyond its shores. Perhaps the evidence of this is seen in the current political climate in Samoa. Despite *aitaumalele* still having *monotaga* through their overseas *tautua*, they are yet being restricted from participating in the Samoan election due to COVID, but also because of the current policy where no absentee votes are allowed.⁵³ One must be registered and live in the country to vote. In spite of this, the voice of disdain towards the current government's policies has increased in diasporic communities, particularly over issues of health and education.⁵⁴ The voices of those who *tautua* in diaspora may consider the traditions and Samoan culture as important, but like my explanation of *faatauvaa*, perhaps not as important as more pressing issues that deserve immediate attention.⁵⁵ Diasporic Samoans ponder over this question, due to the third

---

⁵¹ Phillip Michael Lasater, "No So Vain After All: Hannah Arendt's Reception of Ecclesiastes," *JBRec* 6.2 (2019): 176.
⁵² Lasater, "Not So Vain," 176.
⁵³ Tahlea Aualiitia, and Toby Mann, "Samoa's Government May Be Facing the Biggest Challenge to Its Rule in Forty Years at April's Election," *ABC News—Pacific Beat* 2021, accessed 29 March 2021, https://www.abc.net.au/news/2021-02-14/samoa-hrpp-government-facing-strong-opposition-at-election/13069428.
⁵⁴ Aualiitia, and Mann, "Samoa's Government."
⁵⁵ Cf. Terry Pouono, "Replanting the Transplanted Christian Churches: Missio Dei and the Twenty-First Century Diaspora Samoan Church," *Stimulus: The New Zealand Journal of Christian Thought and Practice* 24.1 (2017): 4. Pouono argues that while the diaspora Samoan Church serves a vital function as a platform for learning the Samoan culture and language, the church should also serve as a prophetic voice for social issues and injustices.

space in which they exist. They may carry the *maota* but transplanting (*tauave*) the *maota* proves difficult and troublesome. As a result, attitudes of resistance and scepticism emerge in response to social injustices and the need for culture to be fluid in new contexts.[56]

Based on this discussion, I reimagine Qohelet (referring to what he did) as a *tautua aitaumalele*. Qohelet's *tautua* (2:4–8) represents that of the *aitaumalele*. Yet, his sceptical attitude towards various aspects of life, particularly his questioning of ancient Jewish wisdom and values, reveals that he also has concern for the homeland, and that he still has *monotaga* with his homeland. This is perhaps why Qohelet, like the *tautua aitaumalele*, shows scepticism, for he is still connected to the *fanua*, the *aiga*, and the *nuu*, but finds that the culture and wisdom is not fluid in diasporic contexts. Ironically, the fact that he is away from his *fanua*, his *aiga*, and his *nuu*, he is able to voice his concerns easily.

In sum, Qohelet's third space in his *Maota Tau Ave* can be expressed through *aitaumalele*. It is the transplanted space of the *tautua* who serves from afar, who uproots their *maota* from their homeland, and ventures out to new lands to resituate their *maota*. Yet it is also a space of tension, because while they are expected by their elders in the homeland to carry their *maota* into foreign territory, the *tautua aitaumalele* realises that relocating the *maota* on diasporic lands is problematic. This is the tension that *aitaumalele* experience with *Maota Tau Ave*, which might also be the tension that Qohelet faces.

REREADING SCEPTICISM IN ECCLESIASTES

Qohelet as *aitaumalele* exists in a third space, and it is a space of tension. When read this way, we may be able to highlight that Qohelet is in conversation with the rest of the Hebrew Bible. Initially, the process of *talanoa* from a diasporic Australian-Samoan perspective has allowed for these conversations to take place. Subsequently, *talanoa* has provided hermeneutical insights for reimagining and resituating Qohelet in a diasporic setting.

The *talanoa* with other Hebrew Bible texts and other intertexts also gives room to reconsider how we read scepticism in Ecclesiastes. Is it part of a walled-off specific class of wisdom literature? I think not. Here, I agree with Kynes in that highlighting scepticism—or any other of the book's themes—"to the detriment of the others will distort the meaning of both that theme and the entire book."[57] Rather, I see scepticism in a *talanoa* with other themes, as a way of viewing scepticism in relation to the whole. As such, it is unfruitful to limit scepticism to a concept within a separate wisdom tradition, because the intertextual framework has revealed new and meaningful insights into why Qohelet was sceptical.

---

[56] Pouono, "Replanting the Transplanted," 4.

[57] Kynes, *Obituary*, 217.

The resonance with the rest of the Hebrew Bible corpus is a testament to the diversity of Qohelet's worldview, which at the same time expands our horizons so that we may unearth Qohelet's complex weaving of the various textual strands. Scepticism is just one of those strands, but in *talanoa*, we need to *tala* (open up) Qohelet's fabric to see how scepticism connects, interacts and is in tension with the other strands. As Kynes argues, "reading the book as *sui generis* blinds readers to the colors Qoheleth weaves into his tapestry,"[58] or in Samoan terms, his mat.

In rereading scepticism, we are reminded of the tension of the *aitaumalele* who struggles to replant their *maota*, in other words, the *aitaumalele* struggles to fit in. This is a tendency of diasporic people, because they may not always experience a seamless transition, particularly if they are to uphold traditions and cultures of the homeland. So, they are in conflict, and it is not necessarily limited to being doubtful of their own traditions being practiced on foreign land, but they may also become cynical to assimilating into the new context. It may well be that Qohelet is an immigrant who struggled to fit within a foreign context.[59] Not only did Qohelet find issue with his own cultural and religious traditions, but he also found the practices of the new context הבל.

Qohelet is also a diaspora work in that as literature, the book struggles to fit into a particular genre. This may be an ideal way of reading Ecclesiastes: to read, as Dell and Kynes propose, intertextually or in conversation with the rest of the Hebrew Bible, but also by means of hard intertextuality, in line with my Samoan perspectives, rather than being confined to a single classification.

Conclusion

This book reconsidered Qohelet's social location and the place from where he raises his voice of scepticism. Based on *talanoa* with other texts in the Hebrew Bible which sought to draw out common religious and cultural concerns within a similar shared culture, it can be concluded that Qohelet was a member of the Jewish diaspora. The analysis also shows that potentially, it is from the diaspora that Qohelet is able to reveal his frustration with certain aspects of life, but also with wisdom discourse.

The diasporic tendencies in Ecclesiastes not only echo a diasporic social setting in tension with the homeland, but also Qohelet's tensions with other parts of Scripture. In this way, rather than being part of a literary genre of wisdom, it can be argued that Ecclesiastes is a book that critiques the teachings found in the rest of the Hebrew Bible, whereby the thought process is articulated through a diasporic worldview.

---

[58] Kynes, *Obituary*, 217.
[59] Cf. Kim, "Ruth vis-à-vis Esther," 20.

To draw out the diasporic attitudes in Ecclesiastes, a hermeneutic of *Maota Tau Ave* perceived the implicit notions of migration in the text, and envisaged Qohelet from an Australian Samoan vantage point as an author who carried his *maota* from his homeland to a diasporic location. As one carries their *maota* to foreign lands, there is bound to be tension and hostility over the conflict between traditional and contemporary values, as well as cultural and intercultural conventions. From this standpoint, it can be argued that Qohelet had a similar experience. Qohelet's *maota* may not have fit in with his diasporic location, and from this conflict comes his agitation.

This understanding not only has ramifications for interpreting Qohelet, but also for reading other texts that question the status quo. This study contends, much like Kynes, that Ecclesiastes might not belong to a particular wisdom genre after all. In fact, the intertextuality of Ecclesiastes reveals the diversity of the book's ideas that perceiving the whole text as wisdom literature seems highly restrictive. The intertextual allusions suggest links between Ecclesiastes and other traditions and thought patterns in the Hebrew Bible, which opens up new possibilities and alternatives in reading. Moreover, the analysis expands its intertextual framework beyond biblical sources to other cultural texts, as a way of accentuating these possibilities in reading and further highlighting the diasporic character of Ecclesiastes.

In turn, for the diasporic reader, I allow for reimagining one's own cultural mandates as they exist in foreign lands. As Qohelet questions his own cultural directives, one might also question the significance of *Maota Tau Ave*. Qohelet carries his *maota* in the following manner: he realises that there is importance in cultural and religious traditions but engages in *talanoa* with these traditions. As argued, *tau ave* is dialogical and continuous, and being dialogical is characteristic of diaspora. Qohelet reveals therefore that the *maota* is not a static platform in the diaspora, but one that constantly twists and turns and evolves through a critical and sceptical outlook.

Bibliography

Afutiti, Levesi Laumau. "Native Texts: Samoan Proverbial and Wisdom Sayings." Pages 53–67 in *Sea of Readings: The Bible in the South Pacific*. Edited by Jione Havea. SemeiaSt 90. Atlanta: SBL Press, 2018.

Airini, Melani Anae, and Karlo Mila-Schaaf. *Teu Le Va—Relationships across Research and Policy in Pasifika Education*. Ministry of Education, New Zealand: The University of Auckland, 2010.

Alama, Samasoni Moleli. "Jabez in Context: A Multidimensional Approach to Identity and Landholdings in Chronicles." PhD Thesis, University of Divinity, 2018.

Allen, Leslie C. *Ezekiel 1–19*. WBC 28. Dalls: Word, 1994.

Alter, Robert. "How Convention Helps Us Read: The Case of the Bible's Annunciation Type-Scene." *Prooftexts* 3.2 (1983): 115–30.

Amit, Yairah. "The Place of Exile in the Ancestors' Narratives and in Their Framework." Pages 131–148 in *The Politics of the Ancestors: Exegetical and Historical Perspectives on Genesis 12–36*. Edited by Mark G. Brett and Jakob Wöhrle. FAT 124. Tübingen: Mohr Siebeck, 2018.

Anae, Melani. "O A'u/I—My Identity Journey." Pages 89–101 in *Making Our Place: Growing up Pi in New Zealand*. Edited by Peggy Fairbairn-Dunlop and Gabrielle Sisifo Makisi. Palmerston North: Dunmore, 2003.

———. "Towards a NZ-Born Samoan Identity: Some Reflections on 'Labels.'" *Pacific Health Dialog* 4.2 (1997): 128–37.

Anderson, James S. "El, Yahweh, and Elohim: The Evolution of God in Israel and Its Theological Implications." *ExpTim* 128.6 (2017): 261–67.

Aualiitia, Tahlea, and Toby Mann. "Samoa's Government May Be Facing the Biggest Challenge to Its Rule in Forty Years at April's Election." *ABC News—Pacific Beat* 2021. Accessed 29 March 2021, https://www.abc.net.au/news/2021-02-14/samoa-hrpp-government-facing-strong-opposition-at-election/13069428.

Auva'a, Gataivai L. Nepo. "A Theological Study of 'Tautua' (Service) in the Light of the Christian Faith, with Special Reference to the Ministry of the Congregational Christian Church in Samoa." Pacfic Theological College, 1990.

Baker, Cynthia M. *Rebuilding the House of Israel: Architectures of Gender in Jewish Antiquity. Divinations: Rereading Late Ancient Religion.* Edited by Daniel Boyarin, Virginia Burrus, Charlotte Fonrobert, and Robert Gregg. Stanford: Stanford University, 2002.

Bal, Mieke. "Between Altar and Wondering Rock: Toward a Feminist Philology." Pages 211–31 in *Anti-Covenant: Counter-Reading Women's Lives in the Hebrew Bible*. Edited by Mieke Bal. Bible and Literature Series 22. Sheffield: Almond, 1989.

———. "Introduction." Pages 11–24 in *Anti-Covenant: Counter-Reading Women's Lives in the Hebrew Bible*. Edited by Mieke Bal. Bible and Literature Series 22. Sheffield: Almond, 1989.

Baldwin, Joyce G. *Esther: An Introduction and Commentary*. TOTC 12. Downers Grove: InterVarsity, 1984.

Barbour, Jennifer. *The Story of Israel in the Book of Qohelet: Ecclesiastes as Cultural Memory*. OTM. Oxford: Oxford University, 2012.

Barr, Lois Baer. "The Jonah Experience: The Jews of Brazil According to Scliar." Pages 33–52 in *The Jewish Diaspora in Latin America: New Studies on History and Literature*. Edited by David Sheinin and Lois Baer Barr. New York: Garland, 1996.

Barstad, Hans M. *The Myth of the Empty Land: A Study of the History and Archaeology of Judah During the 'Exilic' Period*. Symbolae Osloenses Sup 28. Oslo: Scandinavian University, 1996.

Bartholomew, Craig G. *Ecclesiastes*. Grand Rapids, MI: Baker Academic, 2009.

Barton, John. "*Déjà Lu:* Intertextuality, Method or Theory?" Pages 1–16 in *Reading Job Intertextually*. Edited by Katharine Dell and Will Kynes. LHBOTS 574. New York: Bloomsbury, 2013.

———. *Ethics in Ancient Israel*. Oxford: Oxford University, 2014.

Bedford, Peter R. *Temple Restoration in Early Acharmenid Judah*. Leiden: Brill, 2001.

Bendor, Shunya. *The Social Structure of Ancient Israel: The Institution of the Family (Beit 'Ab) from the Settlement to the End of the Monarchy*. Edited by Emunah Katzenstein. Jerusalem Biblical Studies 7. Jerusalem: Simor, 1996.

Bennett, Robert A. "Wisdom Motifs in Psalm 14 = 53—*Nābāl* and *'Ēsāh*." BASOR 220 (1975): 15–21.

Berger, Yitzhak. *Jonah in the Shadows of Eden*. Translated by Jonah in the Shadows. Bloomington: Indiana University, 2016.

Berlin, Adele. "On Writing a Commentary on Lamentations." Pages 3–11 in *Lamentations in Ancient and Contemporary Cultural Contexts*. Edited by Nancy Lee and Carleen Mandolfo. SBLSymS 43. Atlanta: Society of Biblical Literature, 2008.

Berlinerblau, Jacques. *The Vow and the 'Popular Religious Groups' of Ancient Israel: A Philological and Sociological Inquiry*. JSOTSup 210. Sheffield: Sheffield Academic, 1996.

Bernasconi, Rocco. "Meanings, Function and Linguistic Usages of the Term 'Am Ha-Aretz in the Mishnah." *Revue des Études Juives* 170.3–4 (2011): 399–438.

Bhabha, Homi K. *The Location of Culture*. London: Routledge, 1994.

———. "Signs Taken for Wonders: Questions of Ambivalence and Authority under a Tree Outside Delhi, May 1817." *Critical Inquiry* 12.1 (1985): 144–65.

Blagg, Harry, and Thalia Anthony. *Decolonising Criminology: Imagining Justice in a Postcolonial World. Critical Criminological Perspectives*. London: Palgrave Macmillan, 2019.

Blenkinsopp, Joseph. *Ezra-Nehemiah: A Commentary*. OTL. Philadelphia: The Westminster, 1988.

Bloch, Ariel, and Chana Bloch. *The Song of Songs: A New Translation with an Introduction and Commentary*. Berkeley: University of California, 1995.

Blum, Erhard. "The Jacob Tradition." Pages 181–211 in *The Book of Genesis: Composition, Reception, and Interpretation*. Edited by Craig A. Evans, Joel N. Lohr, and David L. Petersen. Leiden: Brill, 2012.

Bolin, Thomas. "The Temple of יהו at Elephantine and Persian Religious Policy." Pages 127–142 in *The Triumph of Elohim: From Yahwisms to Judaisms*. Edited by Diana Edelman. Kampen: Kok Pharos, 1996.

———. *Freedom Beyond Forgiveness: The Book of Jonah Re-examined*. JSOTSup 236. Sheffield: Sheffield Academic, 1997.

Bond, John R., and Faapisa M. Soli. "The Samoans." Pages 240–61 in *People and Cultures of Hawai'i: The Evolution of Culture and Ethnicity*. Edited by John F. McDermott and Naleen Naupaka Andrade. Honolulu: University of Hawai'i, 2011.

Botha, P. J. "Ironie as Sleutel Tot Die Verstaan Van Psalm 14." *Verbum et Ecclesia* 16.1 (1995): 16–27.

Bratcher, Robert G., and William David Reyburn. *A Translator's Handbook on the Book of Psalms*. UBS Handbook Series. New York: United Bible Societies, 1991.

Brekelmans, C. "Wisdom Influence in Deuteronomy." Pages 28–38 in *La Sagesse De L'ancien Testament*. Edited by M. Gilbert. BETL 51. Louvain: Louvain University, 1978.

Brett, Mark G. *Genesis: Procreation and the Politics of Identity*. London: Routledge, 2000.

———. "Interpreting Ethnicity: Method, Hermeneutics, Ethics." Pages 3–22 in *Ethnicity and the Bible*. Edited by Mark G. Brett. Boston: Brill, 1996.

———. *Locations of God: Political Theology in the Hebrew Bible*. New York: Oxford University, 2019.

———. "Whakawhiti Kōrero: Theology and Social Vocation." Pages 214–28 in *Holding Forth the Word of Life: Essays in Honor of Tim Meadowcroft*. Edited by John de Jong and Csilla Saysell. Eugene: Wipf & Stock, 2020.

———. "Yhwh among the Nations: The Politics of the Divine Names in Genesis 15 and 24." Pages 113–30 in *The Politics of the Ancestors: Exegetical and Historical Perspectives on Genesis 12–36*. Edited by Mark G. Brett, Jakob Wöhrle, and Friederike Neumann. Tübingen: Mohr Siebeck, 2018.

Brooker, Peter. *A Glossary of Cultural Theory*. 2nd ed. London: Arnold, 2003.

Bryce, Glendon E. "Better-Proverbs: An Historical and Structural Study." Pages 343–54 in *1972 Society of Biblical Literature Seminar Papers*. Edited by L. C. McGaughy. SBLSP 108. Missoula: SBL, 1972.

Buber, Martin. *I and Thou*. Translated by Ronald Gregor Smith. Edinburgh: T&T Clark, 1937.

Budd, Phillip J. *Numbers*. WBC 5. Dallas: Word, 1998.

Budde, Karl. "Psalm 14 Und 53." *JBL* 47 (1928): 160–83.

Burnett, Joel S. *Where Is God? Divine Absence in the Hebrew Bible*. Minneapolis: Fortress, 2010.

Burns, Alex, Suzanne Morton, and Migrant Resource Centre of Newcastle and Hunter River Region (N.S.W.). *Samoan People of Newcastle N.S.W.* Hamilton: Migrant Resource Centre, 1988.

Burton, Joan B. "Themes of Female Desire and Self-Assertion in the Song of Songs and Hellenistic Poetry." Pages 180–205 in *Perspectives on the Song of Songs/*

Perspektiven Der Hoheliedauslegung. Edited by Anselm C. Hagedorn. Berlin: de Gruyter, 2005.

Cartledge, Tony W. *Vows in the Hebrew Bible and the Ancient Near East*. JSOTSup 147. Sheffield: JSOT Press, 1992.

Chan, Michael J. "Joseph and Jehoiachin: On the Edge of Exodus." *ZAW* 125.4 (2013): 566–77.

Chapman, Cynthia R. *The House of the Mother: The Social Roles of Maternal Kin in Biblical Hebrew Narrative and Poetry*. New Haven: Yale University, 2016.

Cheyette, Bryan. *Diasporas of the Mind: Jewish and Postcolonial Writing and the Nightmare of History*. New Haven: Yale University, 2013.

Christensen, Duane L. *Deuteronomy 21:10–34:12*. WBC 6B. Dallas: Word, 2002.

Clayton, Jay, and Eric Rothstein. "Figures in the Corpus: Theories of Influence and Intertextuality." Pages 3–36 in *Influence and Intertextuality in Literary History*. Edited by Jay Clayton and Eric Rothstein. Madison: The University of Wisconsin, 1991.

Clements, Ronald E. "The Book of Deuteronomy." *NIB* 2:269–538.

Clifford, James. *Returns: Becoming Indigenous in the Twenty-First Century*. Cambridge: Harvard University, 2013.

Connell, John, and Grant McCall. *Islanders in the West: Pacific Island Migrants in Blacktown Local Government Area, Sydney*. Blacktown, NSW: Blacktown Migrant Resource Centre, 1989.

Craigie, Peter C. *Jeremiah 1–25*. WBC 26. Dallas: Word, 1991.

———. *Psalms 1–50*. WBC 19. Dallas: Word, 1983.

Crawford, Sidnie White. "The Book of Esther." *NIB* 3:853–942.

Crenshaw, James L. "Ecclesiastes." Pages 518–24 in *Harper's Bible Commentary*. Edited by J. Crenshaw and J. Willis. San Francisco: Harper & Row, 1988.

———. *Ecclesiastes: A Commentary*. OTL. Philadelphia: Fortress, 1987.

———. *Old Testament Wisdom: An Introduction*. 3rd ed. Louisville: Westminster John Knox, 2010.

———. "Prolegomenon." Pages 46-60 in *Studies in Ancient Israelite Wisdom*. Edited by James L. Crenshaw. LBS. New York: Ktav, 1976.

———. *Qoheleth: The Ironic Wink*. South Carolina: University of South Carolina, 2013.

Crouch, C.L. "Jehoiachin: Not a Broken Vessel but a Humiliated Vassal (Jer 22:28–30)." *ZAW* 129.2 (2017): 234–46.

Dahood, Mitchell. *Psalms I: 1–50: Introduction, Translation, and Notes*. AB 16. New Haven: Yale University, 2008.

Darr, Katheryn Pfisterer. "The Book of Ezekiel." *NIB* 6:1073–1607.

Davies, Philip. "Rough Justice?" Pages 43–56 in *Bible and Justice: Ancient Texts, Modern Challenges*. Edited by Matthew J. M. Coomber. London: Routledge, 2014.

Delkurt, Holger. *Ethische Einsichten in Der Alttestamentlichen Spruchweisheit*. Biblischtheologische Studien 21. Neukirchener: Neukirchen-Vluyn, 1993.

Dell, Katharine. "Exploring Intertextual Links between Ecclesiastes and Genesis 1–11." Pages 3–14 in *Reading Ecclesiastes Intertextually*. Edited by Katharine Dell and Will Kynes. LHBOTS 587. London: Bloomsbury, 2014.

———. *Interpreting Ecclesiastes: Readers Old and New*. Critical Studies in the Hebrew Bible 3. Winona Lake: Eisenbrauns, 2013.

Dell, Katharine, and Will Kynes. "Introduction." Pages xv–xxiii in *Reading Job Intertextually*. Edited by Katharine Dell and Will Kynes. New York: Bloomsbury, 2013.

———, eds. *Reading Ecclesiastes Intertextually*. LHBOTS 587. London: Bloomsbury, 2014.

———, eds. *Reading Job Intertextually*. LHBOTS 574. New York: Bloomsbury, 2013.

Doane, Sébastien, and Nathan Robert Mastnjak. "Echoes of Rachel's Weeping: Intertextuality and Trauma in Jer. 31:15." *BibInt* 27 (2019): 413–35.

Douglas, Mary. *Purity and Danger: An Anlysis of Concept of Pollution and Taboo*. Routledge Classics Edition. New York: Routledge, 2002.

Downs, David J. "The Specter of Exile in the Story of Jonah." *Horizons in Biblical Theology* 31 (2009): 27–44.

Eaton, Michael A. *Ecclesiastes: An Introduction and Commentary*. TOTC 18. Downers Grove: InterVarsity, 1983.

Efi, Tui Atua Tupua Tamasese Ta'isi. "O Samoa O Le Atunuu Tofi, E Lē Se Atunuu Taliola." Paper presented at the NUS Measina Conference, Samoa, 2012.

———. *Su'esu'e Manogi: In Search of Fragrance*. Edited by Tamasailau M. Suaalii-Sauni, I'uogafa Tuagalu, Tofilau Nina Kirifi-Alai, and Naomi Fuamatu. 2nd ed. Wellington: Huia Publishers, 2018.

———. "Whispers and Vanities in Samoan Indigenous Religious Culture." Pages 37–76 in *Whispers and Vanities: Samoan Indigenous Knowledge and Religion*. Edited by Tamasailau M. Suaalii-Sauni, Maualaivao Albert Wendt, Vitolia Mo'a, Naomi Fuamatu, Upolu Luma Va'ai, Reina Whaitiri, and Stephen L. Filipo. Wellington, New Zealand: Huia, 2014.

Eichrodt, Walter. *Ezekiel: A Commentary*. OTL. Philadelphia: Westminster, 2003.

Enns, Peter. *Ecclesiastes. The Two Horizons Old Testament Commentary*. Grand Rapids: Eerdmans, 2011.

Esposito, Thomas. "Echoes of Ecclesiastes in the Poetry and Plays of T.S. Eliot." *Logos* 24.2 (2021): 98–123.

Exum, J. Cheryl. *Song of Songs: A Commentary*. OTL. Louisville: Westminster John Knox, 2011.

Fager, Jeffrey A. *Land Tenure and the Biblical Jubilee: Uncovering Hebrew Ethics through the Sociology of Knowledge*. JSOTSup 155. Sheffield: Sheffield Academic, 1993.

Fairbairn, Ian. "Samoan Migration to New Zealand: The General Background and Some Economic Implications for Samoa." *The Journal of the Polynesian Society* 70.1 (1961): 18–30.

Fanon, Frantz. *The Wretched of the Earth*. Translated by Constance Farrington. New York: Grove Weidenfeld, 1991.

Feinstein, Eve Levavi. *Sexual Pollution in the Hebrew Bible*. Oxford: Oxford University, 2014.

Fidler, Ruth. "Qoheleth in "the House of God" Text and Intertext in Qoh 4:17–5:6 (Eng. 5:1–7)." *HS* 47 (2006): 7–21.

Foi'akau, Inise Vakabua. "Sipora (Zipporah), Both Native and Foreigner: A *Marama Itaukei* Reading of Exodus 4:24–26." Pages 117–30 in *Sea of Readings*. Edited by Jione Havea. Semeia Studies 90. Atlanta: SBL Press, 2018.

Fokkelman, J. P. *Narrative Art in Genesis: Specimens of Stylistic and Structural Analysis*. 2nd ed. Oregon: Wipf & Stock, 2004.
Fox, Michael V. *Ecclesiastes: The Traditional Hebrew Text with the New Jps Translation Commentary*. The JPS Bible Commentary. Philadelphia: The Jewish Publication Society, 2004.
———. "The Meaning of *Hebel* for Qohelet." *JBL* 105.3 (1986): 409–27.
———. *Proverbs 10–31: A New Translation with Introduction and Commentary*. AB 18B. London: Yale University, 2009.
———. *Qohelet and His Contradictions*. JSOTSup 71. Sheffield Almond, 1989.
———. *A Time to Tear Down and a Time to Build Up: A Rereading of Ecclesiastes*. Grand Rapids: Eerdmans, 1999.
Frankel, David. *The Land of Canaan and the Destiny of Israel: Theologies of Territory in the Hebrew Bible*. Siphrut 4. Winona Lake: Eisenbrauns, 2011.
———. *The Murmuring Stories of the Priestly School: A Retrieval of Ancient Sacerdotal Lore*. Leiden: Brill, 2002.
Fredericks, Daniel C. *Coping with Transience: Ecclesiastes on Brevity in Life*. The Biblical Seminar 18. Sheffield: JSOT Press, 1993.
———. *Qoheleth's Language: Re-evaluating Its Nature and Date*. Lewiston: Mellen, 1988.
Fretheim, Terence E. "The Book of Genesis." *NIB* 1:319–674.
Fried, Lisbeth S. "The 'Am Hā'āres in Ezra 4:4 and Persian Imperial Administration." Pages 123–45 in *Judah and the Judeans in the Persian Period*. Edited by Oded Lipschits and Manfred Oeming. Winona Lake: Eisenbrauns, 2006.
Geertz, Clifford. *The Interpretation of Cultures*. New York: Basic Books, 1973.
Gershon, Ilana. *No Family Is an Island: Cultural Expertise among Samoans in Diaspora*. Ithaca: Cornell University, 2012.
Gilroy, Paul. *Against Race: Imagining Political Culture Beyond the Color Line*. Cambridge MA: Harvard University, 2000.
———. *The Black Atlantic: Modernity and Double Consciousness*. London and New York: Verson, 1993.
Goldhill, Simon. *The Temple of Jerusalem*. Cambridge and Massachusetts: Harvard University, 2005.
Gomes, Jules Francis. *The Sanctuary of Bethel and the Configuration of Israelite Identity*. Berlin: de Gruyter, 2006.
Gottwald, Norman K. *The Tribes of Yahweh: A Sociology of the Religion of Liberated Israel 1250–1050 B.C.E.* Maryknoll: Orbis 1979.
Goulder, M. "Behold My Servant Jehoiachin." *VT* 52.2 (2002): 175–90.
Grabbe, Lester L. *Ezra-Nehemiah*. Old Testament Readings. London: Routledge, 1998.
———. "Intertextual Connections between the Wisdom of Solomon and Qoheleth." Pages 201–13 in *Reading Ecclesiastes Intertextually*. Edited by Katharine Dell and Will Kynes. London: Bloomsbury, 2014.
———. "The "Persian Documents" in the Book of Ezra: Are They Authentic?" Pages 531–70 in *Judah and the Judeans in the Persian Period*. Edited by Oded Lipschits and Manfred Oeming. Winona Lake: Eisenbrauns, 2006.

———. "The Reality of the Return: The Biblical Picture Versus Historical Reconstruction." Pages 292–307 in *Exile and Return: The Babylonian Context*. Edited by Jonathan Stökl and Caroline Waerzeggers. Berlin: De Gruyter, 2015.
Greenberg, Moshe. *Ezekiel 1–20*. AB 22. New York: Doubleday, 1995.
Grossman, Jonathan. *Esther: The Outer Narrative and the Hidden Reading*. Siphrut 6. Winona Lake: Eisenbrauns, 2011.
Gruen, Erich S. *Diaspora: Jews Amidst Greeks and Romans*. Cambridge, MA: Harvard University, 2002.
Gunkel, Hermann. "The Literature of Ancient Israel." Pages 26-83 in *Relating to the Text: Interdisciplinary and Form-Critical Insights on the Bible*. Edited by Timothy J. Sandoval and Carleen Mandolfo. JSOTSup 384. London: T&T Clark International, 2003.
Gunneweg, Antonius H. J. ""Am Ha'aretz"—a Semantic Revolution." *ZAW* 95.3 (1983): 437–40.
Gur-Klein, Thalia. *Sexual Hospitality in the Hebrew Bible: Patronymic, Metronymic, Legitimate and Illegitimate Relations. Gender, Theology and Spirituality*. Edited by Lisa Isherwood. London: Routledge, 2014.
Guyette, Fred. "Joseph's Emotional Development." *JBQ* 32.3 (2004): 181–88.
Hacham, Noah. "3 Maccabees and Esther: Parallels, Intertextuality, and Diaspora Identity." *JBL* 126.4 (2007): 765–85.
Hall, Stuart. "Cultural Identity and Diaspora." Pages 222–37 in *Colonial Discourse and Post-Colonial Theory: A Reader*. Edited by Patrick Williams and Laura Chrisman. London: Harvester Wheatsheaf, 1994.
———. *Familiar Stranger: A Life between Two Islands*. Durham: Duke University, 2017.
Hamilton, Victor P. *The Book of Genesis: Chapters 18–50*. NICOT. Grand Rapids: Eerdmans, 1995.
Havea, Jione. "Adjusting Jonah." *International Review of Mission* 102.1 (2013): 44–55.
———. "Bare Feet Welcome: Redeemer Xs Moses @ Enaim." Pages 209–22 in *Bible, Borders, Belonging(S): Engaging Readings from Oceania*. Edited by Jione Havea, David J. Neville, and Elaine M. Wainwright. SemeiaSt 75. Atlanta: SBL Press, 2014.
———. "Diaspora Contexted: Talanoa, Reading, and Theologizing, as Migrants." *Black Theology* 11.2 (2013): 185–200.
Havea, Jione, and Peter H. W. Lau, eds. *Reading Ecclesiastes from Asia and Pasifika*. IVBS 10. Atlanta: SBL Press, 2020.
Hawk, L. Daniel. "Strange Houseguests: Rahab, Lot, and the Dynamics of Deliverance." Pages 89–98 in *Reading between Texts: Intertextuality and the Hebrew Bible*. Edited by Danna Nolan Fewell. Louisville: Westminster John Knox, 1992.
Hundley, Michael B. *Gods in Dwellings: Temples and Divine Presence in the Ancient near East*. WAWSup 3. Atlanta: Society of Biblical Literature, 2013.
Hurowitz, Victor (Avigdor). *I Have Built You an Exhalted House: Temple Building in the Bible in Light of Mesopotamin and Northeast Semitic Writings*. Edited by David J. A. Clines and Philip R. Davies. JSOTSup 115. Sheffield: JSOT Press, 1992.
Ingram, Doug. *Ambiguity in Ecclesiastes*. LHBOTS 431. London: Bloomsbury, 2006.
———. "The Riddle of Qohelet and Qohelet the Riddler." *JSOT* 37.4 (2013): 485–509.
International Business Publications. *Samoa (American): Doing Business, Investing in Samoa (American) Guide—Strategic Information, Regulations, Contacts*. Washington, DC: International Business Publications, 2007.

Ishida, Tomoo. *History and Historical Writing in Ancient Israel: Studies in Biblical Historiography*. Leiden: Brill, 1999.

Janzen, David. "Gideon's House as the אטד: A Proposal for Reading Jotham's Fable." *CBQ* 74 (2012): 465–75.

Janzen, J. Gerald. "Qohelet on Life "under the Sun"." *CBQ* 70 (2008): 465–83.

Japhet, Sara. *I and II Chronicles: A Commentary*. Louisville: Westminster John Knox, 1993.

Jarick, John. "Ecclesiastes among the Comedians." Pages 176–88 in *Reading Ecclesiastes Intertextually*. Edited by Katharine Dell and Will Kynes. London: Bloomsbury, 2014.

Job, John B. *Jeremiah's Kings: A Study of the Monarchy in Jeremiah*. Aldershot, England: Ashgate, 2006.

Jonker, Louis C. *Defining All-Israel in Chronicles*. FAT 106. Tübingen: Mohr Siebeck, 2016.

———. *Reflections of King Josiah in Chronicles: Late Stages of the Josiah Reception in II Chr. 34f.* Gutersloh: Gütersloher Verlagshaus, 2003.

Kaminsky, Joel S. *Corporate Responsibility in the Hebrew Bible*. Sheffield: Sheffield Academic, 1995.

Keck, Elizabeth. "The Glory of Yahweh in Ezekiel and the Pre-Tabernacle Wilderness." *JSOT* 37.2 (2012): 201–18.

Kessler, John. "Persia's Loyal Yahwists: Power Identity and Ethnicity in Achaemenid Yehud." Pages 91–121 in *Judah and the Judeans in the Persian Period*. Edited by Oded Lipschits and Manfred Oeming. Winona Lake: Eisenbrauns, 2006.

Keys, Gillian. *The Wages of Sin: A Reappraisal of the 'Succession Narrative.'* Edited by David J. A. Clines and Philip R. Davies. JSOTSup 221. Sheffield: Sheffield Academic, 1996.

Kidner, Derek. *Psalms 1–72*. TOTC 15. Downers Grove: InterVarsity, 1973.

Kiernan, J.P. "Where Zionists Draw the Line: A Study of Religious Exclusiveness in an African Township." *Africa Studies* 33.2 (1974): 79–90.

Kim, Hyun Chul Paul. "Reading the Joseph Story (Genesis 37–50) as a Diaspora Narrative." *CBQ* 75.2 (2013): 219–38.

———. "Ruth Vis-À-Vis Esther: Reading Intertextually Ruth the 'Widow' and Esther the 'Orphan' as Diasporic 'Immigrants'." *The Korean Journal of Old Testament Studies* 74 (2019): 18–58.

Kim, Jimyung. *Reanimating Qohelet's Contradictory Voices: Studies of Open-Ended Discourse on Wisdom in Ecclesiastes*. Leiden: Brill, 2018.

Klein, Ralph W. "The Books of Ezra & Nehemiah." *NIB* 3:661–851.

Knoppers, Gary. *I Chronicles 1–9: A New Translation with Introduction and Commentary*. AB 12. New York: Doubleday, 2004.

———. *Jews and Samaritans: The Origins and History of Their Early Relations*. New York: Oxford University, 2013.

Knowles, Melody D. *Centrality Practiced: Jerusalem in the Religious Practice of Yehud and the Diaspora in the Persian Period*. ABS 16. Atlanta: Society of Biblical Literature, 2006.

Kolia, Brian Fiu. "'Arriving Like a Fish of the Night' ('Tō'ai faa-I'a le Pō'): An Australian-Samoan Diasporic Reading of Pāsah in Exod 12:12–13 through a Samoan fishing proverb." Pages 102–19 in *Reading the Bible in Australia*. Edited by Barbara Deutschmann, Deborah Storie, and Michelle Eastwood. Eugene: Wipf & Stock, 2024.

Kratz, Reinhard G. "The Second Temple of Jeb and of Jerusalem." Pages 247–64 in *Judah and the Judeans in the Persian Period*. Edited by Odel Lipschits and Manfred Oeming. Winona Lake: Eisenbrauns, 2006.

Kraus, Hans-Joachim. *Psalms 1–59*. A Continental Commentary. Minneapolis: Fortress, 1993.

———. *Theology of the Psalms: A Continental Commentary*. Translated by Keith Crim. Minneapolis: Fortress, 1992.

Kristeva, Julia. *Desire in Language: A Semiotic Approach to Literature and Art*. Translated by Thomas Gora, Alice Jardine, and Leon S. Roudiez. European Perspectives. New York: Columbia University, 1980.

———. *La Révolution Du Langage Poétique*. Paris: Éditions du Seuil, 1974.

Krüger, Thomas. "Die Rezeption Der Tora Im Buch Kohelet." Pages 303–25 in *Das Buch Kohelet: Studien Zur Strucktur, Geschichte, Rezeption Und Theologie*. Edited by Herausgegeben von Ludger Schwienhorst-Schönberger. Berlin: de Gruyter, 1997.

———. *Qoheleth: A Commentary*. Translated by O. C. Dean Jr. Hermeneia. Minneapolis: Fortress, 2004.

Kugel, James L. "Qohelet and Money." *CBQ* 51.1 (1989): 32–49.

Kynes, Will. "Follow Your Heart and Do Not Say It Was a Mistake: Qoheleth's Allusions to Numbers 15 and the Story of the Spies." Pages 15–27 in *Reading Ecclesiastes Intertextually*. Edited by Katharine Dell and Will Kynes. London: Bloomsbury, 2014.

———. "The Modern Scholarly Wisdom Tradition and the Threat of Pan-Sapientialism: A Case Report." Pages 11–38 in *Was There a Wisdom Tradition? New Prospects in Israelite Wisdom Studies*. Edited by Mark R. Sneed. AIL 23. Atlanta: SBL Press, 2015.

———. *An Obituary for "Wisdom Literature": The Birth, Death, and Intertextual Reintegration of a Biblical Corpus*. Oxford: Oxford University, 2019.

———. "The 'Wisdom Literature' Category: An Obituary." *The Journal of Theological Studies* 69.1 (2018): 1–24.

Lasater, Phillip Michael. "No So Vain after All: Hannah Arendt's Reception of Ecclesiastes." *JBRec* 6.2 (2019): 163–96.

Latai, Latu. "Changing Covenants in Samoa? From Brothers and Sisters to Husbands and Wives?" *Oceania* 85.1 (2015): 92–104.

Lefale, Penehuro Fatu. "*Ua 'Afa Le Aso* Stormy Weather Today: Traditional Ecological Knowledge of Weather and Culture, the Samoa Experience." *ClimC* 100.2 (2010): 317–35.

Leithart, Peter J. "Solomon's Sexual Wisdom: Qohelet and the Song of Songs in the Postmodern Condition." Pages 443–60 in *The Words of the Wise Are Like Goads: Engaging Qohelet in the Twenty-First Century*. Edited by Mark J. Boda, Tremper Longman, and Cristian G. Rata. Winona Lake: Eisenbrauns, 2013.

Levenson, Jon D. "The Last Four Verses in Kings." *JBL* 103 (1984): 353–61.

Levine, Baruch A. *Numbers 21–36: A New Translation with Introduction and Commentary*. AB 4A. New York: Doubleday, 2000.

Levine, Étan. "Justice in Judaism: The Case of Jonah." *The Review of Rabbinic Judaism* 5.2 (2002): 170–97.

Levinson, Bernard M. ""Better That You Should Not Vow Than That You Vow and Not Fulfull": Qoheleth's Use of Textual Allusion and the Transformation of Deuteronomy's Law of Vows." Pages 28–41 in *Reading Ecclesiastes Intertextually*. Edited by Katharine Dell and Will Kynes. London: Bloomsbury, 2014.

———. *Legal Revision and Religious Renewal in Ancient Israel*. New York: Cambridge University, 2008.

———. *A More Perfect Torah: At the Intersection of Philology and Hermeneutics in Deuteronomy and the Temple Scroll*. Winona Lake: Eisenbrauns, 2013.

———. "The Reconceptualization of Kingship in Deuteronomy and the Deuteronomistic History's Transformation of Torah." *VT* 51.4 (2001): 511–34.

Liedke, Gerhard. *Gestalt Und Bezeichnung Alttestamentlicher Rechtssätze: Eine Formgeschichtlich-Terminologische Studie*. WMANT 39. Neukirchen-Vluyn: Neukirchener Verlag, 1971.

Lilomaiava-Doktor, Sa'iliemanu. "Beyond "Migration": Samoan Population Movement (Malaga) and the Geography of Social Space (Vā)." *The Contemporary Pacific* 21.1 (2009): 1–32.

Llewellyn-Jones, Lloyd. *King and Court in Ancient Persia 559 to 331 BCE*. Edinburgh: Edinburgh University, 2013.

Lohfink, Norbert. *Qoheleth: A Continental Commentary*. Translated by Sean McEvenue. Minneapolis: Fortress, 2003.

Longman, Tremper. *The Book of Ecclesiastes*. NICOT. Grand Rapids: Eerdmans, 1998.

———. *Psalms: An Introduction and Commentary*. TOTC 15–16. Nottingham: Inter-Vartsity, 2014.

———. "Qoheleth as Solomon: 'For What Can Anyone Who Comes after the King Do?' (Ecclesiastes 2:12)." Pages 42–56 in *Reading Ecclesiastes Intertextually*. Edited by Katharine Dell and Will Kynes. London: Bloomsbury, 2014.

Louw, J. P., and Eugene A. Nida. *Greek-English Lexicon of the New Testament: Based on Semantic Domains*. New York: United Bible Societies, 1988.

Lundbom, Jack R. *Deuteronomy: A Commentary*. Grand Rapids: Eerdmans, 2013.

Ma'ia'i, Semisi. *Tusiupu Samoa: The Samoan Dictionary of Papaali'i Dr Semisi Ma'ia'i*. Vol. 1. Auckland: Little Island, 2010.

Macpherson, Cluny. "From Moral Community to Moral Communities: The Foundations of Migrant Social Solidairty among Samoans in Urban Aoteroa/New Zealand." *Pacific Studies* 25.1–2 (2002): 71–93.

Macpherson, Cluny, and La'avasa Macpherson. *The Warm Winds of Change: Globalisation in Contemporary Sāmoa*. Auckland: Auckland University, 2009.

Mariota, Martin Wilson. "Moses, Both Hebrew and Egyptian: A Samoan *Palagi* Reading of Exodus 2–3." Pages 103–16 in *Sea of Readings*. Edited by Jione Havea. Semeia Studies 90. Atlanta: SBL Press, 2018.

Marlow, Hilary. "Creation Themes in Job and Amos: An Intertextual Relationship?" Pages 142–54 in *Reading Job Intertextually*. Edited by Katharine Dell and Will Kynes. New York: Bloomsbury, 2013.

Matties, Gordon H. *Ezekiel 18 and the Rhetoric of Moral Discourse*. SBLDS 126. Atlanta: Scholars Press, 1990.

May, H.G. "The Book of Ezekiel." Pages 39–338 in *The Interpreter's Bible 6*. Edited by et al. G.A. Buttricke. New York: Abingdon, 1956.

McCann, J. Clinton. "The Book of Psalms." *NIB* 4:639–1280.
McConville, J. Gordon. "Forgiveness as Private and Public Act: A Reading of the Biblical Joseph Narrative." *CBQ* 75 (2013): 635–48.
McNutt, Paula M. *Reconstructing the Society of Ancient Israel*. Edited by Douglas A. Knight. LHBOTS. Louisville: Westminster John Knox, 1999.
Meek, Russell L. "Intertextuality, Inner-Biblical Exegesis, and Inner-Biblical Allusion: The Ethics of a Methodology." *Biba* 95.1 (2014): 280–91.
Mein, Andrew. *Ezekiel and the Ethics of Exile*. New York: Oxford University, 2001.
Meleisea, Malama. *Lagaga: A Short History of Western Samoa*. Suva, Fiji: University of South Pacific, 1987.
Melton, Brittany N. *Where Is God in the Megilloth? A Dialogue on the Ambiguity of Divine Presence and Absence*. Oudtestamentische Studiën. Leiden: Brill, 2018.
Meneses, Eloise Hiebert. "Bearing Witness in Rome with Theology from the Whole Church: Globalization, Theology, and Nationalism." Pages 231–49 in *Globalizing Theology: Belief and Practice in an Era of World Christianity*. Edited by Craig Ott and Harold A. Netland. Grand Rapids MI: Baker Academic, 2006.
Meyers, Carol. *Discovering Eve: Ancient Israelite Women in Context*. New York: Oxford University, 1988.
Milgrom, Jacob. *Numbers*. The JPS Torah Commentary. Philadelphia: The Jewish Publication Society, 1989.
Miller, Douglas B. "Qohelet's Symbolic Use of הבל." *JBL* 117 (1998): 437–54.
———. "Wisdom in the Canon: Discerning the Early Institution." Pages 87–113 in *Was There a Wisdom Tradition? New Prospects in Israelite Wisdom Studies*. Edited by Mark R. Sneed. AIL 23. Atlanta: SBL Press, 2015.
Miller, Geoffrey D. "Intertextuality in Old Testament Research." *CurBR* 9.3 (2011): 283–309.
Miller, Patrick D. "The Book of Jeremiah." *NIB* 6:553–926.
Mills, Mary. "Polyphonic Narration in Ecclesiastes and Jonah." Pages 71–83 in *Reading Ecclesiastes Intertextually*. Edited by Katharine Dell and Will Kynes. London: Bloomsbury, 2014.
Miscall, Peter D. "Isaiah: New Heavens, New Earth, New Book." Pages 41–56 in *Reading between Texts: Intertextuality and the Hebrew Bible*. Edited by Deanna Nolan Fewell. Louisville: Westminster John Knox, 1992.
Mishra, Vijay. *The Literature of Indian Diaspora: Theorizing the Diasporic Imaginary*. London: Routledge, 2007.
Motusaga, Mema. "Women in Decision Making in Samoa." PhD diss., Victoria University, 2016.
Mulitalo-Cheung, Tamari. "*E Lele Le Toloa 'Ae Ma'au I Le Vai*": *Toe Taliu Mai I Fanua Le 'Au Sa'ili Matagi*. National University of Samoa, 2008.
Mulitalo-Lauta, Pa'u Tafaogalupe. "Pacific Peoples' Identities and Social Services in New Zealand: Creating New Options." Pages 247–62 in *Tangata O Te Moana Nui: Evolving Identities of Pacific Peoples in Aotearoa/New Zealand*. Edited by Cluny Macpherson, Paul Spoonley, and Melani Anae. Palmerston North, NZ: Dunmore, 2001.
Murphy, Roland E. *Ecclesiastes*. WBC 23A. Dallas: Word, 1992.

———. "Ecclesiastes (Qoheleth)." Pages 534–40 in *Jerome Bible Commentary*. Edited by Raymond Brown, Joseph A. Fitzmyer, and Roland E. Murphy. Vol. 1. London: Prentice Hall, 1968.

Murray, Donald F. "Of All the Years the Hopes–or Fears? Jehoiachin in Babylon (2 Kings 25:27–30)." *JBL* 120 (2001): 245–65.

Nelson, Richard D. *Deuteronomy: A Commentary*. OTL. Louisville: Westminster John Knox, 2002.

Neuber, Carolin. "'Es Gibt Keinen Gott': Die Möglichkeit Der Gottesleugnung Und Das Gottesbild in Psalm 9/10; 14; 53." *PzB* 29 (2020): 26–46.

Nielsen, Kristin. *Ruth: A Commentary*. OTL. Louisville: Westminster John Knox, 1997.

Nofoaiga, Vaitusi. *A Samoan Reading of Discipleship in Matthew*. IVBS 8. Atlanta: SBL Press, 2017.

Ofo'ia, Numerator. "Revisiting the Babylonian Exile in Jeremiah 29:1–14: A Samoan Latō Reading using an Oceanic Hermeneutic." MTh Thesis, University of Otago 2017.

Ogden, Graham S. "The "Better"-Proverb (Tôb-Spruch), Rhetorical Criticism, and Qoheleth." *JBL* 96 (1977): 489–505.

Ogden, Graham S., and Lynell Zogbo. *A Handbook on Ecclesiastes*. UBS Handbook Series. New York: United Bible Societies, 1998.

———. *A Handbook on the Song of Songs*. UBS Handbook Series. New York: United Bible Societies, 1998.

Olson, Dennis T. "The Book of Judges." *NIB* 2:721–888.

Ostriker, Alicia. "Ecclesiastes as Witness: A Personal Essay." *The American Poetry Review* 34.1 (2005): 7–13.

Oswald, Wolfgang. *Staatstheorie Im Alten Israel: Der Politische Diskurs Im Pentateuch Und in Den Geschichtsbüchern Des Alten Testaments*. Stuttgart: Kohlhammer, 2009.

Otto, Eckart. ""Um Gerechtigkeit Im Land Sichtbar Werden Zu Lassen …": Zur Vermittlung Von Recht Und Gerechtigkeit Im Alten Orient, in Der Hebräischen Bibel Und in Der Moderne." Pages 107–45 in *Recht—Macht—Gerechtigkeit*. Edited by Joachim Mehlhausen. Gütersloh: Christian Kaiser, 1998.

Patton, Matthew H. *Hope for a Tender Sprig: Jehoiachin in Biblical Theology. Bulletin for Biblical Research Supplements*. Winona Lake: Eisenbrauns, 2017.

Pearce, Sarah Judith. "Pity and Emotion in Josephus's Reading of Joseph." *JBL* 133 (2014): 858–62.

Penchansky, David. "Staying the Night: Intertextuality in Genesis and Judges." Pages 77–88 in *Reading between Texts: Intertextuality and the Hebrew Bible*. Edited by Danna Nolan Fewell. Louisville: Westminster John Knox, 1992.

Peleg, Yitzhak (Itzik). *Going up and Going Down: A Key to Interpreting Jacob's Dream (Genesis 28:10–22)*. Translated by Betty Rozen. London: Bloomsbury T&T Clark, 2015.

Pouono, Terry. "Replanting the Transplanted Christian Churches: Missio Dei and the Twenty-First Century Diaspora Samoan Church." *Stimulus: The New Zealand Journal of Christian Thought and Practice* 24.1 (2017): 1–6.

Pratt, George. *A Grammar and Dictionary of the Samoan Language*. London: Trubner 1878.

Prentis, Brooke. "What Can the Birds of the Land Tell Us?" Pages 31–44 in *Grounded in the Body, in Time and Place, in Scripture: Papers by Australian Women Scholars in*

the Evangelical Tradition. Edited by Jill Firth and Denise Cooper-Clarke. Eugene: Wipf & Stock, 2021.
Preuss, Horst Dietrich. *Old Testament Theology*. Translated by Leo G. Perdue. Vol. 1. Lousiville: Westminster John Knox, 1995.
Pummer, Reinhard. *The Samaritans: A Profile*. Grand Rapids: Eerdmans, 2016.
Queen-Sutherland, Kandy. "Ruth, Qoheleth, and Esther: Counter Voices from the Megilloth." *Perspectives in Religious Studies* 43 (2016): 227–42.
Raboteau, Albert J. *Slave Religion: The "Invisible Institution" in the Antebellum South*. Updated ed. Oxford: Oxford University, 2004.
Ramantswana, Hulisani. "Not Free While Nature Remains Colonised: A Decolonial Reading of Isaiah 11:6–9." *OTE* 28.3 (2015): 807–31.
Rofé, Alexander. "An Enquiry into the Betrothal of Rebekah." Pages 27–39 in *Die Hebräische Bibel Und Ihre Zweifache Nachgeschichte: Festschrift Für Rolf Rendtorff*. Edited by Erhard Blum, Christian Macholz, and Ekkehard W. Stegemann. Neukirchen-Vluyn: Neukirchener Verlag, 1990.
Rogerson, John, and Philip R. Davies. *The Old Testament World*. New York: T&T Clark International, 2005.
Rogerson, John W. *Deuteronomy*. Eerdmans Commentary on the Bible. Grand Rapids: Eerdmans, 2003.
Roi, Micha. "Conditional Vows—Where They Are Made and Paid." *BN* 167 (2015): 3–24.
Römer, Thomas. "The Exodus in the Book of Genesis." *SEÅ* 75 (2010): 1–20.
Rosenberg, Gil. "כעת חיה: An Allusion Connecting Genesis 18:10, 14 and 2 Kings 4:16–17." *JBL* 139 (2020): 701–20.
Rothstein, Johann Wilhelm, and Johannes Hänel. *Kommentar Zum Ersten Buch Der Chronik*. Kat 18.2. Leipzig: Scholl, 1927.
Rudman, Dominic. "A Contextual Reading of Ecclesiastes 4:13–16." *JBL* 116 (1997): 57–73.
Ryan, Roger. *Judges. Readings: A New Biblical Commentary*. Sheffield: Sheffield Phoenix, 2007.
Safran, William. "Diasporas in Modern Societies: Myths of Homeland and Return." *Diaspora: A Journal of Transnational Studies* 1 (1991): 83–99.
Said, Edward. *Orientalism*. London: Penguin Books, 2003.
Sarna, Nahum M. *Genesis*. The JPS Torah Commentary. Philadelphia: JPS, 1989.
Sasson, Jack M. *Jonah: A New Translation with Introduction, Commentary, and Interpretation*. AB 24b. New Haven: Yale University Press, 2008.
Scholem, Gershom. "On Jonah and the Concept of Justice." *Critical Inquiry* 25 (1999): 353–61.
Schoors, Anton. "(Mis)Use of Intertextuality in Qoheleth Exegesis." Pages 45–49 in *Congress Volume: Oslo 1998*. Edited by A. Lemaire and M. Sæbø. VTSup 80. Leiden: Brill, 2000.
Schöpflin, Karin. "Political Power and Ideology in Qohelet." *BN-NF* 161 (2014): 19–36.
Sedgwick, Peter. "Essentialism." Pages 113–14 in *Cultural Theory: The Key Concepts*. Edited by Andrew Edgar and Peter Sedgwick. London: Routledge, 2008.
Segovia, Fernando. "Toward a Hermeneutics of the Diaspora: A Hermeneutics of Otherness and Engagement." Pages 57–73 in *Reading from This Place: Social Location and*

Biblical Interpretation in Global Perspective. Edited by Fernando Segovia and Mary Ann Tolbert. Vol. 2. Minneapolis: Fortress, 1995.

———. "Interpreting Beyond Borders: Postcolonial Studies and Diasporic Studies in Biblical Criticism." Pages 11–34 in *Interpreting Beyond Borders*. Edited by Fernando F. Segovia. The Bible and Postcolonialism 3. Sheffield: Sheffield Academic, 2000.

Seitz, Gottfried. *Redaktionsgeschichtliche Studien Zum Deuteronomium Bwant 93*. Stuttgart: Kohlhammer, 1971.

Selvén, Sebastian. "The Binding of Isaac in J.R.R. Tolkien and Stephen King." *BibInt* 28 (2020): 150–74.

Seow, Choon-Leong. "Beyond Mortal Grasp: The Usage of *Hebel* in Ecclesiastes." *Australian Biblical Review* 48 (2000): 1–16.

———. *Ecclesiastes: A New Translation with Introduction and Commentary*. AB 18c. New Haven: Yale University Press, 1997.

Shackleton, Mark. "Introduction." Pages ix–xiv in *Diasporic Literature and Theory—Where Now?* Edited by Mark Shackleton. Newcastle UK: Cambridge Scholars Publishing, 2008.

Sharp, Carolyn J. *Irony and Meaning in the Hebrew Bible*. Bloomington: Indiana University Press, 2009.

Shectman, Sarah. "Israel's Matriarchs: Political Pawns or Powerbrokers?" Pages 151–65 in *The Politics of the Ancestors: Exegetical and Historical Perspectives on Genesis 12–36*. Edited by Mark G. Brett, Jakob Wöhrle, and Friederike Neumann. Fat 124. Tübingen: Mohr Siebeck, 2018.

Shields, Martin A. *The End of Wisdom: A Reppraisal of the Historical and Canonical Function of Ecclesiastes*. Winona Lake: Eisenbrauns, 2006.

Simanu, Aumua Mataitusi, and Luafata Simanu-Klutz. *Sāmoan Word Book*. Honolulu: Bess, 1999.

Smith, Daniel L. *The Religion of the Landless: The Social Context of the Babylonian Exile*. Bloomington: Meyer-Stone Books, 1989.

Smith, Percy S. "Hawaiki: The Whence of the Maori." *Journal of the Polynesian Society* 7 (1898): 135–59.

Smith-Christopher, Daniel L. *A Biblical Theology of Exile. Overtures to Biblical Theology*. Minneapolis: Fortress, 2002.

———. "Introduction." Pages 11–22 in *Text and Experience: Towards a Cultural Exegesis of the Bible*. Edited by Daniel Smith-Christopher. The Biblical Seminar Supplement Series 35. Sheffield: Sheffield Academic, 1995.

———. *Jonah, Jesus, and Other Good Coyotes: Speaking Peace to Power in the Bible*. Nashville: Abingdon, 2007.

———. "Reading Jeremiah as Frantz Fanon." Pages 115–24 in *Jeremiah (Dis)Placed: New Directions in Writing/Reading Jeremiah*. Edited by A.R. Pete Diamond and Louis Stulman. Library of Hebrew Bible/Old Testament Studies 529. New York: T&T Clark, 2011.

Sneed, Mark R. "Is the 'Wisdom Tradition' a Tradition?" *CBQ* 73 (2011): 50–71.

———. *The Politics of Pessimism in Ecclesiastes: A Social-Science Perspective*. AIL 12. Atlanta: Society of Biblical Literature, 2012.

———, ed. *Was There a Wisdom Tradition? New Prospects in Israelite Wisdom*. AIL 23. Atlanta: SBL Press, 2015.

Sommer, Benjamin D. *A Prophet Reads Scripture: Allusion in Isaiah 40–66. Contraversions: Jews and Other Differences*. Stanford: Stanford University Press, 1998.

Southwood, Katherine E. *Ethnicity and the Mixed Marriage Crisis in Ezra 9–10: An Anthropological Approach*. Oxford: Oxford University Press, 2012.

———. "Will Naomi's Nation Be Ruth's Nation? Ethnic Translation as a Metaphor for Ruth's Assimilation within Judah." *Humanities* 3 (2014): 102–31.

Sparks, James T. *The Chronicler's Genealogies: Towards an Understanding of 1 Chronicles 1–9*. Atlanta: Society of Biblical Literature, 2008.

Spivak, Gayatri Chakravorty. "Can the Subaltern Speak?" Pages 66–111 in *Colonial Discourse and Post-Colonial Theory: A Reader*. Edited by Patrick Williams and Laura Chrisman. London: Routledge, 2013.

———. "Diasporas Old and New: Women in the Trasnational World." *Textual Practice* 10.2 (1996): 245–69.

———. "They the People: Problems of Alter-Globalization." *Radical Philosophy* 157 (2009): 31–36.

Stager, Lawrence E. "The Archaeology of the Family in Ancient Israel." *BASOR* 260 (1985): 1–35.

Stanley, Glenda, and Judith Kearney. "The Experiences of Second Generation Samoans in Australia." *Journal of Social Inclusion* 8.2 (2017): 54–65.

Strine, C.A. "Your Name Shall No Longer Be Jacob, but Refugee: Involuntary Migration and the Development of the Jacob Narrative." Pages 51–69 in *Scripture as Social Discourse: Social-Scientific Perspectives on Early Jewish and Christian Writings*. Edited by Jessica M. Keady, Todd E. Klutz, and C. A. Strine. London: T&T Clark, 2018.

Stuart, Douglas. *Hosea-Jonah*. WBC 31. Dallas: Word, 1987.

Su'a-Tavila, Aliitasi. "Contemporary Pacific Values and Beliefs." Pages 25–33 in *Pacific Social Work: Navigating Practice, Policy and Research*. Edited by Jioji Ravulo, Tracie Mafile'o, and Donald Bruce Yeates. New York: Routledge, 2019.

Sweeney, Marvin A. *I and II Kings: A Commentary*. OTL. Louisville: Westminster John Knox, 2007.

Talstra, Eep. "The Name in Kings and Chronicles." Pages 55–70 in *The Revelation of the Name Yhwh to Moses: Perspectives from Judaism, the Pagan Graeco-Roman World, and Early Christianity*. Edited by George H. van Kooten. Leiden: Brill, 2006.

Tauiliili, Pemerika L. *Anoafale O Le Gagana Ma Le Aganuu*. 2nd ed. Keynes: AuthorHouse, 2010.

Tcherkézoff, Serge. *'First Contacts' in Polynesia: The Samoan Case (1722–1848): Western Misunderstandings About Sexuality and Divinity*. Canberra: ANU E Press, 2004.

Thiselton, Anthony C. *New Horizons in Hermeneutics: The Theory and Practice of Transforming Biblical Reading*. Grand Rapids: Zondervan, 1992.

Tigay, Jeffrey H. *Deuteronomy: The Traditional Hebrew Text with the New JPS Translation*. Edited by Nahum M. Sarna. The JPS Torah Commentary. Philadelphia: The Jewish Publication Society, 1996.

Tilburg, Hans K. Van, David J. Herdrich, Michaela E. Howells, Va'amua Henry Sesepasara, Telea'i Christian Ausage, and Michael D. Coszalter. "Row as One! A History of the Development and Use of the Sāmoan *Fautasi*." *Journal of the Polynesian Society* 127.1 (2018): 111–36.

Tiňo, Jozef. *King and Temple in Chronicles: A Contextual Approach to Their Relations*. Göttingen: Vandenhoeck & Reuprecht, 2010.

Tita, Hubert. "Ist Die Thematische Einheit Koh 4,17–5,6 Eine Anspielung Auf Die Salomoerzählung? Aporien Der Religionskritischen Interpretation." *BN* 84 (1996): 87–102.

Tominiko, Seulupe Falaniko, Lupematasila Misatauveve Melani Anae, Muliagatele Vavao, and Malepeai Ieti Lima. "The Transnational Matai and the Foreign Homeland: Does the Toloa Still Return to the Water." Paper presented at the 7th Measina Sāmoa Conference, NUS Fale Samoa, 2016.

Tomlinson, Matt. "Talanoa as Dialogue and PTC's Role in Creating Conversation." *Pacific Journal of Theology* 2/59 (2020): 35–46.

Torres, Amaryllis Tiglao. "Women's Education as an Instrument for Change: The Case of the Philippines." Pages 105–20 in *The Politics of Women's Education: Perspectives from Asia, Africa, and Latin America*. Edited by Jill Ker Conway and Susan C. Bourque. Ann Arbor: The University of Michigan Press, 1995.

Towner, W. Sibley. "The Book of Ecclesiastes." *NIB* 5:265–360.

Trible, Phyllis. "The Book of Jonah." *NIB* 7:461–530.

Trlin, A. D. "Attitudes Towards West Samoan Immigrants in Auckland, New Zealand." *The Australian Quarterly* 44.3 (1972): 49–57.

Trotter, Jonathan R. *The Jerusalem Temple in Diaspora Jewish Practice and Thought During the Second Temple Period*. Leiden: Brill, 2019.

Tull, Patricia. "Intertextuality and the Hebrew Scriptures." *CurBS* 8 (2000): 59–90.

Tuplin, Christopher. *Achaemenid Studies*. Historia Einzelschriften 99. Stuttgart: Franz Steiner Verlag, 1996.

Turner, Marie. *Ecclesiastes: Qoheleth's Eternal Earth*. Earth Bible Commentary. London: Bloomsbury, 2017.

Va'a, Felise. *Saili Matagi: Samoan Migrants in Australia*. Fiji: ISP, 2001.

———. "Searching for the Good Life: Samoan International Migration." Paper presented at the Department of Anthropology Colloquium, University of Hawaii, Honolulu, 27 January, 2005.

Vaka'uta, Nāsili. *Reading Ezra 9–10 Tu'a-Wise: Rethinking Biblical Interpretation in Oceania*. Atlanta: Society of Biblical Literature, 2011.

van der Toorn, Karel. "Yahweh." Pages 910–19 in *Dictionary of Deities and Demons in the Bible*. Edited by Karel van der Toorn, Bob Becking, and Pieter W. van der Horst. Leiden: Brill, 1999.

von Rad, Gerhard. *Das Geschichtsbild Des Chronistischen Werkes*. BWANT 54. Stuggart: Kohlhammer, 1930.

———. *Deuteronomium-Studien*. FRLANT 40. Göttingen: Vandenhoeck & Ruprecht, 1947.

———. *Deuteronomy: A Commentary*. Translated by Dorothea Barton. OTL. Philadelphia: Westminster, 1966.

Waqa, Mariana. "Sophia, Untameable Like Moana: An Oceanic Reading of Sirach 24 with Ecclesiastes 7:10–12." Pages 85–98 in *Reading Ecclesiastes from Asia and Pasifika*. Edited by Jione Havea and Peter H.W. Lau. IVBS 10. Atlanta: SBL Press, 2020.

Webb, Barry G. *The Book of the Judges: An Integrated Reading*. JSOTSup 46. Sheffield: Shefiield Academic, 1987.

Weeks, Stuart. *Ecclesiastes and Sceptism*. New York: T&T Clark International, 2012.
———. *An Introduction to the Study of Wisdom Literature*. New York: T&T Clark, 2010.
Weinberg, Joel. *The Citizen-Temple Community*. Translated by Daniel L. Smith-Christopher. JSOTSup 151. Sheffield: JSOT Press, 1992.
Weinfeld, Moshe. *Deuteronomy and the Deuteronomic School*. Winona Lake: Eisenbrauns, 1972.
———. "Instructions for Temple Visitors in the Bible and in Ancient Egypt." *ScrHier* 28 (1982): 224–50.
Wenham, Gordon J. *Genesis 16–50*. WBC 2. Dallas: Word, 1994.
Wetter, Anne-Mareike. *"On Her Account": Reconfiguring Israel in Ruth, Esther, and Judith*. London: Bloomsbury, 2015.
Wevers, John William. *Ezekiel*. NCB. Greenwood: Attic, 1969.
White, Sidnie Ann. "Esther: A Feminine Model for Jewish Diaspora." Pages 161–77 in *Gender and Difference in Ancient Israel*. Edited by Peggy L. Day. Minneapolis: Fortress, 1989.
Whybray, R. N. *Ecclesiastes*. OTG. Sheffield: Sheffield Academic, 1989.
Williamson, H. G. M. "Ezra and Nehemiah." Pages 426–41 in *New Bible Commentary: First Century Edition*. Edited by D. A. Carson, R. T. France, J. A. Motyer, and G. J. Wenham. Downers Grove: Inter-Varsity, 1994.
———. *Ezra-Nehemiah*. WBC 16. Dallas: Word, 1985.
Wilson, Gerald H. "The Words of the Wise: The Intent and Significance of Qoheleth 12:9–14." *JBL* 103 (1984): 175–92.
Wilson, Ian D. "Joseph, Jehoiachin, and Cyrus: On Book Endings, Exoduses and Exiles, and Yehudite/Judean Social Remembering." *ZAW* 126.4 (2014): 521–34.
———. *Kingship and Memory in Ancient Judah*. New York: Oxford University Press, 2017.
Wilson-Wright, Aren M. "Bethel and the Persistence of El: Evidence for the Survival of El as an Independent Deity in the Jacob Cycle and 1 Kings 12:25–30." *JBL* 138 (2019): 705–20.
Wolff, Hans Walter. *Obadiah and Jonah: A Continental Commentary*. Minneapolis: Augsburg, 1986.
Wolter, Michael. *Theologie Und Ethos Im Frühen Christentum*. WUNT 236. Tübingen: Mohr Siebeck, 2009.
Wright, Jacob L. *Rebuilding Identity: The Nehemiah-Memoir and Its Earliest Readers*. Berlin rk: de Gruyter, 2004.
Yee, Gale A. "'She Stood in Tears Amid the Alien Corn': Ruth, the Perpertual Minority and Model Minority." Pages 119–40 in *They Were All Together in One Place? Toward Minority Biblical Criticism*. Edited by Randall C. Bailey, Tat-siong Benny Liew, and Fernando F. Segovia. Leiden: Brill, 2009.
Young, Ian. "Concluding Reflections." Pages 312–17 in *Biblical Hebrew: Chronology and Typology*. Edited by Ian Young. JSOTSup 369. Sheffield: Sheffield Academic, 2003.
———. *Diversity in Pre-exilic Hebrew* Tübingen: Mohr Siebeck 1993.
———. "Late Biblical Hebrew and Hebrew Inscriptions." Pages 276–311 in *Biblical Hebrew: Chronology and Typology*. Edited by Ian Young. JSOTSup 369. Sheffield: Sheffield Academic, 2003.

Young, Ian, Robert Rezetko, and Martin Ehrensvärd. *An Introduction to Approaches and Problems.* Vol. 1 of *Linguistic Dating of Biblical Texts.* London: Routledge, 2014.

Zimmerli, Walther. *Ezekiel: A Commentary on the Book of the Prophet Ezekiel.* Translated by R. E. Clements. Hermeneia 26. Philadelphia: Fortress, 1979.

———. "Ort Und Grenze Der Weisheit Im Rahmen Der Alttestamentlichen Theologie." Pages 129–36 in *Les Sagesses Du Proche-Orient Ancien.* Paris: Presses Universitaires de France, 1963.

———. "Zur Struktur Der Alttestamentlichen Weisheit." *ZAW* 51 (1933): 177–204.

Scripture Index

Hebrew Bible/Old Testament
Genesis
- 1 — 34
- 1–11 — 38
- 2:7 — 39
- 3:19 — 39
- 7:1 — 53
- 12 — 63, 66
- 16 — 145
- 18:10 — 38
- 18:14 — 38
- 19 — 37
- 19:1–29 — 37
- 20 — 63
- 22 — 41–42
- 22:1 — 42
- 22:20–24 — 58
- 23 — 58
- 24 — 37, 58, 60, 63, 66
- 24:15 — 58
- 24:24 — 58
- 24:28 — 54, 57
- 24:38 — 54
- 24:47 — 58
- 26 — 63
- 28 — 122, 124
- 28:10–22 — 122, 124–25, 134
- 28:13 — 124
- 28:14 — 122, 124
- 28:15 — 124
- 28:16 — 123
- 28:19 — 118
- 28:20–22 — 124
- 31 — 65
- 34 — 61, 64
- 34:17 — 62
- 34:31 — 62
- 35 — 122, 124–25
- 35:9–15 — 124–25, 133
- 45:4–5 — 141
- 45:5 — 142
- 47:21 — 144–45, 152
- 50 — 143
- 50:8 — 53
- 50:15 — 143
- 50:20 — 142–43

Exodus
- 2–3 — 44
- 3 — 43, 119
- 3:12 — 119
- 16:10 — 131
- 18:1–6 — 44
- 34:9 — 149

Leviticus
- 18:20 — 132
- 26 — 155

Numbers
- 5:14 — 132
- 5:20 — 132
- 5:27–29 — 132
- 14:1–4 — 103
- 14:4 — 103
- 14:12 — 104
- 15:39 — 39
- 16 — 104

Deuteronomy		8:22	40
4:27–28	90	8:55	40
5:9–10	139	8:65	40
6:4–5	118		
7:10	139	2 Kings	
11:17	139	4:16–17	38
14:22–26	53	17:21–23	91
19–25	129	21:1–17	91
23:21	121	25:27–30	110
23:21–23	126, 126, 128		
23:22	128–30	1 Chronicles	
23:22 [MT]	121, 127–29, 130	3:17–18	111
23:22–24 [MT]	5, 126–27, 129	6:33	118
23:23 [MT]	127–28, 130	11:3	112
23:24 [MT]	128	28:4	112
28	155		
28:25 [LXX]	10	2 Chronicles	
		36	100, 112
Joshua		36:3	112–13
2:1–24	37	36:4	112–13
6:22–25	37	36:6	112–13
		36:10	113
Judges		36:13	113
6:27	53	36:23	120
9	55		
9:18	53, 55	Ezra	
11:2–11	53	1:2	120
14:15	53	4:1	105
14:19	53	4:2	106
16:31	53	4:3	105
18:31	118	4:4	105–6
		4:5	107
Ruth		4:6	108
1:8	54, 59	4:6–24	105
		4:24	105
1 Samuel		5:11–12	120
2:27–33	53	6	107
17:25	53	6:9–10	120
22:1	53	7:12	120
25:25	146	7:21	120
		7:23	120
1 Kings		9	105
8	39, 120	9–10	107
8:1	40		
8:2	40	Nehemiah	
8:14	40	1:4	120

1:5	120	20:22	90
2	107	24:12	90
2:4	120	25:21	90
2:20	120	27:16	165
		30:4	165

Job

6:26	165	Ecclesiastes	
8:2	165	1	45, 46
9:5	36	1:1	99, 100, 115
9:5–10	36	1:2	48
9:7	36	1:3	1, 167
12:5	36	1:6	45
15:2	165	1:14	48
16:3	165	1:18	48
		2–6	40

Psalms

2:4	120, 145, 137, 141, 145–48, 152–53, 155	2:3	167
		2:4–8	172
14:1	145–46, 149–50	2:18–23	1, 26
14:1–6	148	2:22–23	99
14:2	147–48	2:24–26	99
14:4	146–47	3	45
14:5	146–48	3:1	167
14:5–6	153	3:11	45–46
14:6	147	3:12–13	99
14:7	147–48, 151–52, 159	3:16	168
33:13–14	120	3:20	39
53	150	4:13	100–101
63:1	43	4:13–14	102
63:3	43	4:13–16	100, 114–15
103:19	120	4:14	101
115:2	120	4:15–16	102
115:3	121	4:16	102, 108, 116
123:1	120	4:17	70
137	11	4:17 [MT]	135
		4:17–5:6 [MT]	134

Proverbs

		5	70
1:20–21	2	5:1	135
10:6	90	5:1–2	117
11:29	165	5:1–6	70
11:31	90	5:1–7	117, 134
12:2	90	5:2	120, 136
13:21	90	5:3	129
16:5	90	5:4	125, 129–30
18:10	90	5:4–5	121
19:17	90	5:4–6	128
		5:5	134, 136

5:7	70	Ezekiel	
5:8–20	1	1–24	132
5:17–6:6	171	6	132
7:15	47	8–11	130
8:10	139	10	5, 130
8:11	138–39, 153–54	10:1–2	130
8:12–13	138	10:2	131
8:14	1, 47, 137–40, 144, 149, 152	11:1	131
8:15	46	18	132
8:16	139	18:6	132
8:17	139–40	18:10	132
9:7	171	18:15	132
9:7–10	96		
10:8	46	Daniel	
11:9	39	2:18–19	120
11:9	39	2:37	120
12	7	2:44	120
12:7	39		
		Hosea	
Song of Songs		8:8	109
1:6	60		
3:4	54, 60	Amos	
7:1	63	5:8	36
8:1–2	60	8:9	36
8:2	54		
		Jonah	
Isaiah		1:2	149–50
3:6	53	1:9	120
41:29	165	3:3–5	150
65:17	35	3:4	150
66:22	35	4:2	149
Jeremiah		Micah	
18:18	2	6:8	144
22	108		
22:11	108	Haggai	
22:24	108	2:4	107
22:28	108–9		
27–28	88	Zechariah	
27:1–29:23 [LXX]	110	7:5	107
29:4–7	91		
29:5	11	Deuterocanonical Books	
29:7	11	Sirach	
48:38	109	24	47
		24:2–3	48

Modern Authors Index

Afutiti, Levesi	44
Airini	23–24
Alama, Samasoni Moleli	114
Allen, Leslie C.	133–34
Amit, Yairah	125–26
Anae, Melani	14, 23–24, 26, 106, 162
Anderson, James S.	120
Anthony, Thalia	81, 83
Auva'a, Gataivai L. Nepo	165
Baker, Cynthia M.	53
Bal, Mieke	33
Barbour, Jennifer	50
Barr, Lois Baer	155
Barstad, Hans M.	135
Bartholomew, Craig G.	72, 102, 123
Barton, John	3, 30–32, 42, 145, 147, 149, 159
Bedford, Peter R.	109
Bendor, Shunya	53, 55
Bennett, Robert A.	150
Berger, Yitzhak	154
Berlin, Adele	152
Berlinerblau, Jacques	127
Bernasconi, Rocco	107
Bhabha, Homi K.	24, 73, 76–77, 162
Blagg, Harry	81, 83
Bloch, Ariel	63
Bloch, Chana	63
Blum, Erhard	126–27
Bolin, Thomas M.	122, 155
Bond, John R.	171
Botha, PJ	150–52
Bratcher, Robert G.	151–52
Brekelmans, C.	129
Brett, Mark G.	20, 21, 60, 68, 110, 122, 124, 133, 159
Brooker, Peter	20
Bryce, Glendon E.	103
Buber, Martin	166
Budd, Phillip J.	106
Budde, Karl	50
Burnett, Joel S.	149
Burton, Joan B.	63
Cartledge, Tony W.	127–28, 132, 138
Chan, Michael J.	113
Chapman, Cynthia	10, 53–54, 56, 59–65, 68, 70
Cheyette, Bryan	21
Christensen, Duane L.	129
Clayton, Jay	32
Clements, Ronald E.	128
Clifford, James	74, 79, 80
Craigie, Peter C.	111, 150, 151
Crenshaw, James L.	2, 7–8, 71, 103, 143, 167, 169
Crouch, C. L.	111
Dahood, Mitchell	149
Davies, Philip R.	56, 153, 155–56
Delkurt, Holger	145
Dell, Katharine J.	31–32, 39–40, 137, 167
Doane, Sébastien	30
Downs, David J.	155
Eaton, Michael	169, 171
Efi, Tui Atua Tupua Tamasese Ta'isi	68, 166, 171–72
Eichrodt, Walter	135
Enns, Peter	101–2
Esposito, Thomas	46–47

Fairbairn, Ian	13–14	Kim, Hyun Chul Paul	38–39, 146–48, 177
Fanon, Frantz	73, 77–78		
Feinstein, Eve Levavi	64	Klein, Ralph W.	109–10
Fidler, Ruth	50, 120, 125–26, 137	Knoppers, Gary	116, 121
Foi'akau, Inise Vakabua	45	Knowles, Melody D.	121, 123
Fokkelman, J. P.	124	Kratz, Reinhard G.	110
Fox, Michael V.	2, 8, 10, 72, 101, 103–4, 142, 150, 168, 173	Kraus, Hans-Joachim	152
		Kristeva, Julia	29, 30, 169
Frankel, David	68, 105, 106	Krüger, Thomas	101, 130, 142–44
Fredericks, Daniel C.	168	Kugel, James L.	101
Fretheim, Terence	124–25, 146	Kynes, Will	2–3, 31–32, 39–40, 50–51, 158, 176–77
Fried, Lisbeth S.	108–9		
Geertz, Clifford	19–21, 24	Lasater, Phillip Michael	175
Gershon, Ilana	164, 170	Latai, Latu	174
Gilroy, Paul	74, 78–79, 106	Lefale, Penehuro Fatu	34, 173
Gomes, Jules Francis	54	Leithart, Peter J.	169
Goldhill, Simon	54	Levine, Baruch A.	55–57
Gottwald, Norman K.	55	Levine, Étan	153, 155
Goulder, M.	111	Levinson, Bernard M.	51, 93, 129–32, 143, 157
Grabbe, Lester L.	92, 107–9		
Greenberg, Moshe	134	Liedke, Gerhard	130
Gruen, Erich S.	11	Lilomaiava-Doktor, Sa'iliemanu	163
Gunkel Hermann	2	Lohfink, Norbert	72
Gunneweg, Antonius H. J.	108–9	Longman, Tremper	41, 150
Gur-Klein, Thalia	56	Lundbom, Jack R.	129
Guyette, Fred	148	McCann, J. Clinton	150, 151
Hacham, Noah	39, 42	McConville, J. Gordon	145
Hall, Stuart	22, 73, 75	McNutt, Paula M.	55
Hamilton, Victor P.	125	Macpherson, Cluny	14–15, 17, 162
Hänel, Johannes	113	Macpherson, La'avasa	14–15, 17
Havea, Jione	34, 43–44, 154, 173	Mariota, Martin Wilson	45–46
Hawk, L. Daniel	38	Marlow, Hilary	37
Hundley, Michael B.	124	Mastnjak, Nathan Robert	30
Hurowitz, Victor (Avigdor)	54	Matties, Gordon H.	134
Ingram, Doug	71	Meek, Russell L.	49
Ishida, Tomoo	54	Mein, Andrew	98, 134–35, 149
Janzen, David	57	Meneses, Eloise Hiebert	21
Janzen, J. Gerald	144	Meleisea, Malama	12
Japhet, Sara	113	Melton, Brittany N.	121, 157
Jarick, John	47–48	Meyers, Carol	55, 59
Job, John B.	112	Mila-Schaaf, Karlo	23, 24
Jonker, Louis C.	115	Milgrom, Jacob	138
Kearney, Judith	106	Miller, Douglas B.	167–68
Keck, Elizabeth	133	Miller, Geoffrey D.	31, 36
Kessler, John	109	Miller, Patrick D.	111
Keys, Gillian	56	Mills, Mary	41–42
Kidner, Derek	150	Miscall, Peter D.	30, 36–37, 50
Kiernan, J.P.	88	Mishra, Vijay	80
		Motusaga, Mema	164, 166

Mulitalo-Lauta, Pa'u Tafaogalupe 165
Mulitalo-Cheung, Tamari 165
Murphy, Roland E. 8, 103–4, 123, 128, 142, 144, 167
Murray, Donald F. 112–13
Nelson, Richard D. 128
Neuber, Carolin 150–51
Nofoaiga, Vaitusi 25
Ofo'ia, Numerator 11
Ogden, Graham S. 103, 142
Olson, Dennis T. 120
Ostriker, Alicia 26
Oswald, Wolfgang 54
Otto, Eckart 147
Patton, Matthew H. 110
Pearce, Sarah Judith 148
Peleg, Yitzhak (Itzik) 124
Penchansky, David 35, 38
Pouono, Terry 175–76
Prentis, Brooke 168
Preuss, Horst Dietrich 92
Pummer, Reinhard 121
Raboteau, Albert J. 88
Reyburn, David 151–52
Rofé, Alexander 60
Rogerson, John 56, 131
Roi, Micha 127, 131
Römer, Thomas 149
Rosenberg, Gil 39
Rothstein, Eric 32
Rothstein, Johann Wilhelm 113
Rudman, Dominic 104
Ryan, Roger 120
Said, Edward 73, 74
Sasson, Jack M. 153–55
Schoors, Anton 50
Sedgwick, Peter 20
Safran, William 11
Sarna, Nahum M. 145–46
Scholem, Gershom 154
Schöpflin, Karin 117
Segovia, Fernando 9, 12, 73, 94–96
Selvén, Sebastian 43
Seow, Choon-Leong 1, 8, 71, 103, 120, 123, 142, 168–69, 171
Shackleton, Mark 74
Sharp, Carolyn J. 156
Shectman, Sarah 55, 58, 65–67

Smith-Christopher (also Smith), Daniel L. 4, 58, 70, 72, 84–91, 93–94, 107, 117, 155
Sneed, Mark R. 2, 50, 116, 121, 123
Soli, Faapisa M. 171
Sommer, Benjamin D. 32
Southwood, Katherine E. 61, 97, 109
Sparks, James T. 121
Spivak, Gayatri Chakravorty 22, 80–83
Stager, Lawrence E. 56
Stanley, Glenda 106
Strine, C. A. 125, 136
Stuart, Douglas 122, 153–55, 157
Su'a-Tavila, Aliitasi 163
Sweeney, Marvin A. 93
Talstra, Eep 123
Tauiliili, Pemerika L. 170
Tcherkézoff, Serge 18
Thiselton, Anthony C. 30
Tigay, Jeffrey H. 128, 131
Tiňo, Jozef 114
Tita, Hubert 50
Tominiko, Seulupe Falaniko 165
Tomlinson, Matt 34
Torres, Amaryllis Tiglao 82
Towner, W. Sibley 103, 116–17, 123, 142, 169
Trible, Phyllis 154
Trotter, Jonathan R. 132
Tull, Patricia 31
Turner, Marie 144
Va'a, Unasa L. F. 12, 13, 15–17, 25, 137, 170
Vaka'uta, Nāsili 35
van der Toorn, Karel 121
von Rad, Gerhard 112–13, 128–29
Waqa, Mariana 48–49
Webb, Barry G. 120
Weeks, Stuart 4, 9, 25–26, 50, 72, 102, 117
Weinberg, Joel 57
Weinfeld, Moshe 129
Wenham, Gordon J. 125–27
Wetter, Anne-Mareike 58
White, Sidnie Ann 157
Whybray, R. N. 8
Williamson, H. G. 108, 122
Wilson, Gerald H. 167
Wilson, Ian D. 104–5, 113

Wilson-Wright, Aren M.	120
Wolff, Hans Walter	154
Wolter, Michael	159
Wright, Jacob L.	109
Yee, Gale A.	96–98
Zimmerli, Walther	102–3, 134
Zogbo, Lynell	142

www.ingramcontent.com/pod-product-compliance
Lightning Source LLC
Chambersburg PA
CBHW020837020526
44114CB00040B/1227